Global Environmental Governance, Civil Society and Wildlife

The world is entering a period of unprecedented environmental and political change. By mid-century, climate change will cause dramatic ecosystem shifts. Hundreds, if not thousands, of species will disappear from the earth including icons like polar bears, gorillas, Asiatic lions and bluefin tuna. For many cultures 'species' are 'place'. As our cultivated global community erodes, international triage decisions about species and local ecosystems will commence and if we are not alert, these decisions will be made on our collective behalf, without local perspective or accountability. *Global Environmental Governance, Civil Society and Wildlife* illuminates a clear pathway for the environmental, non-governmental community to transition into a co-governance role. Many NGO diplomats have deeper experience and more technical knowledge about policy discussions than their government counterparts and are unburdened by sovereign constraints. The book puts forward the perspectives of developing world civil society and the case that it must play a more significant role in future decision making. Civil society from around the world must be welcomed by governments at the global environmental governance table if we are to hear birdsong after the storm.

Margi Prideaux is a specialist in wildlife policy development. She has a PhD on the development of wildlife policy and law. Dr Prideaux's research focus is on international policy relating to migratory species conservation, regional agreement development, marine protected areas and the role of local and global civil society in 'track one' and 'track two' international diplomacy. She has participated in more than 20 different international processes, has worked with a number of international conservation organisations and has served as Marine Policy Advisor to the Convention on Migratory Species (CMS). Dr Prideaux is the Policy Director for Wild Migration, a Research Associate with the Indo-Pacific Governance Research Centre and a Member of the Joint IUCN SSC/WCPA Marine Mammal Taskforce and the IUCN WCPA Transboundary Conservation Specialist Group. She writes at www.wildpolitics.co

'An extraordinary book responding with experiential brilliance to the violent storm raging across the whole of planet earth. Writing with the deep knowledge of a scholar, the engaged fervor of a veteran activist, and the wisdom of a poetic visionary Margi Prideaux has produced an inspiring text for our time enlivened by its focus on the frightening ordeal we humans inevitably share with the animal wonders of nature also entrapped in this predatory capitalist world. Without exaggeration, a thrilling and indispensable guide to the future.'

> – Professor Richard Falk, Albert G. Milbank Professor Emeritus of International Law at Princeton University and Fellow of the Orfalea Center of Global Studies at the University of California, Santa Barbara. Author of *Power Shift: On the New Global Order*; and *(Re)Imagining Humane Global Governance*. USA.

'This work by Dr Prideaux, *Global Environmental Governance, Civil Society and Wildlife*, is the exemplar of what happens when you combine two decades of cutting edge conservation at the practical level by a leading NGO, and critical thinking of what solutions, at the theoretical level, to some of the most pressing problems of our generation are required. This book is radical. From the personal journeys at the micro level, to the clashing of states at the macro level, this work will make you think as philosophy, politics and law are all tightly weaved into a convincing narrative. This is an excellent piece of scholarship.'

> – Professor Alexander Gillespie, University of Waikato. Author of *International Environmental Law, Policy and Ethics*; and *Conservation, Biodiversity and International Law*. New Zealand.

'*Global Environmental Governance, Civil Society and Wildlife* offers a call to action. It powerfully makes the case for expanding the parameters of governance beyond states and corporations to include an enhanced, energized, networked civil society capable of caring for local communities and the more-than-human world. Marrying a scholar's analysis with a poet's sensitivity, the book is essential reading for understanding both the constraints and opportunities for creating a more just and ecologically vibrant world. Given that the stakes involve nothing less than the life-support system of the planet, we would be wise to heed Margi Prideaux's deep understanding and astute counsel.'

> – Professor Paul Wapner, American University. Author of *Living through the End of Nature: The Future of American Environmentalism*. USA.

'Margi Prideaux's career of civil society activism gives her profound insights into why so many well-meaning international conservation efforts are failing so many communities and so many species. Her spirited and brave call for truly collaborative governance with local communities deserves a full airing in the boardrooms of the big NGOs.'

> – Professor Peter Dauvergne, University of British Columbia, Canada.

'In this learned and passionate book, environmentalist Margi Prideaux has an indispensable message: a vast ecological storm is coming, and global governance is failing meet it. At once a window onto civil society and a critique of elite diplomacy, this book's powerful call for a new earth-centred democracy cannot be ignored.'

– Professor Anthony Burke, UNSW, Australia.

'Clearsighted, passionate and inspiring, Margi Prideaux has written a vital reimagining of the destiny of environmental activism. *Global Environmental Governance, Civil Society and Wildlife* is a clarion call for civil society to step forward and demand greater power. This important and wise book will reshape the thinking of activists, environmentalists, NGOs and policy makers.'

– Micah White, author of *The End of Protest*, USA.

'Dr Prideaux's life time of work as an environmentalist and community advocate has been combined in this extraordinary book. Passionate, compelling and inspiring. The beautifully told unique stories of people and place and the pathways to the conclusions are compelling and empowering. At a time of global unease with leadership and governance, it challenges the norm and gives hope for the future. It is a book that will stay with you long after you have finished reading.'

– Jayne Bates, OAM, Former Mayor, Kangaroo Island Local Government, Australia.

'A poignant, inspiring, empowering and timely book that shines light on the global conservation issues of our time. It closed the gap between academia and grassroots conservation efforts offering a true insight into the world of those fighting tooth and nail to save our planet. I learned of effort, struggle, triumphs, political and social challenges, but most of all I learned there is hope. This is an outstanding book, written by an extraordinary woman.'

– Donna Mulvenna, author *Wild Roots Coming Alive in the French Amazon*, French Guiana.

'*Global Environmental Governance, Civil Society and Wildlife: Birdsong After the Storm* is a wake-up call on all who are concerned about natures's gift to humanity. The use of birdsong is a metaphor for action. The book is a must read by all nature lovers at all levels.'

– Alfred Oteng-Yeboah, Former Chair of the Standing Committee of the United Nations Environment Programme/Convention on Migratory Species, Germany/Ghana.

'Margi Prideaux has done more than anyone to raise awareness of the need for grassroots voices to be heard in debates over nature, climate change and the environment. She deserves to be widely read.'

– Michael Edwards, Editor of *Transformation*, USA.

Transforming Environmental Politics and Policy

Series Editors
Timothy Doyle, Keele University, UK and University of Adelaide, Australia and Philip Catney, Keele University, UK

Series Blurb

The theory and practice of environmental politics and policy are rapidly emerging as key areas of intense concern in the first, third and industrializing worlds. People of diverse nationalities, religions and cultures wrestle daily with environment and development issues central to human and non-human survival on the planet Earth. Air, Water, Earth, Fire. These central elements mix together in so many ways, spinning off new constellations of issues, ideas and actions, gathering under a multitude of banners: energy security, food sovereignty, climate change, genetic modification, environmental justice and sustainability, population growth, water quality and access, air pollution, mal-distribution and over-consumption of scarce resources, the rights of the non-human, the welfare of future citizens-the list goes on.

What is much needed in green debates is for theoretical discussions to be rooted in policy outcomes and service delivery. So, while still engaging in the theoretical realm, this series also seeks to provide a 'real world' policy-making dimension. Politics and policy making is interpreted widely here to include the territories, discourses, instruments and domains of political parties, non-governmental organizations, protest movements, corporations, international regimes, and transnational networks.

From the local to the global-and back again-this series explores environmental politics and policy within countries and cultures, researching the ways in which green issues cross North-South and East-West divides. The 'Transforming Environmental Politics and Policy' series exposes the exciting ways in which environmental politics and policy can transform political relationships, in all their forms.

For a full list of titles in this series, please visit – https://www.routledge.com/politics/series/ASHSER-1371

Recent titles

Global Environmental Governance, Civil Society and Wildlife

Birdsong After the Storm

Margi Prideaux

LONDON AND NEW YORK

First published 2017 by Routledge

2 Park Square, Milton Park, Abingdon, Oxfordshire OX14 4RN
52 Vanderbilt Avenue, New York, NY 10017

Routledge is an imprint of the Taylor & Francis Group, an informa business

First issued in paperback 2019

British Library Cataloguing in Publication Data
A catalogue record for this book is available from the British Library

Library of Congress Cataloging in Publication Data
Names: Prideaux, Margi, author.
Title: Global environmental governance, civil society and wildlife : birdsong after the storm / Margi Prideaux.
Description: Abingdon, Oxon ; New York, NY : Routledge, [2017] | Series: Transforming environmental politics and policy | Includes bibliographical references and index.
Identifiers: LCCN 2016041436 | ISBN 9781472467744 (hbk) | ISBN 9781315584812 (ebk)
Subjects: LCSH: Environmental policy--International cooperation. | Environmentalism--International cooperation. | Environmental management--International cooperation. | Wildlife conservation-- International cooperation. | Non-governmental organizations.
Classification: LCC GE170 .P745 2017 | DDC 333.7--dc23
LC record available at https://lccn.loc.gov/2016041436

ISBN: 978-1-4724-6774-4 (hbk)
ISBN: 978-0-367-26460-4 (pbk)

Typeset in Times New Roman
by Taylor & Francis Books

Contents

Acronyms

BEES	Benin Environment and Education Society
CBD	Convention on Biological Diversity
CITES	Convention on International Trade in Endangered Species of Wild Fauna and Flora
CIVICUS	World Alliance for Citizen Participation
CMS	Convention on the Conservation of Migratory Species of Wild Animals
CO_2	carbon dioxide
CSO	civil society organisation
DRC	Democratic Republic of the Congo
ECOSOC	United Nations Economic and Social Council
EU	European Union
FAO	Food and Agricultural Organization of the United Nations
G20	Global 20
GNP	gross national product
HLPF	High Level Political Forum on Sustainable Development
IGOs	intergovernmental organisations
INDC	Intended Nationally Determined Contributions
INTERPOL	International Criminal Police Organization
IOP	International Organisation Partner
IPBES	Intergovernmental Science-Policy Platform on Biodiversity and Ecosystem Services
IPCC	Intergovernmental Panel on Climate Change
IUCN	International Union for the Conservation of Nature
IUCN SSC	IUCN Species Survival Commission
MEAs	multilateral environment agreements
NGO	nongovernmental organisation
OECD	Organisation for Economic Cooperation and Development
PES	Payment for Ecosystem Service
PLCN	Prey Lang Community Network
PPP	public private partnerships

R2P	Responsibility to Protect
Ramsar	Convention on Wetlands of International Importance
REDD+	Reducing Emissions from Deforestation and Forest Degradation
SBSTTA	CBD's Subsidiary Body on Scientific, Technical and Technological Advice
SDGs	Sustainable Development Goals
STRP	Scientific and Technical Review Panel
UN	United Nations
UNDESA/DSD	United Nations Department of Economic and Social Affairs/Division for Sustainable Development
UNEA	United Nations Environment Assembly
UNEP	United Nations Environment Programme
UNTOC	Convention against Transnational Organized Crime
USA	United States of America
WCS	Wildlife Conservation Society
WTO	World Trade Organisation
WWF	World Wildlife Fund
WWN	World Wetland Network

Species names and IUCN status

African forest elephant (*Loxodonta cyclotis*)	Not assessed
African savannah elephant (*Loxodonta africana*)	Vulnerable
argali (*Ovis ammon*)	Near threatened
Australian magpie (*Cracticus tibicen*)	Least concern
bharal or Himalayan blue sheep (*Pseudois nayaur*)	Least concern
black-crowned night herons (*Nycticorax nycticorax*)	Least concern
Bornean orangutan (*Pongo pygmaeus*)	Endangered
brown spider monkey (*Ateles hybridus*)	Critically endangered
Bukhara or Yarkand deer (*Cervus elaphus yarkandensi*)	Not assessed
cheetah (*Acinonyx jubatu*)	Vulnerable
chinkara or jebeer gazelle (*Gazella bennettii*)	Least concern
chiru (*Pantholops hodgsonii*)	Endangered
Cross River gorillas (*Gorilla gorilla diehli*)	Critically endangered
forest owlet (*Heteroglaux blewitti*)	Critically endangered
goitered gazelle (*Gazella subgutturosa*)	Vulnerable
Grauer's gorilla (*Gorilla beringei graueri*)	Endangered
hairy-nosed otters (*Lutra sumatrana*)	Endangered
hippopotamus (*Hippopotamus amphibius*)	Vulnerable
ibex (*Capra sp.*)	Least concern – Endangered
kakapo (*Strigops habroptila*)	Critically endangered
kiang (*Equus kiang*)	Least concern
kulan (*Equus hemionus*)	Near threatened
Mongolian gazelle (*Procapra gutturosa*)	Least concern
mountain gorilla (*Gorilla beringei beringei*)	Endangered
Philippine eagle (*Pithecophaga jefferyi*)	Critically endangered
polar bear (*Ursus maritimus*)	Vulnerable
Przewalski's horse (*Equus caballus przewalskii*)	Not assessed

red wolf (*Canis rufus*)	Critically endangered
red-bellied guenon (*Cercopithecus erythrogaster erythrogaster*)	Critically endangered
saiga (*Saiga tatarica* and *S. borealis mongolica*)	Critically endangered
sitatunga (*Tragelaphus spekei gratus*)	Least concern
snow leopard (*Panthera uncia*)	Endangered
southern right whale (*Eubalaena australis*)	Least concern
Sumatran orangutan (*Pongo abelii*)	Critically endangered
Tibetan gazelle (*Procapra picticaudata*)	Near threatened
West African manatee (*Trichechus senegalensis*)	Vulnerable
western lowland gorillas (*Gorilla gorilla gorilla*)	Critically endangered
wild camel (*Camelus bactrianu*)	Not assessed
wild yak (*Bos grunniens*)	Not assessed
yellowfin tuna (*Thunnus albacares*)	Near threatened

Acknowledgments

After more than two decades of writing for others, finally completing my first book is a personal milestone. It is one that humbly borrows from the wisdom of a great many people. I feel indebted to a myriad of faces, voices and sometimes profound and moving comments that have been with me from page one. You are too many to mention, but I have watched you and listened to your courage for decades, as you have advocated for your people (human and non-human) across the table of international affairs.

I extend deep appreciation to Timothy Doyle, Rob Sorsby and Ashgate Publishing for this opportunity. Timothy didn't realise the day I walked into his office and declared I 'wanted to write a book' was the same day I stepped fully into Richard Falk's shadowland. I was greeted with enthusiasm and wise counsel – an insightful gift. Many months later, Kathie Stove's editorial finesse gave me the confidence to finish. The whole team at Taylor & Francis including Claire Maloney, Kevin Selmes and Rebecca Bomford were tremendous. Throughout Nicolas Entrup, Sigrid Lüber, Jayne Bates and Linda Irwin-Oak, and even in his absence the late Peter Pueschal, have kept the fire burning. At a moment of doubt another author, Peter Garrett, called and then the amazing Donna Mulvenna appeared in the final mile. I am humbled by the trust and the personal contributions from Arie Rompas, Armet Memet, Aryo Nugroho, José Truda Palazzo, Jr., Kulbhushansingh Suryawanshi, Lee Tan, Linda Irwin-Oak, Maximin K. Djondo, Norhadie Karben, Yash Veer Bhatnagar and the late Itan Kussaritano. Without each of these connections, this version of this book would not be in front of you now.

Richard Falk's many books have been a constant companion. Likewise, Mac Chapin's bravery in publishing *A Challenge to Conservationists* has spoken to me during each chapter.

Everyone who writes is carried by a web of support – people who touch your life and give you courage. Mine has come from Vera Bügi, Louise Duff, Heidi Frisch, Robyn Handbury, Reiko Hosokawa and John Matheson, Susan Farquhar, Naomi Goto, Leeza Anne Irwin, Minoru Kashiwagi, Peter Lengyel, Fabienne McLellan, Cheryl Merrill, Cara Miller, Claire Mirande, Felipe

Montecito, Cheyne Morris, Giuseppe Notarbartolo di Sciara, Chris Rostron, Tom Shilson, Susan Sorg, Bob and Jennie Teasdale, Melanie Virtue, Kathryn Warhurst, Penny Wright, and my father Paul Blythe.

My innermost message is to Geoff Prideaux – my sentinel, my guide and my soul. This book is written, with deep thanks, for you.

Preface

Numbers can be staggering – some because of the intense compassion they reveal, others for their bleak immensity.

The top trending Twitter hashtags for 2015 included: #JeSuisParis and #PrayForParis, #BlackLivesMatter, #RefugeesWelcome, #IStandWithAhmed, #LoveWins and #MarriageEquality. The online world has a significant capacity to care for something bigger than themselves. #JeSuisParis was included in 3.4 million tweets in the first 24 hours after the terrorist attack. On the other side of the Atlantic #BlackLivesMatter was used over 9 million times during the year. Each of these interactions were moments of compassions that together became something greater, albeit for a fleeting moment.

The year 2015 also brought the news that the International Union for the Conservation of Nature (IUCN) Red List now included 22,784 species that are threatened with extinction. Habitat loss and degradation is identified as the main threat for 85 per cent of all 77,340 species described on the list. 2,300 birds have been identified as particularly vulnerable to climate change. 200 amphibians are already gone. Confronting us – with brittle clarity – that the world is changing. We are not winning the battle.

I want to make a revolutionary case – civil society needs a seat at the governance table. I can feel the visceral reaction from governments and transnational corporations as I type. What I propose erodes the pillars of power that have been so carefully constructed, but this revolution might not be as impossible as we think.

I was first struck with this when I read Clive Hamilton's *Requiem for a Species* and it was reinforced when I recently read Micah White's *The End of Protest*. Both authors advocate disruption. For Clive Hamilton it is civil disobedience and overcoming passivity to collectively build new democracies that can ensure the best defences against a more hostile climate. Micah White challenges us to unleash a spiritual, political and social revolution. Indeed, as I finish this manuscript Anthony Burke, Stefanie Fishel and their colleagues have published *Plant Politics: A Manifesto from the End of IR*, calling for legal and institutional reform of global environmental governance.

The call for revolution is not new for the field of international relations. It has been building for a few decades. In 1983 Richard Falk, who is for many the father of normative international relations, urged normative thinkers to inhabit the 'shadowland' – a conceptual space where one is outraged by contemporary conditions, mindful of past realities and devoted to exploring future possibilities. Slavoj Žižek, in *The Year of Dreaming Dangerously*, picks up this theme as well. He challenges that we have to start from the assumption that the catastrophic future we dread has already happened and work backwards to figure out what we should have done. We then mobilise ourselves to perform the actions that will change that destiny.

So, a few years ago, I allowed the negativity to surface. I stood on the edges of Falk's shadowland with a dash of Žižek. I intentionally engaged in a project born of anger – anger at wasted energy and dismissed action, at bureaucrats who revelled in the power of their position keeping civil society at arm's length to the detriment of the issues we collectively strove to repair, and anger at years upon years of hard won international decisions that were ignored as soon as governments returned home, never to be questioned or considered again.

I hosted a meeting of nongovernmental organisations (NGOs) at an intergovernmental meeting that is held every three years to discuss shared actions for wildlife conservation – the Convention on the Conservation of Migratory Species of Wild Animals (CMS). I made sure the room was filled with diversity. There were professional activists working for the big international NGOs and a few from smaller operations. There were perspectives from Africa, Russia, the United States of America and Latin America, from pro-hunter and pro-welfare worldviews. We discussed what was missing in our relationship with CMS. They told me that civil society is very often the implementer and sometimes even the coordinator of work under the convention and its agreements. Their work is rooted in the cultural context of the places and the people where the conservation action is needed. They were angry that their work remained invisible. It was as if they were busy with 'real world' conservation, while the secretariats and governments, oblivious to this activity, were content to shuffle paper.

Over the next year I interviewed and surveyed more than 100 NGOs and civil society organisations from around the world. Together we formed a series of recommendations for CMS to consider. In 2014, I submitted the report to CMS. With the support of the Government of Ghana we secured a Resolution: *Enhancing the Relationship between the CMS Family and Civil Society*. It established a process for CMS to investigate the recommendations further. The points were made and accepted, at least on the surface, and I was pleased to put down the marker. However, I was still operating within the old rules and present order. Our civil society message was positive, conciliatory and habitually deferential to governments. Even the title of the resolution was soft. Inside, I wanted to thump my fists on the diplomatic table – to make governments hear. I had imagined the dystopian future and worked, stepwise, back to what we should be doing now to change it. I had sought the wisdom of hundreds of colleagues and together we had framed something important. But I had spent my career as a negotiator and NGO diplomat and I realised I wasn't yet brave enough to say it out loud.

So, I ran the process again, with a different group of civil society organisations and a different governance process. This time I focused on the Convention on Wetlands of International Importance (Ramsar) and worked with the World Wetland Network (WWN) – an amazing international collaboration of almost 2,000 small civil society organisations and NGOs from around the world. This time we gathered together 190 surveys.

Without any prompting from me, the message from the CMS and Ramsar groups was the same.

The day I submitted the Ramsar report in early 2015, I fully stepped across into the Falk's shadowland. It was obvious what I needed to write. With the wisdom of hundreds of colleagues alive in my mind, and a feeling of responsibility to be a voice for that collective insight, I was clear that civil society needs to be organised and empowered, and then recognised and respected as an equal at the governance table.

The civil society shared narrative for this book was born.

Margi Prideaux

1 The barometer is rising

A storm is coming

A storm is coming; a maelstrom like we have never experienced before. The combined forces of climate change and political upheaval will play out with more of us aware than at any other time in human history.

Global warming is not hypothetical. It is happening now. Wave after wave of data confirms it. Each of the past several decades has been significantly warmer than the previous ones. The period 2011–2015 was the hottest on record, as was the year 2015 – with an extra boost from a powerful El Niño. The record-breaking trend continued in 2016. Climate change is increasing the frequency and intensity of extreme events like heat waves, droughts and heavy rainfall.[1] The World Meteorological Organization Hurricane Committee reported that the Eastern North Pacific experienced nine major hurricanes (above Category 3) in 2015 – the most since reliable records began in 1971. The Accumulated Cyclone Energy, which measures the combined strength and duration of tropical storms and hurricanes, was about 63 per cent higher than the 1981–2010 average.[2] India and Pakistan suffered the traumatic and devastating effects of heat waves right through 2015. Thousands of lives were lost. The India Meteorological Department has warned of heat-wave conditions still to come.[3] Global average sea level has risen by about 17 cm between 1900 and 2005 at a much faster rate than in the previous 3,000 years.[4] Record rainfall led to flooding that impacted on tens of thousands of people across South America, West Africa and Europe. At the same time, unseasonal dry conditions in southern Africa and Brazil exacerbated multi-year droughts. The global average near-surface temperature for 2015, when the core of this book was written, was the warmest on record by a clear margin.[4]

The first dangerous milestone was crossed in 2013 when Hawaii's Mauna Loa Observatory, a key scientific facility run by the University of California, measured a carbon dioxide (CO_2) concentration in the atmosphere at over 400 parts per million – around 40 per cent higher than before the Industrial Revolution and higher than at any time in human history. That milestone was the trigger for me to begin thinking about this book. The year 2015 was the impetus to start writing. As I write, news has been released that atmospheric

CO_2 concentration of the entire southern hemisphere is now at or above 400 parts per million, much earlier than the experts had predicted. Casey Station on Antarctica exceed 400 parts per million on 10 May 2016.[5] The last time CO_2 levels were this high, some three to five million years ago, the mean global temperature was around 3°C higher than the pre-Industrial average, the sea level was up to 40 metres higher, and the Greenland ice sheet was impermanent. A changing climate has both fast and slow pulses, so temperature shifts and sea-level rise will build momentum in the coming few decades. Our lives and our livelihoods are already changing.

We have absorbed the news of the looming impact of climate change for some time now – like watching a disaster unfold in slow motion. So slow at times that our daily lives continue between the scenes. We are aware of it nonetheless, and for some of us these impacts are already tangible.

On our farm in Australia we now live between two extremes; less rainfall and more very hot days. As I began this book we had just come out of the driest winter in living memory. Without winter rain our reservoirs were dry throughout the summer. There was less green vegetation to sustain the farm. Through spring and summer we anxiously watched the skies for lightning storms on the horizon. When I was a child lightning was exciting. With the long stretches of hot dry days, lightning now means wildfires.

Elsewhere the signs are far worse. Climate change has impacted all continents and all oceans. Arctic sea ice is retreating at a visible rate. Melting around Antarctica is causing sea ice changes which are still not well understood.[6–8] After lifetimes in harmony with the ocean, people of the Pacific and the Indian Oceans already look across the waves to a bleak future. The homes of their ancestors will soon disappear; the sea engulfing their history. Europe's glaciers are retreating. The United Kingdom has been flooding. The Sahara Desert is encroaching on farmland on the African continent, forests are disappearing from Congo to Madagascar and rising sea levels are swallowing homes in West African river deltas. North America faces severe heat, heavy rain and declining snowpack.[6, 9–12] Thirty per cent of the fertile land in the world has vanished in the past 30 years.

Climate change is happening now.

Impacts in the future won't discriminate. Large cities, isolated from the natural world, will be just as susceptible as the ancient Amazon rainforest.[13–16] In the 1970s there were 660 reported disasters around the world including droughts, floods, extreme temperatures events, wildfires and storms. In the 2000s there were 3,322. This is a fivefold increase in just over 30 years.[17] We can expect more climate-related extremes: more heat waves, droughts, floods, cyclones, and wildfires. Competition for water will be intense. In many regions our staple crops and fisheries will diminish.[18] Climate change is expected to reshape the global economy by substantially reducing economic output, reducing average global incomes by roughly 23 per cent by 2100.[19] There will be serious food and water security issues. Violent conflicts, amplified by poverty, will become more common.[6]

While we feel the human impacts, the natural world will also be lurching. The current rates of species extinction are already one thousand times the rate that would be expected if humans were not a factor. In the near future, rapid shifts, caused by climate change, will exceed the ability of many species to migrate or adjust.[6, 20–23] A quarter of the Earth's species could be extinct by midcentury.[24] It is perhaps a sad coincidence that extinction rates will be greatest where the power of people is the least – Latin America, Africa, Oceania.[25] If we continue as we now are, the dawn of the next century will grieve the loss of icons – gorillas, polar bears, lions, tuna, sandpipers and warblers.

The longer the world community dithers, the stronger the likelihood of 'severe, pervasive and irreversible impacts for people and ecosystems'.[18]

The Intergovernmental Panel on Climate Change (IPCC) is the pre-eminent scientific body for climate change. It was established by the United Nations in 1988, at the request of member governments. Its role is to track and advise on matters relating to climate change. There is no higher or more rigorous scientific authority. Their meetings are no side event, nor are they informal gatherings of left-leaning trouble-makers – as the climate sceptics would have you believe.

Every few years 'the best and the brightest' are nominated – by governments – to participate in the IPCC review of the most recent scientific, technical and socio-economic information about the biosphere and to assess what is likely to happen in the decades to come.[26] The scientists involved are all respected, published, acknowledged experts in their fields and their main task is to merge this information into a series of reports for governments to consider. Their reports have always been sobering reading and the fifth formal report does not break the trend.[18]

With the input of thousands of scientists, their message is clear and as solid as science ever gets. Warming of the climate system is unequivocal. Human influence on the climate system is clear, and emissions of greenhouse gases are the highest in history. The atmosphere and ocean have warmed, snow and ice have diminished, and the sea level has risen.[18]

In 2015 the world's governments collectively, finally, agreed that the IPCC is right. The freshly minted Paris Agreement turned a corner on decades of political disregard. Countries agreed to limit emissions, and to continually review and strengthen actions every five years, beginning in 2018. They have set an aspirational goal of 1.5°C that most closely aligns to the scientific recommendations of the IPCC, with a politically expedient target of 2°C, but their pledges (formally called the Intended Nationally Determined Contributions or INDCs) still have the world on a road to between 2.7°C and 3.7°C of warming compared with pre-industrial levels. It is true, this is better than the 4.5°C trajectory before the Paris Summit, but it is significantly short of where we need to be.[27] They won't revisit this figure again until 2020 when their 'five year meeting' to present updated plans on raising their emission cuts begins. Starting in 2023, they will have to update the public on their progress.

The new agreement doesn't take effect until 2020. The window to achieve the 1.5°C goal will have already gone, unless all of the world's largest economies dramatically change course. Emissions levels in 2025 and 2030 will have significant consequences for our ability to limit warming to 2°C. The higher the emissions in the near term, the greater the emissions reduction will be required in later decades.[27, 28]

I have worked in international environmental negations for 25 years. I know that all governments need to do to meet their obligations under the Paris Agreement is to come back in 2023 (and every five years after that) and say they'll do a little more.[28, 29] So long as they do that their peers (i.e., other governments) won't shame them. There is no new money promised to address climate change in developing countries, and discussing loss and damage now or in the future is off limits in order to appease wealthy countries responsible for hundreds of years of emissions that have brought us to this point. The very industries that need to change are absent from the Agreement. Oil, gas, or coal producers have not been told to leave fossil fuels in the ground, and carbon pollution from international shipping and flights don't count as greenhouse gas emissions.[29] The two issues that matter the most – actual emission reductions and financial investment – have no explicit numerical targets for individual countries and no meaningful mechanisms for ensuring accountability.[28]

As part of the Paris deal, governments have put dangerous trust in future technologies – on physically removing huge quantities of carbon dioxide from the atmosphere many decades from today.

It is easy to be swept away in the euphoria of governments achieving even a small level of harmony in Paris. But objective assessment soon dents that high. In the days directly after the Paris Summit, Kevin Anderson wrote:

> If the global community is to maintain emissions with the 2°C carbon budget, there needs to be much greater recognition of the profound and immediate challenges we face. The scale of emission reductions will not be delivered through eloquent speeches, win-win rhetoric and green-growth spin. Zero carbon energy technologies are a prerequisite of a 2°C future – but they are far from sufficient. They will only deliver the necessary levels of mitigation if they are accompanied by fundamental changes to the political and economic framing of contemporary society.[30]

Clive Hamilton makes some sense of the conflict between good news and bad of the Paris Agreement:

> There is good reason to feel, like me and others such as Marlowe Hood, torn in two directions. For those who understand the situation, the polarity sets up a powerful tension. If it's uncomfortable to be suspended between the poles, it's dangerous to go all the way to one or the other ... we have to live between the poles, because it is the tension that allows us

to believe that the great step forward of Paris, while still a long way short of what is needed, could set the world on a path where much more becomes possible.[31]

Commentators are already turning their attention beyond the political class to change driven by society – from cities and regions through to institutions and companies onto local communities and individuals.[32–34] This blanket call is just as precarious and unfounded as government relying on technological solutions in the future. Without fundamental structural change, society's reaction will be *ad hoc* and diffuse, and will very likely fall short, especially because governments are still facilitating the expansion of the fossil fuel industry.

This is not a book about climate change, although that is unmistakably the context from which it is written. There are already many fine books and documents describing what is happening and the steps we need to take to reduce the impact. They should be reading material beside everyone's bed at night, because we simply cannot live in denial any longer. Yet, as I sat and observed the Paris Climate Summit, it was clear that our political class was not prepared to do enough. They still strive to protect the very system that has caused the problem and hope that someone, somewhere, will announce a technological fix that allows the world to continue without change. Perhaps, one day, such solutions will exist. But, we have waited too long before acting to not feel the lashing of the storm. There are profound moral reasons why we must address global warming – crucial issues of ethics and public policy that we ignore at our peril.[35]

This is a book about how we politically adapt in the decades to come, about the choices we make and who is part of making those choices. Using the metaphor of a storm, the impact of climate change is the unstable air mass that will form a dangerous thunderhead. This is a book about how we navigate the storm – it is a book about governance.

I am not alone in turning attention to the failings of our current governance order – the constellation of rules, norms and actions, and the organisation that administers the system.

In the international sphere, these typically operate through multilateral processes, with governments as the primary actors. These processes are proving unequal to the complex challenges facing the modern world – climate change, terrorism, humanitarian catastrophes. While international relations scholars have recently given attention to international governance and the role non-state actors play in influencing debate, the international relations lens has traditionally focused on how states can influence and regulate global norms. Until relatively recently even the discourse on failed, failing or fragile states focused on state building to restore political order. But, in recent years, some academics have adopted a distinctly radical hue. This book is my contribution to the debate. Even as I have finalised this book Anthony Burke, Stefanie Fishel, Audra Mitchell, Simon Dalby and Daniel Levine have published a manifesto of how politics can evolve to respond to changes wrought by the Anthropocene and a changing climate.[36, 37]

In reality, the change has been afoot for some time now. States have been chipping away at their own prominence in the global sphere, creating global or regional institutions to which they cede limited power. Westphalia is breaking, in part by design, in part by the stealth of elite actors and in part because it should.

European States have been engaged in change by design – a project now fully in view with Britain's shock exit from the European Union. European States have consciously given legitimacy to the European Court of Justice in their domestic judicial systems. Similarly, states have given the International Monetary Fund influences to stipulate changes in domestic financial management structures.[38] The controversial international trade agreements currently in negotiation will grant unelected trade tribunal judges, using the provisions of each trade treaty, the capacity to overturn democratically enacted legislation.[39] The myriad of intergovernmental processes that exist to manage world affairs all draw some power away from states. These are tangible, real-world examples of how the international community is consciously and willingly chipping away at the Westphalian world order.

The role of states as pre-eminent actors is also being eroded by failure and non-state actors assuming governance roles. Without doubt, there is a reassurance of intense nationalism and right-wing populism and on the surface many government leaders appear to be responding to their populous be reasserting a Westphalian logic. The voting public may believe the rhetoric, but these political postures are hollow. Below the crust, the right are equally, if not more, committed to the project outsourcing governance to the private sector.

The traditional concept of statehood drew a distinction between the public and private sphere. States have been presumed to govern the public sphere where they are responsible for the delivery of public goods; non-state for-profit corporations and not-for-profit civil society have contributed to the private sphere where individual interests lie. Increasingly these lines are blurred. Militarism is perhaps the one Westphalian vestige that remains.

In many parts of the world non-state actors already provide public goods such as education, health and infrastructure, and many state actors easily exploit state resources for private gain. Where states struggle to maintain governance arrangements, these boundary erosions are easy to detect.[40] But, they are also being dissolved incrementally by non-state actors drawing power away from intergovernmental processes. The Davos World Economic Forum have been quietly progressing the Davos Global Redesign Initiative, as a reflection of how these elites envision the future of governance.[41] They call for a replacement of the intergovernmental decision-making with a system of multi-stakeholder governance – with carefully selected stakeholders.[42] While leaders from most of the economic powers participate in the Davos World Economic Forum, these discussions and decisions are being progressed so far from democratic view that the world community may one day wake to a reality it no longer recognises. The Global Redesign Initiative is centred on the corporation, with stakeholders being constituents associated with the corporation – principally those with commercial ties to the company: customers, creditors, suppliers, collaborators, owners and national economies. Those who would be in charge of the multi-stakeholder governance arrangements would be either appointed by Davos or by self-selection of leading firms interested in managing a particular global challenge with other constituents. There will be no need to wait for the intergovernmental system to come to consensus about acting; the multi-stakeholder governance arrangement will make these decisions itself.

It should be said, shifting the notions of international governance are not necessarily wrong or dangerous. Commentators across agendas have rightly been calling for a revolution in global governance arrangements to reflect the scale of the development challenge and new geopolitical realities.[43–45] Certainly, in the world of my professional focus the current institutional framework for wildlife and environment conservation, born of the Westphalian world order, is deeply inadequate to bring about the swift transformative progress that is needed.[36, 44, 46]

Wildlife are local, but managing impact to this community of wildlife is now unquestionably global. While humans have found ways to shelter or buffer the impacts of human activity, the problems that impact wildlife most severely often come from afar. Industrialized fishing, mining, forestry and mono-agriculture raze areas and replace diversity with a single focus. Often illegal, international trade in the exotic provides a path for the unethical to hunt, kill, package and commodify animals and plants. With a deformed logic, some have convinced themselves that killing for sport is good for conservation. The quest for resource and power floods, burns and devastates whole landscapes. Add climate change and a fragile balance that has existed for millennia is shifted.

We stand at a point in history where kakapo, hairy-nosed otters and red wolves survive with only a shadow of their former numbers.[47–49] Polar bears, forest owlets and Philippine eagles face uncertain futures.[50–52] Lesser known, but just as important species like the brown spider monkey live on the thin margin of survival.[53] Ocean acidification threatens organ damage to yellowfin tuna larvae.[54] And, with each of these species are the communities of humans that share the landscape with them.

When I wake in the morning the sound I hear is a magpie warble. These birds, and their unique and haunting song, as well as the kangaroos that stand on the ridge at dusk are a part of the culture in which I live, and the community to which I belong. People in South Africa, Pakistan, eastern Russia or Ireland will wake to different sounds and have different wildlife as part of their communities. We all know our non-human kin, the animals we live among. We know the seasons we share, what grows when and where. We know the ebb and flow of life in our shared place. For some, our vistas are forests. Others look out to the sea and some on endless frozen horizons. These are not empty places. They are filled with wildlife, with which we commune.[55] There is deeply felt relationality and interconnection between our many intelligences – hunting and foraging intelligences, courting and mating intelligences, migrating and hibernating intelligences and many other ways of being.[56] Many of these are more apparent and obvious to communities less prescribed by anthropocentric reductionism.[57] Even so, scientists are now revealing many nonhuman cultural intelligences as well.[58–60]

For generations we have managed our relationship with this wild part of our community. Some have done better than others. But, the political shift towards globally centralised decisions in the world has taken that association from us. Decisions are now made elsewhere – in an international political space.[61, 62] We have become, in many respects, as helpless as the wild community we live among.

Oran Young, Robert Keohane, Peter Haas and Marc Levy have led a decades-long analysis of multilateral environment regimes, highlighting the emergence of new actors and activities that operate alongside, and in support of, multilateral environment agreements (MEAs).[62–67] They argue that environmental concerns such as climate change or biodiversity loss are more difficult and complex to address than other issues that can be managed completely at the state level or by placing constraint on international corporate activity. They highlight how precarious environmental governance arrangements currently are. They chart the success and failures of many – from acid rain in Europe to vessel pollution on the high seas. There is a great deal of wealth to their analysis of regime effectiveness, increasing compliance and addressing the power imbalances between state actors. For this book, they confirm empirically that MEAs are important mechanisms, providing they recognise themselves as part of a broader political governance arrangement.[62–68] When MEAs do, they level the playing field between powerful and highly organised industry interests and more diffuse public interest and concern.[68]

I will argue that where wildlife conservation is concerned this factor needs to be more aggressively harnessed. Traditional, fragmented government agencies typically struggle with trying to manage across landscapes. Consequently, decisions taken at the international level are often poorly reflected into the national context.[69] Local communities and wildlife often bear the burden of poorly applied implementation. International wildlife conservation needs to better reflect the unique characteristics of 'place' and recognise more fully the overlapping, integrated character of policy decisions, mandates and the desires of those in the communities most affected by policy decisions. International decisions should be meaningful to the local level. Right now, in a great many cases, they are not.

We are hampered by our political commitment to an international system of independent (sovereign) states, with governments programmed to protect their national interest above all else.

Left on our current path, we will fail to protect what we need and what we cherish. And so, continuing with the metaphor of a storm, the desperate grip on the current world order will become the lifting force that feeds the thunderhead. We will have a perfect storm.

I argue that MEAs need to evolve into a collaborative governance space that enhances the resources and knowledge at the table and improves public problem-solving capacity.[70] Collaborative governance requires support and leadership. It needs a dedicated forum. The support identifies the policy problem to be fixed. The leadership gathers the sectors into a forum. Then, the members of the forum collaborate to develop policies, solutions and answers.[71, 72]

I explore the failures of governance in chapters 2, 3 and 4: chapter 2 looks further at how the international system is constructed and at the neoliberal agenda that is progressing beyond our view; chapters 3 and 4 explore the role that transnational corporations, nongovernmental organisations (NGOs) and MEAs currently hold, and how international environmental governance is currently influenced. In chapter 5 I explore how civil society is already mobilising and in chapter 6 I discuss how international environmental governance can be tuned to reflect locally conceived and managed wildlife conservation. In the final chapter (7) I propose a path forward. It is a path that requires considerable behavioural change. Governments need to be prepared to share decision-making and international NGOs need to accept that they must listen to the collective voice of civil society that is already rising up to meet this challenge.

The storm is coming. That cannot be changed now. How we prepare and what we do during the period to coming will dictate what survives the storm. We can choose to have birdsong, but the choice must be a conscious one. This book is my offering towards that goal.

Wandering among wisdom

I am a rōnin, having left behind institutional cover to now freely wander among the wisdom of a great many scholars while I strive to make sense of the world in which I operate. I carry two swords. The first is that I am and will remain, consciously, an actor within my research. The other is that I purposely frame my thinking from minority and majority perspectives. My yumi (bow) is my academic philosophy of normative international relations, informed by rooted cosmopolitanism.

Involvement with the subject

While my work is grounded in academic discipline and understanding, I ask that readers accept my involvement as an actor within this research. I am both an active participant in the story unfolding as well as an observer looking on.

Political and environmental studies have traditionally sought a 'cool separation between objective political analysis and subjective environmental engagement'.[73] As Timothy Doyle notes, this tradition loses a great deal of the texture, flavour and side discussions of many international discussions. All that is left to draw upon are the published and smoothed accounts. But, there is crucial information in the margins as well. I draw on my experience and fully acknowledge that my political insights may be subjective. Significant other works have walked this path and there is no reason to shrink from it. Some of what is contained in this book is born of my first-hand participation, or that of colleagues, in international meetings. Much of what I discuss I know only because of my practitioner insight, reflecting my experience and conversations during specific meetings and events. While not betraying confidences, I draw on the inner workings of international political discourse to help illuminate the discussion.

In addition, I must be transparent and place myself within the world order. I am child of the new world – a Canadian by birth and an Australian for my adult life. I acknowledge that I have a subconscious new world perspective on many points. But, I also believe that life experiences can influence worldviews and I am fortunate to have had a career working with activists and colleagues from many other worldviews. I hope that their worldliness and perspectives have broadened my insights.

Minority and majority worldviews

Understanding how I discuss different groups of people in the world order is important to understanding my core arguments. Again, I draw on Timothy Doyle for a definition of the dualistic division of 'minority' and 'majority' worldviews.[73, 74] I resist using the labels that stem from the colonial and Cold War past (first, second and third world) as well as those that describe our societies according to economic value (developed, developing, less-developed, under-developed). In many cases economically poor countries are countries that have been colonised. Some argue that they continue to be colonised through globalised forms of control.[75, 76] I also resist the grouping of north and south. The labels of north, south, developed and developing each contain inherent internal contradictions. Pockets of human communities everywhere are impoverished and disadvantaged, including acute deprivation in health, education and standard of living.[77, 78]

To avoid contradiction and to speak more clearly about the inequity of the elite deciding outcomes for the majority, I consciously use the groupings of 'minority' and 'majority'. In doing so I am making it clear who should be and who is empowered to participate in international political discussions and who is not.

Minority worldviews encompasses wealthy societies that have, often, historically exploited the majority world – Western Europe, Russia, North America, Australia, New Zealand, South Africa and at times Brazil and China.

Majority worldviews encompasses the vast population of the world that sit outside these wealthy, elite, minority spaces – including Africa, Central and South America, South and South East Asia and the Middle East, and also the pockets of extreme poverty and depravation in Australia, South Africa and Brazil. The majority world is the politically disempowered. Yet, this is also the world that retains the most biodiverse and precious places left on Earth; a factor that is of core importance to this book.

These first two elements – my involvement with the subject, and a minority and majority worldview – led rather naturally to my philosophical home of normative international relations.

Inhabiting the shadowland – normative international relations and rooted cosmopolitanism

Our present-day understanding of politics has become a muted, depoliticised discussion. We have become accustomed to politics focused on the authority of the state and the decisions the state makes on our behalf. We have lost our connection to politics originating with the 'polis', or the political community, as was so eloquently described by Aristotle many years ago.

By muting half of the discussion we have given greater legitimacy to a one-sided consideration. We have hampered our ability to discuss hard questions about agency and authority. We have persuaded ourselves that all problems are addressed through control by the state.[79] Whole academic disciplines have grown around this state-centred perspective. While politics (the ability to decide which things ought to be done) is confined to the state, power (the ability to get things done) is shifting quickly to the transnational.[39] Only a few scholars are examining the capacity and perhaps even the legitimacy of the state system as the sole mediator between the global and the local, especially when the individual capacity of different states is unequal.[80]

Most of us agree that the democratic ideal is that political power and governance at all levels should involve the polis – the people. Yet, beyond the state no such ideals are applied.[45, 81] On the international stage civil society has precious few rights, is mostly forced to request access and has only very limited influence. There is no participatory discussion, no mechanism to seek redress. There is no accountability.[82]

Normative international relations scholars suggest that it is time to reimagine politics: to accommodate changes now and to discuss what we might become. This is an academic tradition focused on the status of moral responsibility in the world system. There are many strands within the tradition. Some focus on understanding the character of moral argument in the context of world affairs. Many are involved in 'engaged scholarship'. To borrow a phrase from Paul Wapner, they 'work not only in the academy but also in the street ... negotiating ways to advance certain political agendas'.[45, 80, 83–85]

I stand among this group of scholars who, united, assert that basic democratic principles should be applied to the international world order as well. Normative international relations scholars contemplate the world from many worldviews, not dominated by United States of America or European perspectives. Indeed, contributions beyond social science are also beneficial, as historical, philosophical and literary approaches add to our shared understanding of world politics.[83, 86, 87]

A great many of the myriad of different environmental issues manifest across boundaries – be they physical, jurisdictional or cultural – and are often addressed by groups of people that come from different countries, regions, language groups or cultural backgrounds.[88] Often they share something in common – the ecological region in which they live.

Species movements and the interconnected nature of ecological systems drive the transnational thinking of people concerned about the environment, but the growth of transnational coordination is unique to our time – borderless communication, broader education, the reach of English as the *lingua franca* and access to information half a world away.[89] There is an explosion of literature on the growth of civil society engagement, and especially global civil society.[90–94] It is increasingly obvious that movements and groups with shared goals are constructing and intentionally working through transnational networks.[88] Understanding how these transnational networks can serve local communities in ecological regions including their wildlife members can be assisted by the concept of cosmopolitanism.

Cosmopolitanism is a philosophy and political theory in dynamic growth,[95–97] with diverse scholars exploring how it applies to contemporary society. Its critics caution that it reflects western values and the interest of the individual, and serves to subjugate the majority world. Indeed, if that was the frame then I would also reject it as a useful lens. Cosmopolitanism has many philosophical roots including Hinduism and Confucius. The Vedic civilisation and Buddhism imagine also the world as one. The idea of belonging to a global community of humankind is neither unique nor exclusive to European civilisation. Originally it probably moved east to west and south to north.[98] It also has many branches: from political cosmopolitanism that seeks a system of nations without nationalism; moral cosmopolitanism that strives to form universal conceptions of justice, equality and virtue;[99] to a number of forms of what the philosopher Anthony Appiah calls rooted cosmopolitanism.[100] This is a form of cosmopolitanism that balances local and larger moral claims while expanding and enriching individuals' understanding of self, the other and the world. Rooted cosmopolitanism includes local communities who reach out to other similar communities half a world away, immigrant activists involved in transnational politics related to their country or origin, activists from the majority world who strategically form ties with activists in the minority world to increase their reach into international institutions and the occasional participants in international protests campaigns.[101] This was packaged in the 1990s by Margaret Keck and Kathryn Sikkink as 'activists without borders'.[91]

I am compelled by the reality that the world has changed. Very few communities are truly isolated now. Information and ideas flow powerfully around the world, with little impediment or control.[102] It is virtually impossible not to know about the diversity of humanity. If we don't consciously empower communities, as means for individual voices to be expressed, we risk the very thing that cosmopolitan critics fear – homogenised culture driven and fed by an elite.

Evaluating stories together is one of the central human ways of learning to align our responses to the world. That alignment of responses is, in turn, one of the ways we maintain the social fabric, the texture of our relationships.[100] By empowering the subjective voices of local, traditional and indigenous people and their often broader perspective about who is within their community, including in many cases non-human animals as well[55] – providing them the space to fuse 'a reflective openness to the new with a reflective loyalty to the known' – ecologically informed management strategies can be formed.[88] The points of entry to these cross-cultural complex conversations are things that are shared by those who are part of the conversation. They do not need to be universal; all they need to be is what these particular people have in common.[100]

In my experience, and that of some scholars, many civil society networks engaged with environmental concerns already ascribed to a form of rooted cosmopolitanism[88] – these are many individuals, more commonly involved in domestic politics or movements, who reach beyond their base to join an international network.[101] They regularly 'meet' either physically or electronically. They share information and draw on international materials from webpages, reports, discussions forums and journals to pursue mutual goals. They respect, listen and learn from the perspectives of their network. They then apply their broader knowledge and the agreement they develop to their localised efforts to protect what is culturally and socially important to their community.[89]

The activities of these network actors are informed and influenced by the social and political systems they seek to influence or work within. Through association with others in their network individuals shape their perspectives and views of their own community and its place in the world. They move, communicate and absorb information from outside, but continue to be linked to their place of origin, their individual social environment and their surroundings that offer meaning as well as resources, experiences and opportunities. Their most important ties are domestic, but they participate in the complex of international society.[89, 100] They are the 'connective tissue' between the global and the local, working as activators, brokers and advocates for claims that are both domestic and international.[103] While a great many rooted cosmopolitan actors focus on domestic issues, some participate in United Nations or MEA processes – which comprise nearly all of the most important environmental negotiations – as a means to pressure for change.

Within civil society organized, often professional, NGOs also operate. Some NGOs deliberately operate within, and engage with, established global environmental governance space that includes governments, intergovernmental organisations (IGOs) and individual experts on a range of issues. Other NGOs maintain a focus on raising public awareness on specific issues.[90, 94] Many specialist NGOs contribute considerable work and effort to policy agendas of these processes. They recognise a role of work within the system and not against it and so adhere to norms, codes of conduct and to be bound to the protocols and the culture of the international diplomatic community, as willing participants in the traditional vertical governance structure. This increases trust and builds important relationships. They consciously nest themselves within the process in which they are working.[62, 104, 105] They typically have capacity and time to focus on the detail of specific issues between and during meetings in ways government delegations, especially those that are small and under-resourced, struggle to match.[90–93] They employ skilled negotiators and diplomats that understand the pulse and process of international policy, many of whom have a longer history of direct experience with key environment conventions and more technical knowledge about the issues being discussed than some of their government counterparts.[70, 106] Much of their diplomacy is focused on leveraging transboundary or 'borderless' information into the essentially state-based system of international governance, but their conception of public diplomacy[101] is more in tune with the social reality of vanishing borders between domestic and international.

When these professionalised NGOs operate as rooted cosmopolitans, working as a part of transnational civil society networks, learning and being influenced by others, there is considerable strength. They increase the power and resources of otherwise marginalised voices.[88] Sadly, this type of partnership is rare. More often than not minority world NGOs choose to operate as autonomous actors serving the mandate of their organisation and the existing global neoliberal power structure. They join the transnational elite. Their positioning reinforces their own construction of nature, the environment and human relationships with the wild, silencing different interpretations and viewpoints.[107] These transnational elite control funding and policy directions, and discipline populations into accepting conditionality attached to aid and support, including a neoliberal market acceptance. They serve a limited, toothless version of environmentalism that ignores the colonial debt of historical resources harvest.[88, 107] Unlike the rooted cosmopolitans above, these actors learn little from others and instead subjugate communities, including the non-human animals members, in their quest for a homogenised world. To borrow from Thomas Berry they cease to be a 'communion of subjects' and become a 'collection of objects'.[108]

Cosmopolitanism responds to the knowledge that there are issues we must grapple with that are beyond the capacity or the powers of states. It provides the principles of building democratic culture from the local to the global – to be a conduit for local information, through the layers of national process and in global governance.[82, 109, 110] Like many international issues, current MEAs are deficient along what David Held has called the democratic fault lines of inclusiveness and accountability.[82]

My thesis is that we must expand political authority beyond the commonly held idea of sovereignty and nation states to include a greater polity that involves, and also attributes rights in, international discourse. My work contributes to the normative international relations tradition as engaged scholarship.

Occupying Richard Falk's shadowland has inspired this book and the metaphor of a storm that carries the thread from this chapter to the end. My overriding intent is to tell the story of my own professional journey and the often bleak conclusions I have personally come to at this unique and important point in human history.

I follow the academic conventions of fair description, analysis and argument. I believe in them. I want, above all, not to disparage the lifelong efforts of many who have advanced the various disciplines I skim over in this book. Nor do I seek to disparage the efforts of activists everywhere who have worked for wildlife conservation. I respect everyone's integrity, commitment and keenness of insight. Yet, I am moved by Herman Daly and John Cobb who, in 1994, wrote:

> [that it was hard] to suppress the cry of anguish, the scream of horror – the wild words required to express wild realities. We human beings are being led to a dead end – all too literally. We are living by an ideology of death and accordingly we are destroying our own humanity and killing the planet.[111]

I cannot find better words to express what compels me to write. Complex ideas are often best illuminated by real world stories. I offer mine while I discuss how we can carve out an alternative for our future.

References

[1] World Meteorological Organization. 2016. State of the Climate: Record Heat and Weather Extremes. Geneva, World Meteorological Organization.

[2] World Meteorological Organization. 2016. Hurricane Committee Reviews 2015 Season, Prepares for 2016 One. [online material]

[3] World Meteorological Organization. 2016. Climate and Health Experts in South Asia Act on Heatwaves. [online material]

[4] Slangen, A. B. A., Church, J. A., Agosta, C., Fettweis, X., Marzeion, B. and Richter, K. 2016. Anthropogenic Forcing Dominates Global Mean Sea-level Rise since 1970. *Nature Climate Change*. [advance online publication]

[5] Krummel, P. and Fraser, P. 2016. Southern Hemisphere Joins North in Breaching Carbon Dioxide Milestone. *The Conversation*. [online material]

[6] Field, C. B., Dokken, D. J., Mastrandrea, M. D., et al., eds. 2014. *Climate Change 2014: Impacts, Adaptation, and Vulnerability. Part A: Regional Aspects*. Edited by Intergovernmental Panel on Climate Change, Contribution of Working Group II to the Fifth Assessment Report of the Intergovernmental Panel on Climate Change. Cambridge: Cambridge University Press.

[7] Douglas, D. C. 2010. Arctic Sea Ice Decline: Projected Changes in Timing and Extent of Sea Ice in the Bering and Chukchi Seas. U.S. Geological Survey Open-File Report, U. S. Department of the Interior.

[8] Bintanja, R., Van Oldenborgh, G. J., Drijfhout, S. S., Wouters, B. and Katsman, C. A. 2013. Important Role for Ocean Warming and Increased Ice-shelf Melt in Antarctic Sea–Ice expansion. *Nature Geoscience*. 6, 5: 376–379.

[9] Kelman, I. 2015. Difficult Decisions: Migration from Small Island Developing States under Climate Change. *Earth's Future*. 3, 4: 133–142.

[10] Weber, E. 2015. Envisioning South-South Relations in the Fields of Environmental Change and Migration in the Pacific Islands – Past, Present and Futures. *Bandung Journal of the Global South*. 2, 1: 6.

[11] Gobiet, A., Kotlarski, S., Beniston, M., Heinrich, G., Rajczak, J. and Stoffel, M. 2013. 21st Century Climate Change in the European Alps – A Review. *Science of the Total Environment*. 493: 1138–1141.

12 Haeberli, W., Hoelzle, M., Paul, F. and Zemp, M. 2007. Integrated Monitoring of Mountain Glaciers as Key Indicators of Global Climate Change: the European Alps. *Annals of Glaciology.* 46, 1: 150–160.

13 Harlan, S. L. and Ruddell, D. M. 2011. Climate Change and Health in Cities: Impacts of Heat and Air Pollution and Potential Co-benefits from Mitigation and Adaptation. *Current Opinion in Environmental Sustainability.* 3, 3: 126–134.

14 Langerwisch, F., Rost, S., Gerten, D., Poulter, B., Rammig, A. and Cramer, W. 2013. Potential Effects of Climate Change on Inundation Patterns in the Amazon Basin. *Hydrology and Earth System Sciences.* 17, 6: 2247–2262.

15 Marengo, J. A., Tomasella, J., Soares, W. R., Alves, L. M. and Nobre, C. A. 2012. Extreme Climatic Events in the Amazon Basin. *Theoretical and Applied Climatology.* 107, 1–2: 73–85.

16 Solecki, W., Leichenko, R. and O'Brien, K. 2011. Climate Change Adaptation Strategies and Disaster Risk Reduction in Cities: Connections, Contentions, and Synergies. *Current Opinion in Environmental Sustainability.* 3, 3: 135–141.

17 Klein, N. 2014. *This Changes Everything: Capitalism vs. the Climate.* New York: Simon and Schuster.

18 Intergovernmental Panel on Climate Change. 2014. Climate Change 2014: Synthesis Report. Contribution of Working Groups I, II and III to the Fifth Assessment Report of the Intergovernmental Panel on Climate Change. Edited by Pachauri, R. K. and Meyer, L. A. Geneva, Switzerland: IPCC: 151.

19 Burke, M., Hsiang, S. M. and Miguel, E. 2015. Global Non-linear Effect of Temperature on Economic Production. *Nature.* [advance online publication]

20 Bellard, C., Bertelsmeier, C., Leadley, P., Thuiller, W. and Courchamp, F. 2012. Impacts of Climate Change on the Future of Biodiversity. *Ecology Letters.* 15, 4: 365–377.

21 Jetz, W., Wilcove, D. S. and Dobson, A. P. 2007. Projected Impacts of Climate and Land-use Change on the Global Diversity of Birds. *PLoS Biology.* 5, 6: e157.

22 Lovejoy, T. and Hannah, L. 2012. *Saving a Million Species: Extinction Risk from Climate Change.* Washington, DC: Island Press.

23 Pimm, S. L., Jenkins, C. N., Abell, R., Brooks, T. M., Gittleman, J. L., Joppa, L. N., Raven, P. H., Roberts, C. M. and Sexton, J. O. 2014. The Biodiversity of Species and Their Rates of Extinction, Distribution, and Protection. *Science.* 344, 6187.

24 Thomas, C. D., Cameron, A., Green, R. E., et al. 2004. Extinction Risk from Climate Change. *Nature.* 427, 6970: 145–148.

25 Urban, M. C. 2015. Accelerating Extinction Risk from Climate Change. *Science.* 348, 6234: 571–573.

26 Intergovernmental Panel on Climate Change. 2015. Organization: Structure. [online material]

27 Levin, K. 2015. Insider: Why Are INDC Studies Reaching Different Temperature Estimates?World Resources Institute. [online material]

28 Selin, H. and Najam, A. 2015. Paris Agreement on Climate Change: The Good, the Bad, and the Ugly. *The Conversation.* [online material]

29 Reyes, O. 2015. Seven Wrinkles in the Paris Climate Deal. Foreign Policy in Focus. [online material]

30 Anderson, K. 2015. The Paris Agreement: 10/10 for Presentation; 4/10 for Content. Shows Promise. UK Tyndall Centre. [online material]

31 Hamilton, C. 2015. Good Deal or Bad? Emotional Turmoil as Paris Climate Talks Draw to a Close. *The Conversation.* [online material]

32 Vale, P. 2015. COP21: Global Climate Agreement Reached at United Nations Talks in Paris. *The Huffington Post*, 12th December 2015.

33 Gore, A. 2012. Statement by Former Vice President Al Gore on the Paris Agreement Reached at the United Nations Framework Convention on Climate Change's 21st Conference of the Parties (COP21). www.algore.com. [online material]

34 Bloomberg, M. 2015. Statement on COP21 Agreement. http://www.mikebloom berg.com. [online material]

35 Lynn, W. 2015. The Ethics of Climate Change: What We Owe People – and the Rest of the Planet. *The Conversation*. [online material]

36 Burke, A., Fishel, S., Mitchell, A., Dalby, S. and Levine, D. J. 2016. Planet Politics: A Manifesto from the End of IR. *Millennium – Journal of International Studies*. 44, 3: 499–523.

37 Crutzen, P. J. 2006. The 'Anthropocene'. In *Earth System Science in the Anthropocene*. Edited by Ehlers, E. and Krafft, T. Heidelberg: Springer: 13–18.

38 Krasner, S. D. 1999. *Sovereignty: Organized Hypocrisy*. Princeton: Princeton University Press.

39 Phillips, L. 2016. The Global Post-Democratic Order. In *State of Power 2016*. Amsterdam: Transnational Institute.

40 Risse, T. 2012. Governance in Areas of Limited Statehood. In *The Oxford Handbook of Governance*. Edited by Levi-Faur, D. Oxford: Oxford University Press: 724–740.

41 Buxton, N. 2014. The Great Divide: Exposing the Davos Class behind Global Economic Inequality. In *State of Civil Society Report: 2014*. Edited by Firmin, A., Pegus, C. M. and Tiwana, M. New York: CIVICUS: World Alliance for Citizen Participation: 145–149.

42 Gleckman, H. 2016. Multi-stakeholderism: A Corporate Push for a New Form of Global Governance. In *State of Power 2016*. Amsterdam: Transnational Institute.

43 Glennie, J. 2015. Financing the Sustainable Development Goals Will Rely Heavily on the Tax Factor. *The Guardian online*, 23th July 2015.

44 Falk, R. 2014. *(Re)Imagining Humane Global Governance*. London: Routledge.

45 Falk, R. and Strauss, A. 2001. Toward Global Parliament. *Foreign Affairs*. 80, 1: 212–220.

46 Biermann, F., Abbott, K., Andresen, S., et al. 2012. Transforming Governance and Institutions for Global Sustainability: Key Insights from the Earth System Governance Project. *Current Opinion in Environmental Sustainability*. 4, 1: 51–60.

47 Robertson, H. A., Dowding, J. E., Elliott, G. P., et al. 2013. Conservation Status of New Zealand Birds, 2012. *New Zealand Threat Classification Series*. 4: 22.

48 Gomez, L., Leupen, B. T. C., Theng, M., Fernandez, K. and Savage, M. 2016. *Illegal Otter Trade*. Selangor: TRAFFIC/Otter Specialist Group.

49 Hinton, J. W., Brzeski, K. E., Rabon Jr, D. R. and Chamberlain, M. J. 2015. Effects of Anthropogenic Mortality on Critically Endangered Red Wolf Canis rufus Breeding Pairs: Implications for Red Wolf Recovery. *ORYX. FirstView*: 1–8.

50 Pilfold, N. W., McCall, A., Derocher, A. E., Lunn, N. J. and Richardson, E. 2016. Migratory Response of Polar Bears to Sea Ice Loss: To Swim or Not to Swim. *Ecography*: n/a.

51 Jathar, G. and Rahmani, A. 2013. Ecology of the Critically Endangered Forest Owlet Heteroglaux blewitti. In *Rare Animals of India*. Edited by Singaravelan, N. Bussum: Bentham Science Publishers: 101–112.

52 Luczon, A. U., Fontanilla, I. K. C., Ong, P. S., Basiao, Z. U., Sumaya, A. M. T. and Quilang, J. P. 2014. Genetic Diversity of the Critically Endangered Philippine Eagle Pithecophaga jefferyi (Aves: Accipitridae) and Notes on Its Conservation. *Journal of Threatened Taxa*. 6, 10: 6335–6344.

53 Marsh, C., Link, A., King-Bailey, G. and Donati, G. 2016. Effects of Fragment and Vegetation Structure on the Population Abundance of Ateles hybridus, Alouatta seniculus and Cebus albifrons in Magdalena Valley, Colombia. *Folia Primatologica*. 87, 1: 17–30.

54 Frommel, A. Y., Margulies, D., Wexler, J. B., Stein, M. S., Scholey, V. P., Williamson, J. E., Bromhead, D., Nicol, S. and Havenhand, J. 2016. Ocean Acidification Has Lethal and Sub-lethal Effects on Larval Development of Yellowfin Tuna, Thunnus albacares. *Journal of Experimental Marine Biology and Ecology*. 482: 18–24.

55 Mendieta, E. 2010. Interspecies Cosmopolitanism. *Philosophy Today*. 54, Supplement: 208–216.

56 Tucker, M. E. 2006. A Communion of Subjects and a Multiplicity of Intelligences. In *A Communion of Subjects: Animals in Religion, Science, and Ethics*. Edited by Waldau, P. and Patton, K. New York, Columbia University Press: 5–10.

57 Knudtson, P. and Suzuki, D. 1992. *Wisdom of the Elders*. North Sydney: Allen and Unwin.

58 Brakes, P. and Dall, S. R. X. 2016. Marine Mammal Behavior: A Review of Conservation Implications. *Frontiers in Marine Science*. 3.

59 Poole, J. H. and Moss, C. J., 2008. Elephant Sociality and Complexity: The Scientific Evidence. In *Elephants and Ethics: Towards a Morality of Coexistence*. Edited by Wemmer, C. and Christen, C. A. Baltimore: Johns Hopkins University Press.

60 Brosnan, S. F., Grady, M. F., Lambeth, S. P., Schapiro, S. J. and Beran, M. J. 2008. Chimpanzee Autarky. *PLoS ONE*. 3, 1: e1518.

61 Nixon, R. 2011. *Slow Violence and the Environmentalism of the Poor*. Cambridge: Harvard University Press.

62 Young, O. R. 1999. *Governance in World Affairs*. London: Cornell University Press.

63 Young, O. R. and Levy, M. A. 1999. The Effectiveness of International Environmental Regimes. In *The Effectiveness of International Environmental Regimes: Causal Connections and Behavioural Mechanisms*. Edited by Young, O. R. Cambridge: MIT Press: 1–32.

64 Keohane, R. O. 1996. Analyzing the Effectiveness of International Environmental Institutions. In *Institutions for Environmental Aid*. Edited by Keohane, R. O. and Levy, M. A. Cambridge: MIT Press: 3–28.

65 Young, O. R. 1994. *International Governance: Protecting the Environment in a Stateless Society*. Ithaca: Cornell University Press.

66 Haas, P. M., Keohane, R. O. and Levy, M. A. 1995. Improving the Effectiveness of International Environmental Institutions. In *Institutions for the Earth: Sources of Effective International Environmental Protection*. Edited by Haas, P. M., Keohane, R. O. and Levy, M. A. Cambridge: MIT Press: 397–427.

67 Haas, P. M., Keohane, R. O. and Levy, M. A. 1995. The Effectiveness of International Environmental Institutions. In *Institutions for the Earth: Sources of Effective International Environmental Protection*. Edited by Haas, P. M., Keohane, R. O. and Levy, M. A. Cambridge: MIT Press: 3–27.

68 Young, O. R. 1999. Regime Effectiveness: Taking Stock. In *The Effectiveness of International Environmental Regimes: Causal Connections and Behavioural Mechanisms*. Edited by Young, O. Cambridge: MIT Press: 249–280.

69 Rogers, E. and Weber, E. P. 2010. Thinking Harder About Outcomes for Collaborative Governance Arrangements. *The American Review of Public Administration*. 40, 5: 546–567.

70 Prideaux, M. 2015. Wildlife NGOs: From Adversaries to Collaborators. *Global Policy*. 6, 4: 379–388.

71 Ansell, C. and Gash, A. 2008. Collaborative Governance in Theory and Practice. *Journal of Public Administration Research and Theory*. 18, 4: 543–571.

72 Emerson, K., Nabatchi, T. and Balogh, S. 2012. An Integrative Framework for Collaborative Governance. *Journal of Public Administration Research and Theory*. 22, 1: 1–29.

73 Doyle, T. 2005. *Environmental Movements in Majority and Minority Worlds: A Global Perspective*. New Brunswick, NJ: Rutgers University Press.

74 Doherty, B. and Doyle, T. 2006. Beyond Borders: Transnational Politics, Social Movements and Modern Environmentalisms. *Environmental Politics*. 15, 5: 697–712.

75 Peña, G. J. 2015. Is Development a Form of Neo-Colonialism? *Dialéctica Libertadora*. 7: 36–42.

76 Obeng-Odoom, F. 2015. Africa's Development post 2015: A Critical Defence of Postcolonial Thinking. *Journal of Pan African Studies*. 8, 1: 37–46.

77 Alkire, S. and Santos, M. E. 2014. Measuring Acute Poverty in the Developing World: Robustness and Scope of the Multidimensional Poverty Index. *World Development*. 59: 251–274.

78 Alkire, S., Roche, J. M., Seth, S. and Sumner, A. 2015. Identifying the Poorest People and Groups: Strategies Using the Global Multidimensional Poverty Index. *Journal of International Development*. 27, 3: 362–387.

79 Walker, R. B. J. 2000. Both Globalisation and Sovereignty: Re-Imagining the Political. In *Principled World Politics: The Challenges of Normative International Relations*. Edited by Wapner, P. and Ruiz, L. E. J. Lanham: Rowman & Littlefield Publishers.

80 Falk, R. 2002. *Reframing the Legal Agenda of World Order in the Course of a Turbulent Century*. New York: Routledge.

81 Strauss, A. J. 2002. Overcoming the Dysfunction of the Bifurcated Global System: The Promise of a People's Assembly. In *Reframing the International: Law, Culture, Politics*. Edited by Falk, R., Ruiz, L. E. J. and Walker, R. B. J. London: Routledge: 83–106.

82 Held, D. 2010. *Cosmopolitanism: Ideals and Realities*. Cambridge: Polity Press.

83 Wapner, P. 2000. Resurgence and Metamorphosis of Normative International Relations: Principles Commitment and Scholarship in a New Millennium. In *Principled World Politics: The Challenge of Normative International Relations*. Edited by Wapner, P. and Ruiz, L. E. J. New York: Rowman and Littlefield: 1–21.

84 Falk, R. 2010. A Radical World Order Challenge: Addressing Global Climate Change and the Threat of Nuclear Weapons. *Globalizations*. 7, 1/2: 137–155.

85 Wapner, P. and Ruiz, L. E. J., eds. 2000. *Principled World Politics: The Challenge of Normative International Relations.* Lanham: Rowman & Littlefield Publishers.

86 Ruiz, L. E. J. 2000. Culture, Politics and the Sense of the Ethical: Challenges for Normative International Relations. In *Principled World Politics: The Challenge of Normative International Relations.* Edited by Wapner, P., Ruiz, L. E. J. Lanham: Rowman and Littlefield: 322–348.

87 Falk, R. 2003. Politically Engaged Spirituality in an Emerging Global Civil Society. *ReVision.* 25, 4: 2–10.

88 Doyle, T. and Doherty, B. 2013. Green Public Spheres and Green Governance: The Politics of Emancipation and Ecological Conditionality. In *Beyond Borders: Environmental Movements and Transnational Politics.* Edited by Doherty, B. and Doyle, T. London: Routledge.

89 Tarrow, S. 2005. *The New Transnational Activism.* Cambridge: Cambridge University Press.

90 Chayes, A. and Chayes, A. H. 1998. *The New Sovereignty: Compliance with International Regulatory Agreements.* Cambridge: Harvard University Press.

91 Keck, M. E. and Sikkink, K. 1998. *Activists beyond Borders: Advocacy Networks in International Politics.* Cambridge: Cambridge University Press.

92 Clark, J. 2003. *Worlds Apart: Civil Society and the Battle for Ethical Globalisation.* London, Earthscan.

93 La Porte, T. 2012. The Impact of 'Intermestic' Non-State Actors on the Conceptual Framework of Public Diplomacy. *The Hague Journal of Diplomacy.* 7, 4: 441–458.

94 Karns, M. P. and Mingst, K. A. 2004. *International Organisations: The Politics and Processes of Global Governance.* London: Lynne Rienner Publishers.

95 Benhabib, S. 2014. Defending Cosmopolitanism without Illusions. Reply to My Critics. *Critical Review of International Social and Political Philosophy.* 17, 6: 697–715.

96 Mendieta, E. 2009. From Imperial to Dialogical Cosmopolitanism? *Ethics and Global Politics,* 2, 3.

97 Prieto-Rios, E. and Koram, K. 2015. Decolonising Epistemologies, Politicising Rights: An Interview with Eduardo Mandieta. *Birkbeck L. Rev.* 3: 13.

98 Leinius, J. 2014. Decolonizing Cosmopolitanism in Practice: From Universalizing Monologue to Intercultural Dialogue? In *Cosmopolitanism and Transnationalism: Visions, Ethics, Practices.* Edited by Kaunonen, L. Helsinki: Helsinki Collegium for Advanced Studies: 39–65.

99 Hansen, D. T. 2010. Chasing Butterflies without a Net: Interpreting Cosmopolitanism. *Studies in Philosophy and Education.* 29, 2: 151–166.

100 Appiah, K. A. 2006. *Cosmopolitanism: Ethics in a World of Strangers.* London: Allen Lane.

101 Tarrow, S. and Della Porta, D. 2005. Conclusion: 'Globalization,' Complex Internationalism, and Transnational Contention. In *Transnational Protest and Global Activism.* Edited by Della Porta, D. and Tarrow, S. Lanham: Rowman & Littlefield: 227–246.

102 Kahne, J., Middaugh, E. and Allen, D. 2015. Youth, New Media, and the Rise of Participatory Politics. In *From Voice to Influence: Understanding Citizenship in a Digital Age.* Edited by Allen, D. and Light, J. S. Chicago: University of Chicago Press.

103 Tilly, C. and Tarrow, S. G. 2015. *Contentious Politics.* Oxford: Oxford University Press.

104 Young, O. R. 1989. *International Cooperation: Building Regimes for Natural Resources and the Environment.* London, Cornell University Press.

105 Young, O. R. 2008. The Architecture of Global Environmental Governance: Bringing Science to Bear on Policy. *Global Environmental Politics.* 8, 1: 14–32.

106 Betsill, M. M. 2008. Reflections on the Analytical Framework and NGO Diplomacy. In *NGO Diplomacy: The Influence of Nongovernmental Organisations in International Environmental Negotiations.* Edited by Betsill, M. M. and Corell, E. Cambridge: MIT Press: 177–206.

107 Doherty, B. and Doyle, T. 2013. *Environmentalism, Resistance and Solidarity: The Politics of Friends of the Earth International.* New York: Springer.

108 Berry, T. 2006. Prologue: Loneliness and Presence. In *A Communion of Subjects: Animals in Religion, Science, and Ethics.* Edited by Waldau, P. and Patton, K. New York: Columbia University Press: 5–10.

109 Held, D. 2009. Restructuring Global Governance: Cosmopolitanism, Democracy and the Global Order. *Millennium-Journal of International Studies.* 37, 3: 535–547.

110 Held, D. 2013. Cosmopolitanism in a Multipolar World. In *After Cosmopolitanism.* Edited by Braidotti, R., Hanafin, P. and Blaagaard, B. London: Routledge: 28–39.

111 Daly, H. E. and Cobb, J. B. 1994. *For the Common Good: Redirecting the Economy toward Community, the Environment and a Sustainable Future.* Boston: Beacon Press.

2   Storm on the horizon

Gorillas in Rwanda – a personal journey

It was a hot and muggy day in November 2005. I stood in the terminal of Kigali Airport, Rwanda, my energy frayed. Seven days of intense intergovernmental discussions in Kenya had taken a toll. The organisation I worked for had boldly and optimistically reached for recognition of nongovernmental organisation (NGO) work in conserving wildlife. Our case had been months in careful preparation and I had rolled up my sleeves for the contest.

In honesty, I still went into the meeting expecting defeat. Governments don't usually like to recognise that NGOs contribute much value to the world. So, I was still reeling from our unexpected, albeit incremental, success and hadn't adjusted my disbelief yet. It was surreal to now be standing at the border to Rwanda; like moving from one waking dream into another.

Border control ushered through all my colleagues from Europe and North America without delay or question. Yet, here I was with my Australian papers, a headache and exhausted legs that were threatening to crumble beneath me at any moment. An eternity seemed to pass with each page turn. Never before has a passport been so closely studied. I was so tired.

Rwanda was then and now a country deep in unimaginable pain – slowly adjusting to being demographically young, after the massacre of its mature and wise population just 11 years earlier. During the Rwandan Genocide 500,000–1,000,000 Tutsi and moderate Hutu were slaughtered by their countrymen between April and July of 1994. This was probably 20 per cent of the country's total population and 70 per cent of the Tutsi then living in Rwanda. Coverage of the Rwandan civil war and the genocide received a few mentions through international media, but it was a war half a world away for many. As I stood at this fragile county's border I knew that many people in Europe, North America and Australia had already forgotten the tragedy.

At last I stepped across into the country and directly onto a small bus that bounced over the rutted road of Kigali and swiftly out into the countryside. After months of anticipation we were on our way to see mountain gorillas.

Hours of thin roads snaked through crop-covered hillsides. Men, woman and children stood by the road in occasional groups. It took some time for me to be conscious of the missing element. There was almost no-one with age etched into their face. No creases echoed back wisdom or experience. I wondered how a country bereft of its elders could cope in the world.

The slow punctuation of simple one-room mud huts and makeshift stock yards, eventually gave way to a denser rural population. Dozens of tightly grouped shanties were separated by small fields of sustenance crops. The earth was rich and dark. The cropping was basic human toil. An agrarian snapshot most of us recognise, but vicariously. Adults bent double, tending their daily food.

I guiltily smiled at the too-familiar scene of children chasing the bus yelling 'pen – pen – pen'. In my travels around the world I knew this chant very well. Poverty asked for such small tokens of progress.

In time the human density grew thicker, and people now hung even closer to the road. The casual ease of their nearness to the dangers of a bouncing, bounding bus was unsettling. Mothers stood in door frames with infants on their hips. Behind them, in small, dark rooms other women bent over cooking fires.

Hut after hut passed, and I sank deep into thought.

My internal reflections were splintered as we turned into a driveway and through a tall gate. Suddenly we were still. At rest, in a serenely quiet compound. Large trees on the edge of dense woodland marked the boundary. An oasis of soundless shade. The children's voices were silent echoes in my mind. Ahead, hushed and large, was our hotel.

It was beautiful. Yet my heart flipped in my chest as I realised that this town of people, tilling the soil as their children ran after the bus, was a constellation around a space designed for wealthy gorilla trekkers. We were an island of the 'minority' standing in a sea of the 'majority'.

Was this what it meant to save gorillas? My soul ached at the thought.

The next morning had us back in our bounding bus for a short ride to the interpretive centre. Earnest, educated and articulate locals explained the plight of the gorillas and the international conservation efforts on their behalf. They spoke of researchers from Europe and America. They spoke of international campaigns. They didn't mention the community surrounding the centre. We heard nothing about their crops or their lives. The signs and the materials were handmade, raw and genuine, yet I recognised the 'westernness' of the message they contained, planted there by NGOs from afar.

Without doubt, questions were influencing my experience of the day. I love wildlife and have invested my life in wildlife protection, without compromise. But by 2005 I was starting to question the wisdom of imposing solutions on people from other worldviews. I was also uneasy about the conservation movement developing tourism dependency in communities, without a corresponding conservation commitment that would endure if the tourism evaporated. I came to this gorilla trek with these questions in mind. Aware that I was taking part in the system I was self-consciously interrogating, I wanted to experience another layer. I wanted to understand whether the conservation effort was serving the gorillas and the community. Without doubt, it was to be a memorable day and would change me profoundly.

After another short bus ride we began our trek up the first of many hills; led by confident and quiet local guides. They kept each other's company rather than engaging with the trekkers. Notably these fit and agile men carried guns. The trek went on for hours as we climbed one hill after the next, tumbling into the valleys between. At times we walked sideways around the hillsides, following signs of the gorillas – their beds from the previous night, their breakfast grazing, the echo of a youngster's somersault tumble in the vegetation. Occasionally the guides called out a series of deep, resonant sounds. It was a shared language between humans and these gorillas, they shyly explained. They were letting the silverback know we were approaching. They were seeking his permission to come closer. I asked what would happen if he said 'no'. 'We would leave' was the assured answer.

The jungle around us was dense, lush, expansive and alive. In truth I would have been happy to have just been on this mountain. The trip would have been worthwhile. Birds and insects hummed and buzzed, called and sang everywhere that my senses reached.

Then it rained. Distant views disappeared and the world contracted to a series of beautiful rain-soaked trees around us. Between raindrops the air was thick mist, almost as if we had been transported to a cloud.

We crouched huddled for a while. The dialogue between our guides and gorillas began again. The family was approaching. Two of our guides disappeared quietly through the curtain of rain. When they returned we were edged quietly out and onto a tangle of vines growing from the side of a steep hill. The rain eased.

Inept in this environment, I focused on finding a foothold and readied myself to scan for gorillas some distance away. When I looked up, it was directly into eyes that touched my soul. Only metres away, she was one of the elders of the group. I could recognise so much in that gaze. My mind tumbled with a complex mixture of guilt and awe. I was overwhelmingly grateful for the honour of meeting her and deeply apologetic for invading her family's peace and space.

To my left was her family. A young mother sat contentedly with an infant in her arms. Nearby a few youngsters were absorbed in their meal, their dark heads cloaked in a twinkling blanket of water droplets. Further along the hill were more black shapes, gorillas huddled in the mist. To my right sat the silverback; on a branch he had bent to serve as a throne. He was huge. A majestic sovereign. It was indubitable that we were in his family's presence with his permission. His posture clearly communicated the limit of this permission. Subconsciously, I registered the continuing dialogue he was having with our guides and would recall it later.

A youngster rolled down the hill from above our heads, reaching out to touch my boot as he tumbled past – a simple, but forbidden, act for us both. His freedom and joy tugged at my heart. I knew the risks his family faced every day. I knew of their precarious survival on the slimmest edge of what could sustain them. I knew the risk of disease trekkers brought. I knew of the poachers who sought to hunt them.

Tears welled while I sank into the beauty of the scene and I lost time for a while.

A guide gently touched my shoulder – a signal to move quietly back the way we had come. The audience was over.

Feeling a chasm of loss already swelling inside, I turned to go, but looked back at the eyes that had captured me moments ago. She blinked, held my gaze and imprinted a gift in my heart. It sustains me to this day.

I silently, gratefully, thanked her, and we left.

The return trek was shorter and more direct, but still took some hours and included many hills. At the foot of the mountain we clamoured over a rough stone fence that marked the boundary between wildness and fields of crops. I asked a guide what the fence was for. He explained it marked a demarcation between the gorillas and the people. Did the gorillas ever come into the croplands, I asked? He said no. I wondered, to myself, if people ventured often into the mountains. A short while later I gently asked about the guns. He replied they were for poachers on the border. I knew what this meant and didn't need to ask more. His eyes spoke volumes of the dangers he faced.

My experience transitioned somewhere in the mountains to something more reflective of the guides and their community. When we met the gorilla family it was tangible and honest. The pride the guides had in their relationship with these animals was real. The understanding between these brave young men and the silverback was their own. Unquestionably, these men knew each gorilla personally. I was confident that they shared the highs and lows of life and death with these animals. I suspected that they planned to do this work for their lifetime.

But, I was still haunted by the fact that that gorilla trekkers were being served. The whole scene – the village around the hotel, the guides and the gorillas – was for our enjoyment, like a massive amusement park for wealthy tourists. Would it endure if tourism stopped? Was this what it took to save gorillas?

Serving the minority

At one point in conservation history, tourism funding wildlife conservation was new. In countries where there was little economic incentive to protect wildlife, conservation organisations across the world understandably turned to a market-based answer. It was a good answer at the time. It provided an education opportunity for both the local community and the tourists visiting the wildlife. Without doubt, awareness about the unique and often problematic conservation needs of many species took a massive leap forward. I commend those who developed these programmes for overcoming the complications and difficulties they faced. I do not question the motivation, the integrity or the intent of any of these efforts, or the commitment of individuals involved every day. I am sure that a great many of these ventures will continue to provide an economic incentive for the future.

This is especially so for wildlife targeted by illegal hunting and trade: elephants, gorillas and many of the birds of prey. In these instances, the monetary gain of hunting and trading animal parts can easily outweigh any altruistic motivation, especially when communities are bitterly poor. The economic gain from tourism can provide a balance and offer opportunities.

But, has tourism become an easy conservation end? Have the communities surrounding wildlife asked for help or put forward their own solutions? Perhaps the most important question is if tourism evaporated would these communities still feel a commitment to protect these species? I recognise these are thorny and difficult questions. Some people will feel hurt when reading them. They are important questions to ask, because the second of those questions speaks to a bigger problem about how we govern our world in the future. Who is empowered in that world? To what extent will their guardianship endure? Will the wildlife we care so deeply about have surety as well?

The case of gorillas in Africa is a starting point for this investigation. Gorillas are found naturally in ten African countries and are protected by law in all of them. Both species are also listed in Appendix I of the Convention on International Trade in Endangered Species of Wild Fauna and Flora (CITES), which bans all forms of commercial trade in live gorillas or gorillas parts. Despite the impressive legal coverage, gorillas continue to be threatened throughout their range.[1]

Over the past 100 years, gorillas have been confronted by: disease brought in by humans; destruction and fragmentation of their habitats through logging, mining and burning; direct hunting for bushmeat; or being killed at random in ongoing conflicts, by booby traps or anti-personnel mines placed on natural travelling routes used by gorillas and man, as well as occasionally being hunted for meat.[1, 2] Theirs is a dire world.

What we think of as 'gorilla' is more complicated that just one species. The western gorilla consists of two recognised subspecies: western lowland gorillas and Cross River gorillas – both critically endangered.[3] The eastern species of gorilla consists of two subspecies, the mountain gorilla and Grauer's gorilla – both endangered.[2] I had the fortune to meet a family of mountain gorillas.

The area most critical to mountain gorilla tourism lies at the centre of the Great Lakes region of Africa – the Virunga mountain range, shared by Rwanda, Uganda and the Democratic Republic of the Congo (DRC). Each of these three countries shares borders and a transboundary park that is broken into each country's own protected area. These are Parc National des Volcans in Rwanda, Mgahinga Gorilla National Park in Uganda and Parc National des Virunga in the DRC – the last a World Heritage Site since 1979 and added to the sites of World Heritage in Danger in 1994.[4] The shared park contains about half of the region's mountain gorilla population. The Bwindi Impenetrable

National Park in Uganda is home to the other half of the mountain gorilla population.

Rwanda, Uganda, and the DRC are among the poorest countries in the world, and population densities surrounding the parks are among the highest in the world – up to 700 people per square kilometre.[5, 6] There are few places that encapsulate the concept of the disempowered majority world better than this region.

Although the Virungas were given national park status in 1925, major conservation programmes only began in the 1970s, concentrating on three broad issues: developing sustainable and economically viable gorilla-based tourism; supporting anti-poaching programmes; and launching conservation education for the local communities around the Virunga mountain range. According to a 2005 African Wildlife Foundation study, gorilla tourism in this region generates US$20.6 million per year in benefits, with 53 per cent benefiting the government and agencies, 41 per cent international actors (including funders and NGOs) and 6 per cent local communities.[7] Anecdotally I know these percentages more or less hold today.

In Rwanda, where I visited the gorillas, the reports certainly indicate that protected area forests generate positive benefits, both tangible and intangible, for the local community. There are financial gains from the sale of products to visitors and some support through national and regional revenue-sharing schemes. Miko Maekawa and colleagues reported in 2013 that the revenue-sharing scheme had disbursed an estimated US$1,830,000 to community projects since 2005. Ten schools had been constructed accommodating approximately 3,640 pupils; 88 water tanks were built providing water to around 40,000 people; and ten community associations were supported to build income-generating activities. Other community projects have included health facilities, local tile and brick factories, bee-keeping projects, seed production and storage projects, agroforestry and tree planting.[8] Similar results were reported by Ritah Tusabe and Straton Habyalimana in 2010, although they noted that at the time their report was being written the government had still not collected baselines to measure improvements in biodiversity conservation and community livelihoods. Some community members were still weighing individual benefits from poaching against the possible benefits from the collective projects.[9]

If they stand alone on the page these community benefits sound impressive. But, when the sheer population of Rwanda and the actual local community share of the benefit generated by gorilla-based tourism are considered, the gains look considerably more modest. When averaged by population, the benefits account for around US$6 per person in Rwanda.[8] Indeed, the bulk of the revenue benefits from gorilla tourism is enjoyed by the international community.[7]

Researchers found, when they interviewed the local community in neighbouring Uganda, that locals saw the park as potential gain because it helped to bring revenue to the community, but were disappointed with the amount of economic benefit it actually brought.[10] They didn't speak of protecting the gorillas because they were committed to the rights of the species to have a home. They had come to see the gorillas as a commodity.

Ambivalence cuts both ways. Other research has revealed that the trekkers – from the wealthy minority world – are not particularly interested in the community benefits either. In the main, the percentage of park revenue used to enhance local community development within the park doesn't have a significant effect on tourism demand. Gorilla trekkers go to see the gorillas, nothing more.[11]

This is a fragile situation, without deep commitment from either side. Given this, the most concerning reaction – from my perspective at least – was the high levels of community dissatisfaction with local influence in decision-making about the trekking tourism.[10]

Without doubt, the international community should be paying a greater share of the benefits directly to the local community, especially investing in local smallholder agricultural livelihoods. But, will this be enough? There are few other regions of the world so beset by environmental crime as this one.[12] Transnational environmental crime includes the obvious national illegal activities; activities with a cross-border transference and an international or global dimension; and crimes against wildlife (such as illegal hunting). I believe it also includes transgressions that are harmful to humans, environments and wildlife, regardless of legality per se, including environment-related harms that are facilitated by the state, corporations and other powerful actors. Logging, looting and destruction of gorilla habitat is an international concern, with transnational networks operating openly, illegal activity continuing with little action, and the protection of the gorilla habitat left as a local law enforcement issue.[13–15] Over the last 20 years, 140 rangers have been killed in the line of duty. Armed poachers and roving militias – who have been warring in the park since the 1990s – outnumber park rangers ten to one.[16] Oil companies are now circling and African governments say they have a moral obligation to pursue anything that might lift their countries out of grinding poverty, including drilling for oil in pristine natural environments. Villagers who have opposed oil projects in the DRC have been beaten by government soldiers.[17–19]

Conservationists, trapped inside a world order that leaves them few options, call again and again for law enforcement training, financing and particularly transboundary coordination with the judicial system, customs and international collaboration to become effective in uncovering environmental crime where it is happening.[1] Few have the capacity and depth of understanding to tackle the problem where it is controlled – in the minority world. This is because environmental crime relies on individual states to implement national legislation and actively enforce against environmentally criminal behaviour as it occurs within their own borders. Thus the minority world has extensive and impressive legislative regimes for environmental crime, but low conviction rates for crimes that have happened on the other side of the world – the majority world.[20] Minority world NGOs advocate for more action in CITES to the extent that the threats relate to illegal trade of wildlife or their parts. Some give attention to the International Criminal Police Organization (INTERPOL) and some even focus on the Convention against Transnational Organized Crime (UNTOC). Very few seek to connect local communities to these processes. Mostly, they represent their own organisational positions or perspectives.

Meanwhile, this region and many just like it suffer from 'economic leakage', where economic benefits flow to external transnational interests.[21] This fuels the engine of crime because the benefits of the criminal road outweigh the conservation one. The international NGOs invested in the ecotourism ventures could, if they chose, redress the social justice elements of the trekking businesses. Perhaps this is within reach of the community. But, denting the world of corrupt transnational actors is far beyond their reach, and their closest allies are focused on increasing border controls in situ. The community have neither distributive justice through access to natural resources and distribution of economic benefits from the gorilla tourism, nor procedural justice with any level of meaningful involvement in the process through which environmental decisions are made.[22] The community is woefully disempowered and dependent on external stakeholders.[21] What happens when times get tougher?

I left after my time with gorillas with more empathy and understanding for the commitment of the local guides directly involved with the gorillas, but my underlying concerns remained. If the decision was placed in the hands of the community – right now – what would their solution be? In the minority world, where we are focused in large cities and have absorbed generations of scientific reductionism, it is easy to forget that these discussions are not really about gorillas. They are about 'place' as a 'lived' environment, and a community's connection to that place.[23–25] They are about a communion of subjects unique to this region. People living on the hillside of Virunga know the mountains, and the species who live on them, in detail. Protecting gorillas means protecting this landscape and all the resources it offers. When a park is imposed over this landscape and people are ushered into other areas, they become reliant on the trickle down from ecotourism. It is a solution imposed from elsewhere – someone else's vision. If there is a down-turn in gorilla trekker tourism, either a result of global economic upheaval or a new fad sweeping the wildlife watching world, will the gorillas continue to enjoy the same level of protection for the community that surrounds them? Or, will poverty drive the local community back into the last remnants of forests and to perhaps succumb to illegal wildlife trade by hunting the few animals that are left?

And, with the Paris Agreement now locked in, Rwanda's meagre aid funding will be increasingly linked to climate resilience and low carbon development. Does gorilla trekking, an activity heavily dependent on international air travel, even fit this model? Since the gorillas are confined to a relatively small habitat within a high altitudinal range, changes to the habitat could have severe impacts on their population. As John Platt has aptly put it: 'When you live on the top of a mountain, you don't have many places to run if the environment of that mountain habitat changes.'[26] The future may bring pressure for both subsistence systems and cash crops such as tea and coffee that are currently produced on the lower slopes around the montane forests to move upwards to maintain suitable agro-ecological zones.[27]

The minority world NGOs involved in gorilla ecotourism may feel they are bringing the plight of the animals and the community to the attention of international process. In truth, they raise the issues, but they speak as themselves, and they stand outside of the governance process. They don't have a way of genuinely and defensibly representing the voices of the community. In my experience, NGO voices are small and easily sidelined.

As I left Rwanda I took with me the thought that, while admirable and well meaning, the gorilla tourism industry wasn't truly local nor was it independently sustainable. Gorilla trekking was a minority world solution imposed on the majority.

It was not rooted cosmopolitanism.

The Westphalian world order

To understand how such a misfit as I have described can exist requires understanding the system in which the minority world NGOs operate, their context and what influences their programmes. This requires a step back in time.

Many centuries ago the European world was carved up into parcels of land and, where land met the oceans, the adjoining sea was included as territory. Borders were agreed and within these borders, various systems of governance were formed – monarchies, dictatorships, democracies, theocracies and a myriad of other formulations. These parcels and their governance system became known as sovereign states.

Wars were fought. Borders were moved. States were subsumed into other states. States divided and became new states. All the while European mercantilism, colonialism and imperialism stretched out to subjugate the rest of the world. Gradually, the international system of sovereign states we know today took shape.[28–30]

It is unlikely that the moment happened suddenly, but many international relations scholars symbolically anchor the evolution to the Peace of Westphalia – a series of peace treaties signed between May and October 1648 in the Westphalian cities of Osnabrück and Münster. These treaties ended the Thirty Years' War (1618–1648) in the Holy Roman Empire, and the Eighty Years' War (1568–1648) with Spain formally recognising the independence of the Dutch Republic.[31]

The Peace of Westphalia established an important precedent of peace by 'diplomatic congress' – meaning officials from each of the states met to agree mutual terms. Time progressed and this new system of political order in central Europe, became known as Westphalian sovereignty, based upon the concept of co-existing sovereign states. Aggression between states was, more or less, held in check by a balance of power and a norm established against interfering in another state's domestic affairs. It is easy to slip into the fable that this took root because enlightened Europeans sought peace. In truth, it took root because it provided stability for commerce between states.

As European influence aggressively spread across the globe, the Westphalian principles of sovereignty and inter-state commerce became central to international law and to the prevailing world order.[31–33] Eventually they overtook all other pre-existing systems outside Europe. A number of treaties articulated greater levels of regulation and control on how states relate to each other and finally influenced the creation of the United Nations (UN) directly after World War II, which maintains the Westphalian principles.[34]

Most international relations scholars know this truncated version of history well, but for other disciplines it is useful to recount if only to point out that the current world order is recent and that is has facilitated the growth of economies as the primary driver for international affairs.

Even as colonised populations have thrown off the shackles of their oppressors in Africa, Asia, the Americas and the Pacific, these same populations have had little choice but to cast their newly independent 'nation states' according to the Westphalian world order. They are then pitted against economically powerful countries that have had centuries to hone their systems and establish their relationships with the economic engine. It is no wonder they struggle.

This is a simplistic snapshot of the evolution of the current order. I wish it could remain so simple, but human affairs never are. Over this same period the simple idea of sovereignty has been more carefully defined, and in seeking the definitions, many forms of sovereignty have been legally identified, each with its own rules and norms. In its simplest form Westphalian sovereignty is about the authority and legitimacy of the state, and the exclusion of external actors, whether de facto or de jure, from the territory of that state. When states are focused on exercising their authority on the population they govern, they are engaged in domestic sovereignty. When recognition is extended to territorial entities that have formal juridical independence, it is called international legal sovereignty. When states regulate movements across their borders, it is called interdependence sovereignty.[35] I mention all of these only to be clear that the world has evolved since 1648, and the rules have had to evolve with it. The evolution has still encompassed the basic principles that the states are in control, and their priority is to gain economic advantage and maintain national security to protect that advantage.

The Westphalian world order has not evolved because diplomats are all inherently selfish. Our world order emerged through the political negotiations in the 1600s, long before there was recognition of the need for collective actions.[32] Between Westphalia and now we have facilitated expanding capitalist production across the globe, by strategic integration between banks and industry, the export of capital, accelerated technological innovation, a now permanent military economy, the growth of transnational corporations and the expansion of credit, with resultant global indebtedness. The corporate actors involved in this dance have risen to prominence through neoliberal privileged access relationship they hold with states.

Obviously there is more to life than protecting borders and making money. There are global norms that we all share about human rights and dignity; the myriad of cultural expressions; the shared desire to control pandemics, nuclear weapon possession and ozone depletion; to manage harvesting the wealth of the high seas; and the existential need to address climate change to name only a few. New shared concerns are emerging fast including synthetic organisms, human cloning and artificial intelligence.

Enter the United Nations

Against this backdrop, it is then heartening to know that one counterpoint – the UN – has been established to promote international cooperation for the benefit of all humanity. A replacement for the ineffective League of Nations, the UN was formulated and negotiated among delegations from the Soviet Union, the United Kingdom, the United States of America and China at the Dumbarton Oaks Conference in 1944, to prevent another conflict like World War II, and opened its doors in 1945. The first meetings of the General Assembly, with 51 nations represented, and the Security Council, took place in London in early 1946. There are elements of the power structure of the UN that are unattractive, including the veto power that was given to the Security Council's five permanent members (now China, France, Russia, United Kingdom and the United States), enabling them to prevent the adoption of any substantive decisions. Germany has now been added to the five. The geopolitical leverage these six governments exert through this power is a carryover of the Westphalian state-centric structure. None-the-less, the UN is one of the few international spaces where small nations have a say. The General Assembly selected New York City as the site for the UN headquarters.[36] The site – like UN buildings in Geneva, Vienna and Nairobi – is designated as international territory. There are now 193 member states.

While a great deal of the UN's attention is focused on the Security Council, beyond that body the early years of the UN were focused on the most pressing needs of the day, and flavoured with a distinctly cosmopolitan tone: disarmament, refugees and stateless persons, ongoing disputes and genocide.[37] The first Universal Declaration was about Human Rights (1948),[38] and it was soon followed by a Declaration of the Rights of the Child (1959),[39] and the Declaration on the Granting of Independence to Colonial Countries and Peoples (1960). The third was perhaps the most significant strike against the old Westphalian world order. Captured in the statement is a '[recognition] that the peoples of the world ardently desire the end of colonialism in all its manifestations'.[40] The 1960s became known in UN circles as the Decade of Decolonization, with 42 countries gaining independence and UN membership. By the mid-1970s most colonial areas had achieved independence, leaving only a few smaller micro-states which, because of size and small populations, would take longer to work through.[37]

The UN continued to expand its reach, each time chipping away at Westphalian sovereignty. By the time the Declaration on the Rights of Indigenous Peoples was adopted in 2007, there was solid recognition of 'the urgent need to respect and promote the inherent rights of indigenous peoples which derive from their political, economic and social structures and from their cultures, spiritual traditions, histories and philosophies, especially their rights to their lands, territories and resources'. The Declaration articulates that indigenous peoples have the right to freely determine their political status and freely pursue their economic, social and cultural development, including autonomy or self-government if they want this. They may not be forcibly removed from their lands or territories, and relocation can only take place with free, prior and informed consent. Equally, free, prior and informed consent is required before states adopt and implement legislative or administrative measures that may affect them. Articles 18 and 21 of the Declaration are particularly pertinent for this book:

> Indigenous peoples have the right to participate in decision-making in matters which would affect their rights, through representatives chosen by themselves in accordance with their own procedures, as well as to maintain and develop their own indigenous decision-making institutions
>
> (Article 18)

> Indigenous peoples have the right to the conservation and protection of the environment and the productive capacity of their lands or territories and resources
>
> (Article 29.1)[41]

However, there is a tension inherent in having a world order split in two directions – with Westphalian sovereignty and the more recent rise of the neoliberal economic agenda on one side, pulling against the more universal humanitarian UN agenda on the other.

A system failing modern times

Westphalia is breaking, in part by design, in part by the stealth of elite actors and in part because it should. Commentators across agendas have rightly been saying that we need a revolution in global governance arrangements to reflect the scale of the development challenge and new geopolitical realities.[42–44] The centuries-old system of sovereign states is unfit or unable to address humanity's most urgent challenges.[43, 45, 46]

Make no mistake, I am a fan of the current Westphalian order dissolving. Many activists and academics are. The current institutional framework for wildlife and environment conservation, born of this system, is deeply inadequate to bring about the swift transformative progress that is needed.[43, 47] Stephen Krasner calls Westphalian sovereignty 'organised hypocrisy'. He rightly points out that rulers adhere to conventional norms or rules when it provides them with the resources and support (both material and ideational) to continue the economic agenda and violate the norms in equal measure for exactly the same reasons.[35] What I am concerned about is what we replace sovereignty with.

His core point is well made. There is clearly flexibility in this system. It is rulers, not states – and not the international system – that make choices about actions, policies, rules and institutions. There is, in truth, no rulebook that prescribes what can and cannot be done. The international canons are not so fixed as to prevent evolution. The interpretation of issues and the decisions that follow are made by people, very often bureaucrats acting on behalf of heads of states. So it is rulers who decide who and what to include, and who and what to exclude from their policy deliberations.[35] It is also rulers who hang on, with a vicelike grip, to the posture that states should be the only actors allowed at the decision-making table. States profess to represent the interests of us all. But, in the international sphere, their activities are often opaque to us.

In truth they have already allowed another player to join them at the table, granting them more and more power and influence as the decades have unfolded, while keeping other non-state actors at arm's length. This is a significant act because it has set the world on a particular neoliberal path. The other player at their table is transnational corporations.[48–50] In the following pages I will explain why many feel deeply worried about this partnership, which is doing as much to erode Westphalian sovereignty as anyone.

Governments behaving badly

A quest for monetary wealth has built the global system, so it is not a surprise that the same quest is now being used to erode it.

Financial institutions, ranging from large institutional investors to investment banks, have important social and ecological impacts at a global level through their investment decisions.[51] International development banks and transnational corporations are pushing an expansion of megahydroelectric dams at a rate never seen before, as a source of cheap energy, and branded as a solution to poverty and the climate crisis. Often, these dams displace communities; destroying large areas of biodiverse regions and the local social fabric that have ties to this land.[52] They lead to privatisation of land and water, and are very often used to power mining and fossil fuel extraction.[53, 54] In tropical regions they are a major source of the potent greenhouse gas methane.[55, 56]

Disappointingly, wealthy governments demonstrated their reluctance to curb the growth and power of corporations when the opportunity to do so presented itself during the Financing for Development meeting in 2015. More than 100 majority world countries still remain excluded from decision-making processes when global tax standards and rules are being decided. Neither the United States of America or any of the EU member states has challenged this approach and, as a result, decision-making on global tax standards and rules remains within a closed 'club of rich countries'.[57] Spain remains by far the most aggressive tax treaty negotiator, and has managed to lower majority country tax rates by an average 5.4 percentage points through its tax treaties. Recently new tax treaties between Spain and Nigeria, and Spain and Senegal have secured significantly reduced tax rates. The Spanish Government has established a special regime for the Canary Islands that will allow investors in West Africa a low-tax platform.[57] But Spain is not alone. The United Kingdom has aggressively promoted tax competition and France has consistently protected business interests; both have firmly blocked the creation of a global tax body to allow developing countries an equal voice.[57]

Governments appear to remain equally blinkered about financial reform. With the interests of finance capital now the driving force of the big Western democracies, and virtually unchecked, the question is not if another bubble will burst but when.[58] Despite the scandal of the 2008 crash, banks today are bigger and more opaque than ever, and they continue to trade in derivatives in much of the same way they did before the crash, but on a larger scale and with precisely the same unknown risks. Derivatives trading now totals, in notional amount, more than US$700 trillion – more than ten times the size of the entire world economy.

The situation is not helped by minority world countries maintaining legal loopholes that encourage illegal inflows. Gaps are left in statutes that keep open the doors to criminal and tax-evading money. As a result, every western nation fails in its anti-money laundering efforts.[59] The World Investment Report – Reforming International Investment Governance released in mid-2015 by the UN Conference on Trade and Development (UNCTAD) estimated that majority countries lost around US$100 billion per year in revenues due to tax avoidance by transnational enterprises, and as much as $300 billion in total lost development finance. The report release was timed to inform discussions at the UN's Third International Conference on Financing for Development.[60]

Jesse Griffiths, Director of the European Network on Debt and Development told the media before that Financing for Development meeting in mid-2015 that domestic resources raised by majority world countries are the largest single resource for funding development in most countries, but that this funding is being 'tragically undermined' by international tax evasion and avoidance, which cost majority world countries hundreds of billions of dollars every year.[61]

The European Network on Debt and Development report, *The State of Finance for Developing Countries*, makes the alarming point that the poorest countries have lost just over twice as much as they have gained since 2008. Not all of this is because of interest repayments on foreign debt. Illicit financial flows, profits taken out by foreign companies and lending to rich countries, is responsible for most of the outflow. Illicit financial flows accounted for US $634 billion in 2011. This is unrecorded private financial outflows involving capital that is illegally earned, transferred or utilised.[62]

Abusive tax avoidance – where companies dodge taxes through complex internal structures and by finding loopholes in tax laws – is also a significant problem. Taxes on transnational corporations have been significantly reduced through the proliferation of tax breaks, tax deals and other tax 'incentives' offered by majority world countries to transnational companies. This 'race to the bottom' – where countries compete with each other to offer lower tax rates to attract transnationals – is compounded by the difficulty majority world countries face when trying to levy taxes in the first place.[60, 62]

I was amazed to discover that governments in the majority world have been lending to the minority world, on a significant scale, for years. Over the five years between 2008 and 2012, close to US$2.5 trillion was lent by the majority world, including low-income countries, to wealthy countries, in particular to the United States of America.[62] Since 2006, there has been a sharp increase in new debt taken on by majority countries, driven by middle-income countries. Majority country debt stocks reached their highest level ever in 2012 – US$4.8 trillion, according to the World Bank – which was largely driven by increases in indebtedness by private actors.[62, 63]

Compounding all these inequities, the governments of the 20 major world economies (G20) are providing support to the very industry that is fuelling the thunderhead of climate change. Subsidies of around US$452 billion a year are provided for the production of fossil fuels, in effect propping up the production of oil, gas and coal, most of which can never be used if the world is to avoid dangerous climate change,[64] while diverting investment away from low-carbon alternatives such as solar, wind and hydro-power, and civil society conservation activities. Breaking it down, the United States of America provides more than US$20 billion in national fossil fuel production subsidies each year. The United Kingdom continues to encourage offshore oil and gas in the North Sea, giving national subsidies to fossil fuel production at an annual average of US$9 billion in 2013 and 2014. Australia and Brazil provide national subsidies of US$5 billion on average annually, including for the development of fossil fuel resources in increasingly remote and challenging areas (inland and offshore).[64]

Fossil fuel subsidies are probably one of the clearest examples of the folly of the current world order. Governments acting with self-interest continue support for fossil fuel production that risks 'carbon lock-in'. This means that once certain carbon-intensive development pathways are chosen and capital-intensive investments are made, fossil fuel dependence, and the carbon emissions that come with it, can become immovable and the investment required up to 2035 to achieve low-carbon objectives will increase by a factor of four.[64, 65] International Energy Agency analysis from 2012 found 'almost four-fifths of the CO_2 emissions allowable by 2035 are already locked-in by existing power plants, factories, buildings' to achieve limiting the increase in global temperatures to within the 2°C target. Yet, despite the urgency of the carbon lock-in risk, subsidies to fossil fuel producers persist, while simultaneously reducing public resources available to support low-carbon alternatives.[64, 66, 67]

In addition to the risk of carbon lock-in, a significant portion of subsidies to fossil fuel producers supports exploration for new fossil fuels; yet according to the IPCC, as of 2014, at least three-quarters of proven reserves of oil, gas and coal are already unburnable[68] – they must stay in the ground for Earth to have a two-in-three chance of remaining below the 2°C climate change threshold.

Responsibility for our current woes does not wholly rest at the feet of the minority world. The majority world suffers the 'resource curse' – a paradox where the countries often richest in natural resources tend, with sadly too few exceptions, to be badly governed, prone to violent conflict and impoverished. In many of these counties, governments sell natural resources worth hundreds of billions of dollars, with little trickle-down to their citizens.[69] The reasons are many and complex. Where governments don't need to rely on citizens to provide a tax base, they have little incentive to be accountable. In the absence of accountable governance, it is easier for natural resources to be mismanaged, poorly invested or siphoned off to an elite that seeks to concentrate power.[70] If that money was moved into the public domain and spent properly, the impacts on tackling poverty and environmental degradation would be that much easier. To give an idea of the potential benefit: in 2011 oil, gas and mineral exports from Africa were worth US$382 billion – more than eight times the value of official development aid received by African countries that year.[71]

Public sector corruption isn't simply about taxpayer money going missing. Broken institutions and corrupt officials fuel inequality and exploitation – keeping wealth in the hands of an elite few and trapping many more in poverty.

It is difficult to get a snapshot of levels of nepotism and corruption without relying on civil society to gather the data. Governments, not surprisingly, are reluctant to gather the data on themselves. Transparency International regularly publishes high quality information, and their 2015 Corruption Perceptions Index makes sobering reading.

Latin America continues to be beset with corruption trouble. Brazil faces its largest-ever corruption scandal around Petrobras. In Argentina, Mexico and Venezuela long-standing corruption has led to a desperate lack of investment in security, education and health. Malaysia's '1Malaysia Development Bhd' state fund scandal and the Prime Minister's inability to answer questions on the US $700 million that made its way into his personal bank account sets the contemporary tone for the region. India, Sri Lanka, Indonesia and China are inactive on their corruption problems. Bangladesh and Cambodia are exacerbating corruption by clamping down on civil society. Afghanistan and Pakistan's failure to tackle corruption is feeding ongoing vicious conflict. Eastern European and Central Asian, Hungarian, Polish and Turkish politicians and their cronies are increasingly hijacking state institutions to shore up power, a worrying trend also affecting the Balkans. It's even grimmer in Azerbaijan, Kazakhstan, Russia and Uzbekistan where governments are restricting, if not totally stifling, civil society and the free media. In the Middle East and North Africa, the devastating conflicts in Iraq, Libya and Sudan, Syria and Yemen, have pushed efforts to strengthen institutions and break from cronyism beyond view. The rise of ISIS and the ensuing fight against terrorism have been used by many governments as an excuse to crack down on civil liberties and civil society. In Sub-Saharan Africa, 40 out of 46 countries have serious corruption problems. Facing a myriad of threats in

2015, from the Ebola epidemic to rising terrorism, some governments have taken steps to reduce risks for business, but there has been little change for civil society. Police and courts have the highest rates of bribery. In Angola, Burundi and Uganda, there has been a documented failure to prosecute corrupt public officials on the one hand, and intimidation of citizens who speak out against corruption on the other.[72]

This deep level of inherent corruption across the majority world has a very direct and devastating impact on conservation efforts. Illegal harvesting of timber, and international illegal timber trade, continues to thrive in many regions. This trade does not just cause environmental damage, it deprives countries of millions in lost revenue, causes loss of livelihoods to forest dwelling communities, and leads to other criminal activities and, often, armed conflict. The power that politicians have in many countries is exploited by companies looking to operate illegally or without following rules that ensure sustainable forestry.[73] Most of the logging companies operating in the Congo Basin in the 1990s to 2000s were based in the European Union, including companies from Denmark, France, Italy and Germany, many with local and subsidiary companies operating in the Congo Basin countries. In 1998, 61 per cent of Cameroon's logs were exported to the European Union. Mining is a similar story, with British companies complicit in funding the regional conflict, including one that was found by the British Government in 2008 to be in breach of the Organisation for Economic Cooperation and Development (OECD) Guidelines for Multinational Enterprises for buying from suppliers who made payments to a rebel group. US-based companies are equally complicit. Add to this unethical mixture uncritical markets that ensure there are buyers for goods at the right price, regardless of how they are obtained, processed or transported and the region will never be able to climb out of this difficult mess. Transnational corporations keep the lid tightly fastened by building political networks of directors who later become top government officials.[1, 14]

Another resource curse relates directly to the emerging low-fossil carbon economy and biofuels. Many majority world governments, including China, India and Brazil, have established targets and mandatory quotas for biofuels in transportation. This could require an additional 118–508 million hectares on existing cropland, carrying with it a range of impacts on local communities.[70, 74] In recent cases in Asia, Africa and South America, governments and community officials have facilitated land deals with foreign companies that plan to produce crops for export, with limited economic and social value for local communities. Biofuel production in countries including Tanzania, Mozambique, India, Indonesia and Colombia has generated reports of land acquisition through illegitimate land titles, water access being denied to local farmers and the displacement of local communities by force. In February 2010, Sierra Leone signed a US$400 million land deal with a bioenergy company to cultivate sugarcane for bioethanol production – a deal that will displace dozens of villages.[70, 75]

Mineral mining for microelectronic devices and batteries is another area of corruption. The industry is believed to be one of the business sectors most likely to bribe public officials or to influence political processes. Katanga, in the south-east of the DRC, is one of the world's richest copper and cobalt producing areas, and a significant proportion of the copper and cobalt is mined and exported illegally. Government officials collude with trading companies in circumventing control procedures and the payment of taxes. The profits line the pockets of a small but powerful elite – politicians and businessmen who are exploiting the local population and subverting natural riches for their own private ends. Militarisation of mining is well documented and illegal trade revenues have been linked to the financing of civil war activities. Global Witness has documented how, in the course of plundering these minerals, rebel groups and the Congolese army have used forced labour (often in extremely harsh and dangerous conditions), carried out systematic extortion and imposed illegal 'taxes' on the civilian population. They have also used violence and intimidation against civilians who attempt to resist working for them or handing over the minerals they produce.[76, 77]

Corporations behaving badly

Since European countries reached out and gripped the distant lands through colonial control the majority world has been a 'hinterland' for the global capitalist system, transferring value from poor to rich countries.[78] The power relationship between global corporations and weak nation-states is imbalanced and local communities suffer. Community development programmes constructed by corporate entities have caused disastrous outcomes.[78–82]

Around the world, oil and mining operations continue to be the focal point of community concerns, protests and, in some cases, outright opposition. Local communities often strongly oppose new mining projects on the grounds of environmental, ethical and economic concerns. The industrial-scale extraction of natural resources generates significant social and environmental impacts. It is simply not possible to construct massive open-pit mining operations or build thousands of miles of pipeline without causing disturbances.[83–87]

In addition to their poor record environmental management, corporate dirty money, the spoils of corrupt or criminal activities and of systematic tax evasion, is another means of controlling the world. An entire structure of entities and mechanisms has been created to defraud and cheat the majority world global community. This structure is used by drug dealers, criminal syndicates, terrorists, corrupt officials, corporations, CEOs and tax evaders.[59] As Raymond Baker has eloquently said: 'In a process that parades as agreeable enterprise, illegal money in the trillions of dollars flows effortlessly. The money streams through mechanisms designed by western countries to bring hundreds of billions annually into western coffers.'[59]

The oldest – and ultimately the only sustainable – source of development finance is taxation in poor countries themselves, not permanent aid dependence. For minority world government revenues to be put on a sustainable footing tax evasion and tax avoidance have to be overcome. While the Panama Papers have recently exploded public debate and discussion, the system has been a long time in the making. Transnational corporations routinely engage in a range of actions aimed at reducing their tax burden to the lowest level possible. They include transfer pricing, nominal transfers, under-reporting, bribery of tax officials, refusal to pay, lobbying of governments to reduce tax liability, and lobbying by transnationals to pressure governments directly or through international institutions (IMF, World Bank, WTO) to achieve similar effects.

The scale of tax-avoidance activity has become so enormous that it can fairly be described as a shadow economy operating across globalised sectors. The sectors include the extractive industries, banking and finance, aviation, shipping, communications, pharmaceuticals, media, commodities and the weapons industry. Transnational companies make use of aggressive tax-planning strategies because they are able to operate in the legal vacuum that exists between nation states.[88] Analysis by Global Financial Integrity shows that, of the annual US$1 trillion in illicit flows leaving majority world countries, over 83 per cent is due to fraudulent trade misinvoicing. Trade misinvoicing is a form of trade-based money laundering where trading partners write their own trade documents, or arrange to have the documents prepared in a third country (typically a tax haven).[89–92] Manipulating price, quantity or quality of a good or service on the invoice 'allows criminals, corrupt government officials, and commercial tax evaders to shift vast amounts of money across international borders quickly, easily, and nearly always undetected.'[93]

The figures are not to be glossed over. Between 2004 and 2013 Sub-Saharan Africa accounted for 8.6 per cent of cumulative illicit financial flows, of which 71.5 per cent, or US$482.4 billion, was due to trade misinvoicing. In the same period Asia accounted for 38.8 per cent of cumulative illicit financial flows, with trade misinvoicing accounting for 83.6 per cent or US$2.5 trillion. Eastern Europe accounted for 25.5 per cent of cumulative illicit financial flows, almost exclusively due to trade misinvoicing, which averaged 88.8 per cent or US$1.8 trillion cumulatively of the region's yearly outflows. The Middle East, North Africa, Afghanistan and Pakistan accounted for 7.1 per cent of cumulative illicit financial flows with 63.6 per cent due to trade misinvoicing, totalling US$354.1 billion. South America accounted for 20.0 per cent of cumulative illicit financial flows, with trade misinvoicing accounting for 88.4 per cent or US$1.4 trillion cumulatively.[93]

Ila Patnaik, Abhijit Sen Gupta and Ajay Shah found that trade misinvoicing was not only as a result of overt corruption. Capital account openness (easing restrictions on capital flows across borders), interest rate differentials and the exchange rate regime also play a role.[91]

In July 2015, the Addis Ababa Action Agenda of the Third International Conference on Financing for Development committed all governments to 'redouble efforts to substantially reduce illicit financial flows by 2030, with a view to eventually eliminating them.'[94] We will have to wait to see if much happens.

We are left with a conundrum. Minority world governments are focused on self-interest, and while they have the power and influence to fix inequities, it serves them to let the situation continue. Majority world governments are beset by corruption and corporations are happy to exploit their low levels of accountability and loopholes to benefit their own ends.

There are bad people everywhere. But, there are good people everywhere as well. The situation we now face is shared by us all. If history evolved in a different direction it could just as easily been Europe or North America that evolved on the back foot, and Africa or Asia or Latin America that dominated the world. This isn't about culture, religion, education or regional tendencies. This is about what we share – the layers of human nature.

So, as a global community we have some decisions to make. One of these is how much more power do we want to allow our current world order to shift towards corporations.

The advance of a neoliberal plan

Government agencies have long been on a quest to access transnational funding for development infrastructure, and have been facilitating corporate actor involvement for decades.[95] The current buzz phrase for this corporate involvement is 'multi-stakeholder initiatives'.

The OECD wants multi-stakeholder consultations to implement the new Sustainable Development Goals (SDGs); minority world governments are pushing for multi-stakeholder consultations to open up US$100 billion per year for climate-related issues.[96] Indeed, commentators and scholars have argued for nearly a decade that the transnational arena of climate governance requires a remapping of public and private 'authority' over climate issues.[96–99] Without doubt, accessing the capital of the private sector holds promise. It also comes with risks including poor accountability, gaming the system and free riding.[100–103]

We have trialled the exercise already and founding it wanting. The first wave of private sector involvement in the public sphere has been through the widespread adoption of public private partnerships (PPPs) that involve a contract between a public sector authority and a private party. PPPs were proposed at the Rio Earth Submit in 1992 and have since become an increasingly mainstream approach.[95] They give private consortia of banks, constructors and service suppliers a concession to invest in new or existing public infrastructure. Concession periods are 15 years or more, granting private parties operation monopolies to enable them to recover their investments.[104, 105] This is increasingly promoted as a way to finance development projects,[106] and donor governments and financial institutions, such as the World Bank, have set up multiple donor initiatives to promote changes in national regulatory frameworks to facilitate PPPs.[107]

As time passes and critical assessment of PPPs becomes possible, they are revealed to be expensive and risky ways of financing public services and have significantly increased the costs to the public purse, often with higher construction and transaction costs than was planned. Inequity and environmental impact very often result. The evidence of the benefit is increasingly weak and their low transparency and limited public scrutiny undermines democratic accountability.[107] Experience following the wave of water services privatisation through the 1990s, mostly in majority world countries, shows that global water corporations have not brought the promised improvements in public water utilities. Instead of lower prices, large volumes of investment and improvements in the connection of the poor to water and sanitation, water tariffs have increased and are out of the reach of poor households.[108–111] Yet, there has still been a strong push to promote PPPs as a key tool to reach SDGs.[106, 107] This is a mere precursor to the next step towards privatising the world.

Davos multi-stakeholder governance agenda

In 2008, the world economic system stood at the edge of an abyss. The international community was confronted by the biggest economic crisis since the Great Depression of the 1930s. Instead of pursuing isolated national strategies the international community reacted with a series of world economic summits. Economic support measures on an unprecedented scale were agreed in order to rescue the world economy. What was special about this was that in this crisis, for the first time, the leaders of ten emerging economies were also welcomed at the negotiating table on an equal footing. A new powerful forum was born: the first summit of heads of state or government of the 20 most prosperous economies, the so-called G20, convened in 2008. Its leaders announced in September 2009 that the group would replace the G8 as the main economic council of wealthy nations. The members include 19 individual countries – Argentina, Australia, Brazil, Canada, China, France, Germany, India, Indonesia, Italy, Japan, South Korea, Mexico, Russia, Saudi Arabia, South Africa, Turkey, the United Kingdom and the United States of America – along with the European Union. The UN administration had initially embraced the notion of a G20, including a tentative offer of the UN's New York headquarters as the summit site, but the overture was declined and the UN was gradually marginalised from the process.[112] This should have rung alarm bells. It seems that the G20 wanted to dabble with new relationships, unhindered by the democracy of the UN. What this has meant for all of us is no transparency, no reports.

Into the check and balance vacuum created by the G20 stepped the Davos World Economic Forum. In 2009 Davos responded to the G20's longing looks for transnational capital and started to frame their suggested path forward.[113] This is, of course, perfectly understandable and reasonable from their perspective,[95] but the Davos worldview should not simply be adopted without careful scrutiny and conversation.

Davos represents the world's super wealthy elite – the Davos Class. A report by the Transnational Institute reveals that the world's wealth is concentrated even more than is popularly understood – not in the 1 per cent but the 0.001 per cent. A mere 111,000 people control a fifth of the world's gross national product (GNP) – US$16.3 trillion.[114]

The Davos Class has been quietly progressing what it calls the Davos Global Redesign Initiative, as a reflection of how these elites envision the future of governance. Nick Buxton characterises the motivations well: 'In the world of Davos, the tired old slow world of democratic demands channelled through states is replaced by a slicker, fast moving, corporate-led governance.'[115]

They want to replace of intergovernmental decision making with a system of multi-stakeholder governance, with carefully selected stakeholders.[116]

While most of the G20 leaders participate in the Davos Round, these discussions and decisions are being progressed so far from democratic view that the majority world may one day wake to a reality it no longer recognises. I felt the chill wind of the storm when I read Harris Gleckman's summary of the Davos Global Redesign Initiative:

> What is ingenious and disturbing is that the [World Economic Forum] multi-stakeholder governance proposal does not require approval or disapproval by any intergovernmental body. Absent any intergovernmental action the informal transition to MSG [multi-stakeholder governance] as a partial replacement of multilateralism can just happen.[116]

The Global Redesign Initiative is centred on the corporation, with stakeholders being constituents associated with the corporation – principally those with commercial ties to the company: customers, creditors, suppliers, collaborators, owners and national economies. Those who would be in charge of the multi-stakeholder governance arrangements (an important, but subtle evolution of the terminology) would be either appointed by Davos or by self-selection of leading firms interested in managing a particular global challenge with other constituents. There will be no need to wait for the intergovernmental system to come to consensus about acting; the multi-stakeholder will make these decisions themselves. The first transformative step proposed in the Global Redesign Initiative is to:

> redefine the international system as constituting a wider, multifaceted system of global cooperation in which intergovernmental legal frameworks and institutions are embedded as a core, but not the sole and sometimes not the most crucial, component.[116]

There are many layers of concern with this proposal, but an acute concern from the perspective of this book is who decides who is included and who is excluded. At the moment, the selection process is biased toward those with an explicit stake (presumably economic) in the outcome and other categories of stakeholder who are likely to agree with the approach of the sponsor of the multi-stakeholder governance arrangement. It is also not yet determined how the balance of power of the multi-stakeholder participants will be established. There are already strong reasons for concern when looking at a number of the existing multi-stakeholder initiatives including for palm oil,[82] biofuels[117] and forestry.[118]

Proponents argue that spanning the public–private domain can harness the essence of 'governance from below', counter the participation gap and address the implementation gap in global environmental politics. Just as many critics argue that these partnerships consolidate the privatisation of governance and reinforce dominant neoliberal modes of globalisation.[119] They lack accountability and legitimacy.[120, 121] I lean towards the critics. At its core, multi-stakeholder governance is proposing a route past the limits of multi-lateralism, where Westphalian-based intergovernmental diplomacy alone has proved it cannot grapple with the pressing problems and complex dimensions of sustainable development.

The Davos agenda exposes the incremental challenge to Westphalia already in play. Governments are speeding their own redundancy. Caught within short political-term timelines and ongoing financial crises, they are contracting the budgets and mandates for all the issues that sit outside the market, throwing away important detail and replacing it with broad sweeping global statements that cost little and achieve less. At some point soon the result of the governance retreat will become publicly evident. The Davos Class will be welcomed with desperate arms.

I believe there is another option. A different post-Westphalian rooted cosmopolitan option to reform multilateral environment agreements (MEAs) to give civil society a formal seat at the decision-making table.

*** *** ***

I think back to my trek to see gorillas in Rwanda and the gorilla who held my gaze and touched my heart.

In many ways she is my guide through the metaphorical storm of this book.

I imagine that I am standing on the edge of a field of golden wheat, watching the sky. It is big and blue. The breeze light and cool. The sun shines and it is easy to presume it will be this way tomorrow.

The gorilla sits alone, surrounded by the gentle swaying stalks. An idyllic scene. She seems content.

As I watch, deep grey clouds slide towards us, gliding on a pane of glass. The air becomes still and heavy. As the clouds advance the light dims.

My imagined gorilla is unsettled now. Occasionally she glances up. Something is happening, but she is not sure what is wrong.

I ache that she is so vulnerable.

References

1. Nellemann, C., Redmond, I. and Refisch, J. 2010. *The Last Stand of the Gorilla: Environmental Crime and Conflict in the Congo Basin*: UNEP/Earthprint.
2. Robbins, M. and Williamson, L. 2008. Gorilla beringei. *The IUCN Red List of Threatened Species*. Version 2015.2., Downloaded on 06 September 2015.
3. Walsh, P. D., Tutin, C. E. G., Oates, J. F., et al. 2008. Gorilla gorilla. *The IUCN Red List of Threatened Species*. Version 2015.2., Downloaded on 06 September 2015.
4. World Heritage Convention. 1979. Virunga National Park. UNESCO World Heritage Centre. [online material]
5. Tusabe, R. and Habyalimana, S. 2010. From Poachers to Park Wardens: Revenue Sharing Scheme as an Incentive for Environment Protection in Rwanda. *Mountain Forum Bulletin*.
6. World Bank. 2016. *Country Data*. [online material]
7. Hatfield, R. 2005. Economic Value of the Bwindi and Virunga Gorilla Mountain Forests. African Wildlife Foundation.
8. Maekawa, M., Lanjouw, A., Rutagarama, E. and Sharp, D. 2013. Mountain Gorilla Tourism Generating Wealth and Peace in Post-conflict Rwanda. Paper presented at the Natural Resources Forum.
9. Musahara, H., Musabe, T. and Kabenga, I. 2006. *Economic Analysis of Natural Resource Management in Rwanda*. Kigali: UNDP, UNEP and REMA.
10. Tumusiime, D. M. and Svarstad, H. 2011. A Local Counter-narrative on the Conservation of Mountain Gorillas. Paper presented at the Forum for Development Studies.
11. Nielsen, H. and Spenceley, A. 2011. The Success of Tourism in Rwanda: Gorillas and More. World Bank and Netherlands Development Organisation.
12. Milburn, R. 2014. Gorillas and Guerrillas: Environment and Conflict in the Democratic Republic of Congo. In *Environmental Crime and Social Conflict: Contemporary and Emerging Issues*. Edited by Brisman, A., South, N. and White, R. Farnham: Ashgate Publishing: 57–74.
13. Stoett, P. J. 2015. *The Evolution of and Future Prospects for Transnational Environmental Crime Prevention*. New York: Commission of Global Security, Justice and Governance.
14. Elliott, L. 2012. Fighting Transnational Environmental Crime. *Journal of International Affairs*: 87–104.
15. White, R. 2009. Researching Transnational Environmental Harm: Toward an Eco-Global Criminology. *International Journal of Comparative and Applied Criminal Justice*. 33, 2: 229–248.
16. Kowalczyk, P. 2015. These Park Rangers Would Die (and Have) to Save Mountain Gorillas. CNN. [online material]
17. Gettleman, J. 2014. Oil Dispute Takes a Page from Congo's Bloody Past. *The New York Times*, 15th November.
18. Graeber, D. J. 2015. SOCO Gives up Oil License in Protected DRC Park. UPI. [online material]
19. Starr, A. 2015. Congolese Activists Honored for Fighting Oil Exploration in Virunga National Park. NPR. [online material]
20. Wright, G. 2011. Conceptualising and Combating Transnational Environmental Crime. *Trends in Organized Crime*. 14, 4: 332–346.

21 Lee, S. and Jamal, T. 2008. Environmental Justice and Environmental Equity in Tourism: Missing Links to Sustainability. *Journal of Ecotourism.* 7, 1: 44–67.

22 Turner, R. L. and Wu, D. P. 2002. Environmental Justice and Environmental Racism: An Annotated Bibliography and General Overview, Focusing on US Literature, 1996–2002. Paper presented at the Berkeley Workshop on Environmental Politics, Institute of International Studies.

23 Turton, D. 2011. Wilderness, Wasteland or Home? Three Ways of Imagining the Lower Omo Valley. *Journal of Eastern African Studies.* 5, 1: 158–176.

24 Kaltenborn, B. P. 1998. Effects of Sense of Place on Responses to Environmental Impacts: A Study among Residents in Svalbard in the Norwegian High Arctic. *Applied Geography.* 18, 2: 169–189.

25 Stedman, R. C. 2003. Sense of Place and Forest Science: Toward a Program of Quantitative Research. *Forest Science.* 49, 6: 822–829.

26 Platt, J. R. 2013. How Will Climate Change Affect Mountain Gorillas? *Scientific American.* [online material]

27 Stockholm Environment Institute. 2009. Economics of Climate Change in Rwanda.

28 Philpott, D. 2001. *Revolutions in Sovereignty: How Ideas Shaped Modern International Relations.* Princeton: Princeton University Press.

29 Bull, H. 1977. *The Anarchical Society: A Study of Order in World Politics.* New York: Columbia University Press.

30 Elias, J. and Sutch, P. 2007. *International Relations.* New York: Routledge.

31 Krasner, S. D. 2001. Sovereignty. *Foreign Policy:* 20–29.

32 Osiander, A. 2001. Sovereignty, International Relations, and the Westphalian Myth. *International Organization.* 55, 02: 251–287.

33 Ling, L. H. M. 2013. *The Dao of World Politics: Towards a Post-Westphalian, Worldist International Relations.* Abingdon: Routledge.

34 United Nations. 1945. Charter of the United Nations. In *1 UNTS XVI.* San Francisco: United Nations.

35 Krasner, S. D. 1999. *Sovereignty: Organized Hypocrisy.* Princeton: Princeton University Press.

36 Schlesinger, S. C. 2003. *Act of Creation: The Founding of the United Nations.* Cambridge: Westview Press.

37 Gorman, R. 2001. *Great Debates at the United Nations: An Encyclopaedia of Fifty Key Issues, 1945–2000.* Westport: Greenwood.

38 United Nations. 1948. *Universal Declaration of Human Rights.* New York: United Nations.

39 United Nations. 1959. *Declaration of the Rights of the Child.* New York: United Nations.

40 United Nations. 1960. *Declaration on the Granting of Independence to Colonial Countries and Peoples.* New York: United Nations.

41 United Nations. 2007. *United Nations Declaration on the Rights of Indigenous Peoples.* New York: United Nations.

42 Glennie, J. 2015. Financing the Sustainable Development Goals Will Rely Heavily on the Tax Factor. *The Guardian Online,* 23th July 2015.

43 Falk, R. 2014. *(Re)Imagining Humane Global Governance.* London: Routledge.

44 Falk, R. and Strauss, A. 2001. Toward Global Parliament. *Foreign Affairs.* 80, 1: 212–220.

45 Falk, R. 2010. A Radical World Order Challenge: Addressing Global Climate Change and the Threat of Nuclear Weapons. *Globalizations.* 7, 1/2: 137–155.

46 Falk, R. 2002. *Reframing the Legal Agenda of World Order in the Course of a Turbulent Century.* New York: Routledge.

47 Biermann, F., Abbott, K., Andresen, S., et al. 2012. Transforming Governance and Institutions for Global Sustainability: Key Insights from the Earth System Governance Project. *Current Opinion in Environmental Sustainability.* 4, 1: 51–60.

48 Falk, R., Ruiz, L. E. J. and Walker, R. B. J. 2002. The International and the Challenge of Speculative Reason. In *Reframing the International: Law, Culture, Politics.* Edited by Falk, R., Ruiz, L. E. J. and Walker, R. B. J. London: Routledge: ix–xiii.

49 Walker, R. B. J. 2002. After the Future: Enclosures, Connections, Politics. In *Reframing the International: Law, Culture, Politics.* Edited by Falk, R., Ruiz, L. E. J. and Walker, R. B. J. London, Routledge: 3–25.

50 Strauss, A. J. 2002. Overcoming the Dysfunction of the Bifurcated Global System: The Promise of a People's Assembly. In *Reframing the International: Law, Culture, Politics.* Edited by Falk, R., Ruiz, L. E. J. and Walker, R. B. J. London, Routledge: 83–106.

51 Galaz, V., Gars, J., Moberg, F., Nykvist, B. and Repinski, C. 2015. Why Ecologists Should Care about Financial Markets. *Trends in Ecology & Evolution.* 30, 10: 571–580.

52 de Boissière, P., Cabello, J., McDonagh, T., Orellana López, A., Shultz, J., Sabido, P. and Tansey, R. 2014. *Corporate Conquistadors: The Many Ways Multinationals Both Drive and Profit from Climate Destruction.* San Francisco: The Democracy Center, Corporate Europe Observatory (CEO) and The Transnational Institute (TNI).

53 de Boissière, P. and Cowman, S. 2016. For Indigenous Peoples, Megadams Are 'Worse than Colonization'. *Foreign Policy in Focus.*

54 World Commission on Dams. 2000. *Dams and Development: A New Framework for Decision-Making.* London: Earthscan.

55 Kemenes, A., Forsberg, B. R. and Melack, J. M. 2007. Methane Release below a Tropical Hydroelectric Dam. *Geophysical Research Letters.* 34, 12.

56 Lima, I. B. T., Ramos, F. M., Bambace, L. A. W. and Rosa, R. R. 2007. Methane Emissions from Large Dams as Renewable Energy Resources: A Developing Nation Perspective. *Mitigation and Adaptation Strategies for Global Change.* 13, 2: 193–206.

57 d'Edimbourg, R. (ed). 2015. *Fifty Shades of Tax Dodging: The EU's Role in Supporting an Unjust Global Tax System.* Brussels: European Network on Debt and Development.

58 Bello, W. 2016. The Tyranny of Global Finance. In *State of Power 2016.* Amsterdam: Transnational Institute.

59 Baker, R. W. 2005. *Capitalism's Achilles Heel: Dirty Money and How to Renew the Free-market System.* Hoboken: John Wiley & Sons.

60 Division on Investment and Enterprise. 2015. *World Investment Report 2015 – Reforming International Investment Governance.* Geneva: United Nations Conference on Trade and Development.

61 Anderson, M. and Ní Chonghaile, C. 2015. Addis Ababa Development Finance Summit: All You Need to Know. *The Guardian Online,* 13th July 2015.

62 Giffiths, J. 2014. *The State of Finance for Developing Countries.* Brussels: European Network on Debt and Development.

63 World Bank. 2014. *International Debt Statistics 2014*. Washington DC: World Bank.

64 Bast, E., Doukas, A., Pickard, S., Van Der Burg, L. and Whitley, S. 2015. *Empty Promises: G20 Subsidies to Oil, Gas and Coal Production*. London: Overseas Development Institute.

65 Erickson, P., Lazarus, M. and Tempest, K. 2015. *Carbon Lock-in from Fossil Fuel Supply Infrastructure*. Seattle, Stockholm Environment Institute.

66 International Energy Agency. 2013. *Redrawing the Energy-Climate Map: World Energy Outlook Special Report*. Paris: International Energy Agency.

67 International Energy Agency. 2012. *World Energy Outlook 2012*. Paris: International Energy Agency.

68 Intergovernmental Panel on Climate Change. 2014. *Climate Change 2014: Synthesis Report. Contribution of Working Groups I, II and III to the Fifth Assessment Report of the Intergovernmental Panel on Climate Change*. Edited by Pachauri, R. K. and Meyer, L. A. Geneva, IPCC: 151.

69 Robinson, J. A., Torvik, R. and Verdier, T. 2006. Political Foundations of the Resource Curse. *Journal of Development Economics*. 79, 2: 447–468.

70 Bringezu, S. and Bleischwitz, R. 2011. Preventing a Resource Curse Fuelled by the Green Economy. In *Global Corruption Report: Climate Change*. Edited by Sweeney, G., Dobson, R., Despota, K. and Zinnbauer, D. London: Earthscan.

71 Hayman, G. 2014. Reversing the Curse: The Global Campaign to Follow the Money Paid by Oil and Mining Industries. In *State of Civil Society Report: 2014*. Edited by Firmin, A., Pegus, C. M. and Tiwana, M. New York: CIVICUS: World Alliance for Citizen Participation.

72 Beddow, R. 2015. *2015 Corruption Perceptions Index*. Berlin: Transparency International.

73 Transparency International. 2012. *Tackling Forestry Corruption Risks in Asia Pacific*. Berlin: Transparency International.

74 Bringezu, S., Schütz, H., O'Brien, M., Kauppi, L., Howarth, R. W. and McNeely, J. 2009. *Towards Sustainable Production and Use of Resources: Assessing Biofuels*. London: UNEP/Earthprint.

75 Shepard, D. and Mittal, A. 2010. *(Mis) Investment in Agriculture: The Role of the International Finance Corporation in Global Land Grabs*. Oakland: The Oakland Institute.

76 Global Witness. 2009. *"Faced with a Gun, What Can You Do?": War and the Militarisation of Mining in Eastern Congo*. London: Global Witness.

77 Global Witness. 2006. *Digging in Corruption: Fraud, Abuse and Exploitation in Katanga's Copper and Cobalt Mines: a Report by Global Witness, July 2006*. London: Global Witness.

78 Maconachie, R. and Hilson, G. 2013. Editorial Introduction: The Extractive Industries, Community Development and Livelihood Change in Developing Countries. *Community Development Journal*. 48, 3: 347–359.

79 Akiwumi, F. A. 2012. Global Incorporation and Local Conflict: Sierra Leonean Mining Regions. *Antipode*. 44, 3: 581–600.

80 Ackah-Baidoo, A. 2013. Fishing in Troubled Waters: Oil Production, Seaweed and Community-level Grievances in the Western Region of Ghana. *Community Development Journal*. 48, 3: 406–420.

81 Triscritti, F. 2013. Mining, Development and Corporate–community Conflicts in Peru. *Community Development Journal*. 48, 3: 437–450.

82 Köhne, M. 2014. Multi-stakeholder Initiative Governance as Assemblage: Roundtable on Sustainable Palm Oil as a Political Resource in Land Conflicts Related to Oil Palm Plantations. *Agriculture and Human Values*. 31, 3: 469–480.

83 Slack, K. 2012. Mission Impossible?: Adopting a CSR-based Business Model for Extractive Industries in Developing Countries. *Resources Policy*. 37, 2: 179–184.

84 Farrell, L. 2004. *Dirty Metals: Mining, Communities, and the Environment*. Boston, MA: Oxfam America and Earthworks.

85 Obi, C. 2007. Oil and Development in Africa: Some Lessons from the Oil Factor in Nigeria for the Sudan. In *Oil Development in Africa: Lessons for Sudan after the Comprehensive Peace Agreement*. Copenhagen: Danish Institute for International Studies Report.

86 Hilson, G. and Yakovleva, N. 2007. Strained Relations: A Critical Analysis of the Mining Conflict in Prestea, Ghana. *Political Geography*. 26, 1: 98–119.

87 Mutti, D., Yakovleva, N., Vazquez-Brust, D. and Di Marco, M. H. 2012. Corporate Social Responsibility in the Mining Industry: Perspectives from Stakeholder Groups in Argentina. *Resources Policy*. 37, 2: 212–222.

88 Christensen, J. and Murphy, R. 2004. The Social Irresponsibility of Corporate Tax Avoidance: Taking CSR to the Bottom Line. *Development*. 47, 3: 37–44.

89 Qureshi, T. A. and Mahmood, Z. 2015. *The Size of Trade Misinvoicing in Pakistan*. Islamabad: National University of Science and Technology.

90 Boyce, J. K. and Ndikumana, L. 2012. Capital Flight from Sub-Saharan African Countries: Updated Estimates, 1970–2010. In *Political Economy Research Institute Working Papers*. Amherst: University of Massachusetts.

91 Patnaik, I., Sen Gupta, A. and Shah, A. 2011. Determinants of Trade Misinvoicing. *Open Economies Review*. 23, 5: 891–910.

92 Jha, R. and Truong, D. N. 2015. Estimates of Trade Mis-invoicing and Their Macroeconomic Outcomes for the Indian Economy. *Review of Economics & Finance*. 5: 19–34.

93 Kar, D. and Spanjers, J. 2015. *Illicit Financial Flows from Developing Countries: 2004–2013*. Washington DC: Global Financial Integrity.

94 United Nations General Assembly. 2015. Addis Ababa Action Agenda of the Third International Conference on Financing for Development (Addis Ababa Action Agenda). In *A/69/313*. New York: United Nations.

95 Clapp, J. and Meckling, J. 2013. Business as a Global Actor. In *The Handbook of Global Climate and Environment Policy*. Chichester: John Wiley & Sons Ltd: 286–303.

96 Pattberg, P. and Stripple, J. 2008. Beyond the Public and Private Divide: Remapping Transnational Climate Governance in the 21st Century. *International Environmental Agreements: Politics, Law and Economics*. 8, 4: 367–388.

97 Bernstein, S. 2010. When is Non-State Global Governance Really Governance? *Utah Law Review*. 1: 91–114.

98 Climate Change Support Team of the United Nations Secretary General. 2015. *Trends in Private Sector Climate Finance: Climate Change Support Team of the United Nations Secretary General on the Progress Made since the 2014 Climate Summit*. New York: United Nations.

99 Brown, J. and Jacobs, M. 2011. *Leveraging Private Investment: The role of Public Sector Climate Finance*. London: Overseas Development Institute.

100 Ostrom, E. 2010. Polycentric Systems for Coping with Collective Action and Global Environmental Change. *Global Environmental Change*. 20, 4: 550–557.

[101] Bäckstrand, K. 2008. Accountability of Networked Climate Governance: The Rise of Transnational Climate Partnerships. *Global Environmental Politics.* 8, 3: 74–102.

[102] Matisoff, D. C. 2012. Privatizing Climate Change Policy: Is There a Public Benefit? *Environmental and Resource Economics.* 53, 3: 409–433.

[103] Lyon, T. P. 2013. The Pros and Cons of Voluntary Approaches to Environmental Regulation. Paper presented at the Reflections on Responsible Regulation Conference.

[104] Koppenjan, J. F. M. 2015. Public–Private Partnerships for Green Infrastructures. Tensions and Challenges. *Current Opinion in Environmental Sustainability.* 12: 30–34.

[105] Koppenjan, J. F. M. 2008. Public–private Partnership and Mega-projects. In *Decision-making on Mega-projects.* Cheltenham: Edward Elgar Publishing: 189–212.

[106] Green Growth Action Alliance. 2013. The Green Investment Report: The Ways and Means to Unlock Private Finance for Green Growth. Geneva: World Economic Forum, Green Growth Action Alliance.

[107] Romero, M. 2015. *What Lies Beneath? A Critical Assessment of PPPs and their Impact on Sustainable Development.* Brussels: European Network on Debt and Development.

[108] Nugroho, R. 2012. Public Private Partnership as a Policy Dilemma. *Bisnis & Birokrasi Journal.* 18, 3.

[109] Effah Ameyaw, E. and Chan, A. P. C. 2013. Identifying Public-private Partnership (PPP) Risks in Managing Water Supply Projects in Ghana. *Journal of Facilities Management.* 11, 2: 152–182.

[110] Nastar, M. 2014. What Drives the Urban Water Regime? An Analysis of Water Governance Arrangements in Hyderabad, India. *Ecology and Society.* 19, 2: 57.

[111] Kayser, G. L., Amjad, U., Dalcanale, F., Bartram, J. and Bentley, M. E. 2015. Drinking Water Quality Governance: A Comparative Case Study of Brazil, Ecuador, and Malawi. *Environmental Science & Policy.* 48: 186–195.

[112] Cooper, A. F. and Helleiner, E. 2010. *The G-20: A 'Global Economic Government' in the Making?* Bonn, Germany: Friedrich Ebert Stiftung: 4.

[113] Sogge, D. 2014. State of Davos – The Camel's Nose in the Tents of Global Governance. In *State of Power 2014.* Amsterdam: Transnational Institute: 16–20.

[114] Buxton, N. 2014. *State of Power 2014.* Amsterdam: Transnational Institute.

[115] Buxton, N. 2014. The Great Divide: Exposing the Davos Class behind Global Economic Inequality. In *State of Civil Society Report: 2014.* Edited by Firmin, A., Pegus, C. M. and Tiwana, M. New York: CIVICUS: World Alliance for Citizen Participation: 145–149.

[116] Gleckman, H. 2016. Multi-stakeholderism: A Corporate Push for a New Form of Global Governance. In *State of Power 2016.* Amsterdam: Transnational Institute.

[117] Selfa, T., Bain, C. and Moreno, R. 2014. Depoliticizing Land and Water "Grabs" in Colombia: The Limits of Bonsucro Certification for Enhancing Sustainable Biofuel Practices. *Agriculture and Human Values.* 31, 3: 455–468.

[118] Moog, S., Spicer, A. and Böhm, S. 2014. The Politics of Multi-stakeholder Initiatives: The Crisis of the Forest Stewardship Council. *Journal of Business Ethics.* 128, 3: 469–493.

119 Bäckstrand, K. 2006. Multi-stakeholder Partnerships for Sustainable Development: Rethinking Legitimacy, Accountability and Effectiveness. *European Environment.* 16, 5: 290–306.

120 Risse, T. 2004. Global Governance and Communicative Action. *Government and Opposition.* 39, 2: 288–313.

121 Nanz, P. and Steffek, J. 2004. Global Governance, Participation and the Public Sphere. *Government and Opposition.* 39, 2: 314–335.

3 Lightning cracks

Southern right whales – José Truda Palazzo, Jr

After a successful 60 million years, less than two centuries of industrial whaling brought the southern right whale to the edge of survival. By the 1970s fewer than 400 individuals were thought to survive.

Majority country participation in the whale hunts was shaped and directed from far beyond their geographical, political and social boundaries. Indeed, the Latin American relationship with industrial whaling was established by North American and European fleets well before the 1946 Convention for the Regulation of Whaling was even drafted. These whalers decimated southern right whales in the western South Atlantic as early as the eighteenth century, and Norwegian whalers operated in the region in the early twentieth century. Without question, this was a minority world, capitalist agenda. Most of these whaling grounds were taken over by Japanese whaling companies in the third-quarter of the twentieth century, promoted into Japan as economic and food relief by the United States of America after World War II.[1]

But against the odds, when whaling was banned and small groups of committed individuals fought to protect ancient calving grounds from other threats, southern right whales slowly made a comeback. In the mythology of the conservation movement, there is a tendency to believe these individuals were all from the 'enlightened west' – the United States, the United Kingdom and Australia. What few consciously recognise is that a brave few also turned the tide of political momentum for Latin America, from whaling and towards a deep appreciation for whales.

Giant and beautiful, southern right whales spend their summers deep in the vastness of the Southern Ocean feeding on tiny crustaceans. We know little about their activities during this season, except that they are building blubber insulation from the cold and vital food reserves for their annual northbound migration to give birth to the next generation.

In 1996 José Truda Palazzo, Jr, one of the southern right's most stalwart and tenacious champions, floated in the coastal waters off Santa Catarina, Brazil waiting to welcome the return of a precious few heavily pregnant whales to their calving ground. He was with the journalist Todd Lewan who captured the moment:

> Her bulk is black and oily smooth and tapered like a submarine. And when she crashes back into the sea, the spray roars up in a curtain of crystalline drops ... She submerges in a slow slant, then rises again, the hump of her back awash as she breaks the surface to breathe. Up goes a spout, high, pluming like a geyser.
>
> 'For the love of God,' gasps Palazzo. 'She's got to be 40, no, 50 feet long.'
>
> Suddenly, there is another boil in the water – a four-ton calf jumping. He leaps on his mother's back and rolls about, butting his blunt head against her.
>
> Today the right whales are making a comeback off Brazil's southern seaboard, thanks largely to Palazzo's crusade to protect them and their underwater world.
>
> 'It's really gratifying to see them here, in Imbituba,' Palazzo says, 'since this is where thousands of whales were butchered at the local whaling station ... When we started, we knew almost nothing about them. Even now, we still don't know basic things, like their complete migration routes or the dangers they face.'[2]

I first stood on a cliff to watch southern right whales in southern Australia about two years before this interview, so I feel a strong connection with Todd's words and José's reaction. Whales in this region as well have been making a slow, tentative return. There is something profoundly moving about being near these animals when they are in shallow water. By anyone's standards, they are huge – around 17 metres long and weighing up to 80 tonnes. They might be heavily pregnant and about to give birth, tenderly nursing newborn infants or watching their youngsters explore movement in the soft caress of the surf and the sea. At this time and in this environment these mothers move with slow, powerful grace. Watching them, the world seems to turn more slowly.

As social communicators, much of these whales' histories would have been lost to them when whaling decimated their families, their communities. It has long been thought that mothers come back to the same bay to give birth and raise each calf, often the bay where they themselves were born. So, calving grounds and migration routes have been empty for generations. But slowly, in their own time and their own way, they are rediscovering these important places and returning to continue the cycle of life.[3] By the time I had my first encounter with whales, José was in his second decade of dedication to these animals, having met his first southern right in the 1970s.

While writing this book I had the good fortune to be face to face with this activist. I have known José long enough to have watched his influence fundamentally change the politics of key wildlife issues in Latin America. He is one of the few people in my orbit who understands the mechanics of campaigning in both the minority and majority worlds, having worked within both. Aside from sharing a love for the big mammals of the sea, his perspective was a wellspring for me to tap. He also knows what it means to campaign in dangerous circumstances.

Activists in Latin America bravely face odds many of us can only imagine. Conflicts with corporate interests over the ownership and use of land, particularly in the face of expanded mining, logging and large-scale agribusiness activities, spawn a dangerous atmosphere for environmental action. In 2014, 29 environmental activists were murdered in Brazil – 477 have been killed since 2002. Almost half of them were indigenous peoples fighting for their own survival and their community's way of life, illustrating how the fight to protect the natural world and indigenous rights are often one and the same.

This dire situation resonates across the region. Brazil is the worst hit by this scourge, but Honduras, Peru, Columbia and Guatemala are chasing the honour.[4, 5] So, interviewing José, a survivor in a troubled region, was an opportunity.

A career as long and committed as José's becomes difficult to capture because of its enormity. Shortening the account robs the person of recognition for their sustained and constant work, yet a long list of achievements becomes disconnected from the passion. Who he is and what he has achieved is illustrative of the professionalism that exists outside the minority world – professionalism and experience that is often overlooked by international nongovernmental organisations (NGOs) in Washington, Brussels and London.

In the 1970s, when Brazil was still under a military dictatorship, José became one of Brazil's leading voices against Japanese whaling in its waters. Brazil's connection with whaling ended in 1985. In a ceremony to mark the transition from hunters to protectors, Brazil's President Sarney recognised José's work. In the meantime, he and a group of local volunteers had rediscovered a breeding population of southern right whales in Southern Brazil in 1982. For 27 years José led a research and conservation project which ensured the recovery of the species, securing its recognition as State Natural Heritage in 1995 and secured a Federal Environmental Protection Area for their breeding grounds in 2000.

José served for two decades as an official Brazilian representative at the International Whaling Commission as well as strengthening the Latin bloc of countries against whaling. It was in this capacity that we first met, straddling the disparate world of NGO whale politics and government pragmatism. But, his activism was always bigger and broader than the whales and whaling. José also led campaigns for the successful establishment of three separate protected areas, one of which is also now a World Heritage Site, created a whole new diver network for shark conservation, authored key legal and policy initiatives, and served on a number of institute and non-profit boards. As if that isn't enough, he is also an accomplished writer.

Few in the minority world even register that this remarkable career has been predominantly self-funded. Like most activists in the majority world, José lives hand-to-mouth to continue his work, raise his family and maintain his life. He has never wavered from his path and he remains fearless in calling his government to account for their recent deconstruction of national environmental policy and the blatant corruption of environmental regulation.

In 2009 political elites sought to sideline José, angry that he would not cease his sharp public criticism about the Brazilian Government and Petrobras. One evening while he and his family were resting after a day of right whale research, José opened the door to a long-term colleague without a single thought that anything was wrong. He was viciously beaten, with no warning or defence – his physical pain was only tempered by the relief that his partner had grabbed his two children and was now locked in the next room calling the police. The emotional pain of the incident would linger for much longer.

The motivation of his attacker will likely never be fully understood although, instead of being prosecuted for the grievous assault, the perpetrator was appointed as the Director of the Right Whale Project soon afterwards.

When violence didn't work, the elites tried to discredit José through the courts and he found himself fighting for his reputation through the legal system. He won. His name was cleared, but sadly the Right Whale Project crumbled in the wake of this bad press. Yet, José remains philosophical. The protection measures the project secured have allowed at least three generations of right whales to be born in safety. While many of us from wealthier, safer surroundings would be deeply traumatised by this treatment, José continues his quest for marine conservation in defiance of that day in 2009. He is glad to still be alive, and proudly wears the banner of 'troublemaker' bestowed on him by the environmental journalist Marcos Sá Corrêa for his uncompromising defence of nature.[6] In an interview with Marcos, José said: 'Environmental activism is a constant space filled with powerful enemies … It is important to create trouble to get results … NGOs should not submit to censorship, should not allow their silence to be bought.'[7]

In telling his story he recounted another where good fortune ran tragically dry. In 2012 Almir Nogueira de Amorim and João Luiz Telles Penetra, artisanal fishermen and members of AHOMAR (Associação Homens e Mulheres do Mar, or Association of Sea Men) in Guanabara Bay, were murdered for their struggle against Brazilian government activities in the Guanabara Bay. Almir's body was found submerged and tied to his boat and João Luiz was found soon after with his hands and feet tied in the foetal position. It is not as if the authorities had no warning. Two other members of the AHOMAR resistance, Paulo Santos Souza and Márcio Amaro, were killed in 2010. Paulo was beaten and shot in front of his family. Márcio was also murdered in front of his mother and wife. Other AHOMAR members have received death threats. To this day the courts have failed to prosecute anyone for these crimes.[8–10] As I said, José is lucky to be alive.

The violence faced by activists in this region alone should command our respect for them. But it seems that minority NGOs exacerbate the injustice with our own blind determination to force the world to conform to our worldview. We don't recognise the harm we cause and the extent to which we undermine people. We don't recognise how much we don't know.

I was especially interested get José's impression of the structure and focus of campaigns in both worldviews and to hear if he could identify clear differences. Reflecting a lifetime of experience, he smoothly identified two.

The first is that funding from the minority world facilitates big NGOs to infiltrate and control majority world government agencies with large programmatic grants and seconded staff. These relationships with government are often close and serve the interests of the NGO well, but lock local NGOs out of discussions. Without the same close access local NGOs become distrusted despite garnering considerably more public support and influence in the country. These minority NGOs usually make no attempt to work with or connect with the local NGO community, which only deepens the mistrust and divisions that communities have with their own government. With characteristic humour, José chuckled that when these same NGOs turn their attention to their own governments in North America or Europe they strike very different postures, 'respectfully influencing through their national democratic process' rather than 'infiltrating the heathens'.[11]

His other significant point of difference was that the perspectives of local NGOs were frequently dismissed as irrelevant, unsophisticated or unimportant. Indeed, often they were not even asked. The situation was marginally better when the minority world NGOs invested in establishing offices in majority world countries and hired local activists. At least in these instances there was better communication and engagement with local networks, even if the headquarters forbade it. Campaigners had an opportunity to become deeply familiar with the subjects and were able to freewheel more. But, even this arrangement was not ideal. Frequently the headquarters would send expat staff to hold senior positions or would fly in their senior team (minority world) to meet with government officials. Our blindness and prejudice can run deep.

All this costs money. We agreed the investment could be much better spent. We could both name dozens of international meetings, often held in the majority world, where the public relations budgets of the minority world NGOs for the meeting alone grossly outstripped the budgets of local activists for the whole year. In José's words: 'people are dying around them, activists have lost their lives for less, yet they don't see'.

Sadly, both flawed models reek of tokenism. We have both been around long enough to watch the boom bust cycle of our sector, and know too well that when these big international NGOs (often referred to as BINGOs in the majority world) feel financial strain both of these models are the first to be cut. The movement always shrinks back to Washington, Brussels and London – reinforcing our point that the majority world is a second-order priority to minority world NGOs.

Despite a burning anger about injustice, José remains a remarkably centred and morally balanced individual – and he still harbours a deep love for the southern right whales that visit his coastline each year.

*** *** ***

I offer José's story to demonstrate that majority world perspectives should not be considered simplified or unsophisticated. Nor should they be sidelined because they don't conform to the marketing priorities of minority world NGOs. Nonetheless they often are.

José's professionalism and career experience is reflective of a great many other majority world activists. Given my rough treatment of governments and corporations in chapter 2, it is appropriate to also shine a light on the minority world NGO sector. Investigating what has created a disconnect between NGOs in the minority and majority world is an important exercise to better understand how we can overcome it.

Losing way through the storm

Although the influence of identifiable NGOs in domestic environmental policy dates back more than a century, minority world NGOs have come into their own as major players in international environmental discussions since the 1960s,[12, 13] when conservation was projected onto the world stage. Their early roots can be traced back to the late nineteenth century, when 'men of privilege' sought to protect their favourite wilderness spots as havens for hunting, fishing and hiking. Modern minority world conservation NGOs have grown on the foundations of older national NGOs such as Flora and Fauna International, the Royal Society for the Protection of Birds, the Sierra Club, the World Wildlife Fund (WWF; also known as the World Wide Fund for Nature) and the quasi-NGO the International Union for the Conservation of Nature (IUCN).

The term NGO is a post-World War II expression that was initially coined by the United Nations to describe a specific subset of civil society. Kerstin Martens provides a succinct definition: 'NGOs are formal (professionalised) independent societal organizations whose primary aim is to promote common goals at the national or the international level'. NGOs are neither part of government nor conventional for-profit activities. They originate from the private sphere and are formal organisations because they have – at the least – a minimal organisational structure which allows them to provide for continuous work. International NGOs are composed of members from at least two countries and they often engage in activities across many countries.[14, 15]

NGOs do not gain their influence from delegation by states. Any influence they have is achieved through the attractiveness of their ideas and values – influence that must constantly be earned. The drive for influence has shaped the NGO agenda.

The Stockholm Conference (United Nations Conference on the Human Environment) in 1972 reported the attendance of over 400 representatives from intergovernmental and nongovernmental organisations. Conservation NGO influence emerged in a more obvious way during the first Earth Summit (United Nations Conference on Environment and Development) in 1992. Before the meeting NGOs from around the world marshalled a significant international awareness campaign to help set the conference agenda. Around 1,400 NGO representatives were accredited to attend the Earth Summit[16] with an additional 17,000 representatives taking part in the parallel NGO 'Global Forum'.[17–20]

There was a surge of global awareness about the state of the environment during the Earth Summit. Overwhelmed with the task ahead, many minority world NGOs believed they had little to counterbalance the might of capitalism, so the reaction was to allow the ideology of 'sustainability' to be reduced to 'acceptable cost' and they bonded with the economic system run by the corporate elite. This fateful step has meant that many of the larger minority world NGOs have lost their moral centre. Minority world conservation NGOs have ceded power to the plutocracy and now see the market as the only path.[21] They have lost sight of the path through the storm and are now racing in a direction that makes the storm worse. To understand how this happened requires some explanation.

Speaking for ecosystems and the services they provide

About 30 years ago a brilliant and insightful group of ecological economists worked out that the services provided by ecosystems should be described with a monetary value for what they contribute to the healthy function of the biosphere. Their intention was that damage to these services would have a reciprocal cost. I was first introduced to this concept by Herman Daly and John Cobb in 1995 in their book *For the Common Good: Redirecting the Economy towards Community, the Environment, and a Sustainable Future.* [22] By then the book was already it its second edition, having first been released in the eighties. Their partnership – an economist and theologian – produced a profound thesis that opened a generation of activists' minds to the flaws of the current economic order. A philosophical thread about community and connection ran through the pages – about how much we needed the natural world but have failed to value it for what it provides us. It was inspiring to read then, and it still is now.

In 1997, another published piece of work from Robert Costanza and a large group of his colleagues crunched the numbers about what 'natural capital' was actually worth. I remember being stunned by the numbers and revisiting these papers has taken me back into my dusty and rarely opened filing cabinet to retrieve them. Thumbing through the folders, past faded faxes, hand scribbled notes in the margins of old photocopies, and articles I recall waiting impatiently for weeks to receive, reminds me of how we processed information in that time. There was time to think, reflect and deeply consider implications.

I remember these works having a significant impact on the direction of my career, because they revealed what the market was doing to the world. They estimated the economic value of the Earth's biosphere to be in the range of US$16–54 trillion (recalling this was 20 years ago), most of which sat outside of the market system.[23, 24]

There was much more than raw number crunching in this collective work. Herman Daly, John Cobb and Robert Costanza, and the tribe of economists working together on this project, were trying to make a point – one that has sadly been lost as time has moved on – that the economic system should not be allowed to 'externalise' the costs of impact. That the cost of a degraded natural system should be factored into the cost of production. For instance, a mine that proposes to use the ecosystem services of a river to dispose of its tailing waste should factor in the ecosystem service impact costs to the river and the ecosystem and the communities it supports, all the way down to the wetland and the river that flows out to sea, where the freshwater and salt water mix to feed the marine ecosystem. Rather than the cost to the mine being focused on a few pipes and a media blackout campaign about the impact of the tailings, the company should have to 'internalise' the economic value of their damage to the ecosystem services the entire way through. It doesn't take too much imagination to build a picture of what the cost of the mining commodity would truly be – should truly be.[24]

With academic clarity and care, they made the case that if the ecosystem damage was actually paid for, in terms of their value and contributions to the global economy, the price of commodities using or damaging these services would be much greater. The structure of the economy from payments, including wages, interest rates and through to profits would change dramatically. World gross national product (GNP) would be very different in magnitude and composition.[23, 24]

As time has moved on, the foundation work of these ecological economists has been rolled into something very different and minority world NGOs have been complicit in the reinterpretation. Ecosystem services programs now involve evaluating the monetary value to society of natural services, such as clean water, biodiversity or reduced atmospheric carbon, and then compensating people who manage land that provides these services. There is rarely any thought or connection given to community and communion with the natural world. And, sadly, the vision of the market internalising the cost of the damage it causes has not come to fruition. Instead, what we have now is a focus on retaining a few landscape level systems as intact, by making payment to governments, and sometime communities, for the ecosystem service they provide.

The reinterpreted ideology is a brand of neoliberal market environmentalism which has been promoted since the late 1980s, when minority world NGOs began to look for market-led ways to solve the world's development and environmental problems. Essentially, market environmentalism promotes the pricing of nature's services, the assignation of property rights and the expansion of commodity markets into the realm of nature's services.[25] Often, as envisaged by the Reducing Emissions from Deforestation and Forest Degradation (or REDD+) scheme, the flow of money is from richer countries to poorer ones in market-based Payment for Ecosystem Service (PES) schemes. PES, REDD+, carbon trading, conservation marketing and conservation finance mechanisms such as biodiversity derivatives and species banking are just some of the market mechanisms that have soared in popularity in recent decades.[26]

I don't argue against the real costs to providing and protecting ecosystem services, and I recognise we must develop suitable mechanisms for paying for them. Ideally, the funds would be enough to provide people with the option of choosing a more sustainable livelihood than, say, agriculture requiring expansion into forests.[27] But, we have lost our way in a tangled interpretation. PES has been built on market economics to determine a fair price for the ecosystem services in formal Wall Street-type exchanges, where services go to the highest bidder. Ecosystems have been turned into a commodity. Doing this has robbed the discussion of the understanding of the inherent complexity of ecosystems and the myriad non-economic values they also contain.

Majority world activists have a different, and perhaps more legitimate, perspective – that ecosystem services are co-produced by nature and communities and that their value is not derived from market prices of their services but instead from their contributions to communities and livelihoods, their food production, biodiversity and wider social benefits that cannot be quantified or sold.[28, 29]

We should have known better. In our folly, power has been systematically transferred to the corporate elite.

Sustainability is merged with development

Alexander Gillespie warned us about the risks in two important academic works. Nearly 20 years later we are seeing his warning borne out. In 1997 he made the case that self-interest, which is the major driving force propelling the market, cannot be relied upon for the greater good. And, placing an economic value on the environment may serve some aspects, but the value of the whole system cannot easily be captured by economic instruments.[30] In 2001, he investigated the root of the sustainability concept failure. Like ecosystem services, the original concept of sustainable development was about limiting activity to restrict it to within ecological and social means, and do no harm. Over time the ideology has been hijacked and is now intrinsically linked to the conventional ideology of economic growth (as well of population growth). Economic growth, in its present form, requires production, resource use and consumption. Those seeking economic gain have a direct interest in promoting resource use and production, while marketing their case as 'green' with remarkable effectiveness to almost all governments, everywhere.[31] The social and environmental dimension of sustainable development has become little more than lip-service.

Writing after the World Summit on Sustainable Development (also known as the Rio+10) in 2002, Paul Wapner captured the emerging conflict at a key moment. The majority world articulated a belief that ecological protection was the grounding for economic well-being and development. Whereas the minority world shift dramatically to become pro economic development.[21, 32] As Paul Wapner reported:

> the US and a number of other Northern governments proposed economic globalization as the answer to the world's environmental and development challenges. They argued that further opening-up of markets, lowering tariffs, privatizing public land and holdings, and so forth would improve the lot of the poor and, at the same time, improve environmental conditions.[32]

It is interesting to reflect on this again, 14 years later, because with time we can see how the ripples have shaped new shorelines and the neoliberal market environmentalism agenda has become mainstream in the minority world.[33, 34] Meanwhile, the majority world interpretation is left calling into the wind.

Philanthrocapitalism steps in

Emboldened with their new market friendly veneer, minority world NGOs were well placed to pursue major funding. This funding shapes whole programmes today,[35] directed for the attention and focus of foundations as well as wealthy social entrepreneurs and venture philanthropists, otherwise known as philanthrocapitalists, who loan their name and wealth to large-scale and often simplistic solutions that may inhibit real change and strengthen the status quo.[36, 37] So long as sustainable development continues to mouth the words minority world conservation NGOs want to hear; as long as it is written into every treaty, every agreement and every government commitment, the illusion is maintained.

Philanthrocapitalism is straight from the neoliberal textbook. It purports that social good can be supported by privatisation, deregulation, free trade and reductions in government spending to enhance the role of the private sector in the economy. To do good socially the neoliberal ideology believes that you must do well financially: public and private interest are promoted as intrinsically mutually compatible.[35, 38] The focus is often on big prizes or big goals, and not on the day-to-day that is required to keep the world functioning. This is not limited to attractive strap lines.

Philanthrocapitalists tend to differentiate themselves from the rest of civil society claiming they are 'results based' or 'high performance', implying that everyone else is not.[39] As Peter Dauvergne and Jane Lister argue, marketing your solution as sustainable gives market advantage to your brand, and helps to shape the agenda along the way. That the solution is dreamt up in the corporate board room or a CEO's head matters little, especially if the business is able to enlist green support from NGOs.[40]Aside from being absurd – and arrogant – this message has a trickle-through effect that skews which proposals the big NGOs pursue. Michael Edwards warns about the serious bias this creates. As part of the process of legitimising capitalism, philanthropy favours certain forms of environmentalism – those that are friendly to capitalism, or at least not directly threatening to it.[33] Minority world NGOs arrange 'results based prizes', like protected areas over large, pristine and fragile areas in the majority world. The intent is to lock precious places away from harm, yet the action ignores the inconvenient knowledge that these areas exclude local communities – people who have lived in these pristine places for generations and are just as wronged by big business as wildlife are.[41]

Legally ambiguous land rights are already a global crisis – for the millions of indigenous peoples and local communities who risk losing their lands and livelihoods, undermining their collective ability to confront climate change, food insecurity, poverty and political instability, and to protect wildlife and wild places.[42, 43]

The high performance principle sounds great on paper. In practice it is problematic. It not only shifts power to minority world donors, corporations, NGOs and wealthy individuals, it increases market incentives for governments to displace local communities.[44–47]

Courting capitalism also means you have to lower your standards. The Nature Conservancy, Conservation International and WWF each have significant and long-term relationship with coal, petroleum or minding companies.[48] Conservation International has relationships with Wal-Mart, Monsanto, Toyota and McDonalds.[49] In *This Changes Everything*, Naomi Klein reveals that many of the big organisations invest in the dirtiest polluters through their endowment funds or from foundations that invest in the major polluters.[49] She rightly comments that the hypocrisy is staggering. A coalition of US conservation NGOs even created a pro-free trade organisation called the Environmental Coalition for NAFTA. The members included the National Wildlife Federation, Environmental Defence Fund, Conservation International, National Audubon Society, Natural Resources Defence Council and World Wildlife Fund.[50] While pro-trade agreement coalitions have not been created for the big new trade deals, I have been dismayed to watch many minority world NGOs active in the lobbying for the Trans-Pacific Partnership and Transatlantic Trade and Investment Partnership to secure wildlife trade provisions, while remaining silent on the grave risks of environmental harm to wildlife habitat. The achievements are important, but many commentators argue they are effectively eroded by measures that weaken domestic legislation.

With large scale philanthropic funding, the five largest US conservation NGOs – The Nature Conservancy, Conservation International, Wildlife Conservation Society, WWF–US and The Conservation Fund – spend more than US$1 billion each year on conservation work outside of the United States of America. Estimates are that a further US$6 billion each year is invested in maintaining protected areas outside of the United States. The senior staff of these organisations command salaries comparable with major transnational corporations, more than six times the US median household earning.[48] With such significant funding it is difficult to avoid capture.

In 2015 the Global Policy Forum, an international watchdog group, released a report on the growth of philanthropic influence in global policy agenda setting. The report by Jens Martens and Karolin Seitz warns that the scope of influence by a few very large foundations is fully equal to, and in some cases goes beyond, that of other private actors. In 2012, the 1,000 largest US foundations gave US$5.9 billion, or about 27 per cent of their grants, to international activities. Prominent foundations were actively involved in the debates on what a future UN development agenda could look like. They influenced the process through their funding, their advocacy activities and direct interventions, and will continue this influence through the process of implementing the 2030 Sustainable Development Agenda.[51] The World Bank rather glowingly says:

> Use of venture capital or private equity style decision-making is increasingly widespread within philanthropy, but with a focus on development objectives rather than the expected financial return on investment. ... The blending of business approaches within philanthropic models is mirrored by a blending of philanthropic and corporate objectives. For a growing number of firms, philanthropy is no longer considered outside of corporate strategy.[52]

Conservation NGOs have also entered the market by selling 'adoption products' and 'travel experiences'; smoothing the ripples in marketing messages so as to not offend supporters (viewed as clients) with difficult or bad news; marketing departments are increased and conservation teams are shrunk, outsourcing knowledge and expertise because it makes business sense. Many minority world NGOs have adopted the posture and attributes of the very thing – capitalism, consumerism and the market – that is also doing the damage.

We could overlook these failings if the conservation they achieved was great. Instead, their attention is deflected from harmful corporations, and toward demonising people who have lived for millennia beside elephants and tigers, sharks and turtles. Rather than supporting these communities to fend off palm oil or industrialised fishing fleets, communities are cast as selfish when they plant short-term cash-crops or hunt or fish for species they have not caught before – because they are hungry. Eyes are averted from the systemic causes for elephant poaching or shark finning. Stands of forests are traded for agreement not to rail against dams that will flood whole valleys. Nicole Aschoff says it well:

> When we channel our desire to end global warming or rainforest destruction or species extinction through corporations, our desires end up getting absorbed into business strategies for growth and expansion, strengthening the production-for-profit architecture that's consuming and destroying the world's resources.[53]

If the majority world remains impoverished, the ramifications for wildlife and people are already dire. But, it will become even worse if the corporate elite garner even more power.[54–60]

Blinded by our own spin

Through these three decades, many minority world NGOs have developed a layer or arrogance that matches their major funders. From the safety of Washington, Brussels or London they believe their wisdom is sufficient to encompass the world. Franchising their global brands, they have manoeuvred themselves to capture the flow of financing and support, crowding out majority world voices.[61]

In the previous two chapters I levelled the accusation of nepotism, corruption and self-interests at governments and corporations. But, we are all part of an international system that no longer works, and neoliberal market environmentalists and some philanthrocaptialists also contribute hubris to the failing mix. It is conceited to presume that majority world perspectives are simple, unsophisticated or small. Indeed, the economic standing of a country in the global community rarely reflects the sophistication of its citizens. Where communities and indigenous peoples have secure land tenure they are often the most capable custodians of the planet's natural capital. A review of 130 local studies in 14 countries, conducted jointly by the Rights and Resources Initiative and the World Resources Institute, found that community-run forests suffer less deforestation and store more carbon than other forests.[62] This evidence contradicts decades of conservation thinking, which has believed that forest communities were widely responsible for deforestation through shifting cultivation. Yet, the minority conservation NGOs persist in their 'command and control' approach.[42]

I can hear the howls of furious objection from conservationists in the minority world to these comments. But I also hear the quite thanks of conservationists and community leaders almost everywhere else.

I wish it wasn't possible to defend this statement as easily as it is. Unfortunately minority world NGOs have left a trail of incriminating evidence behind them.

Coopting funding

An incredible power has grown in a few large NGOs, particularly in the United States. This problem was cracked open in 2004, when Mac Chapin of

the World Watch Institute released a discussion paper that confirmed many of
our fears and shook the ground under our feet. He begins:

> In June 2003, representatives of major foundations concerned with the
> planet's threatened biodiversity gathered in South Dakota for a meeting
> of the Consultative Group on Biodiversity. On the second evening, after
> dinner, several of the attendees met to discuss a problem about which
> they had become increasingly disturbed. In recent years, their foundations
> had given millions of dollars of support to nonprofit conservation
> organizations, and had even helped some of those groups get launched.
> Now, however, there were indications that three of the largest of these
> organizations – World Wildlife Fund (WWF), Conservation International
> (CI), and The Nature Conservancy (TNC) – were increasingly excluding,
> from full involvement in their programs, the indigenous and traditional
> peoples living in territories the conservationists were trying to protect.[63]

Mac Chapin bravely went on to reveal a disturbing underbelly to a movement
many of us had invested our lives in. Not only was funding being funnelled to
these few organisations, but their agendas were dictating what many local
NGOs were able to work on. The intent of the foundations had been that
these big NGOs would re-grant to local NGOs, to ease the foundation's
paperwork, but it gave these NGOs considerable power over where money was
directed. In dealing with local NGOs they either used their 'sheer heft' to use
Chapin's language or they starved groups out of existence. Frequently, they
created whole new local organisations – so-called spinoffs – implanting these
with expat staff, making them extensions of the parent. Meanwhile, they
actively distanced themselves from local civil society and in so doing
swamped the policy landscape with agenda and directions that were devoid of
these voices.[63]

The World Watch Institute website archived the discussion and maintained
a section they reserved for comments on Mac Chapin's controversial paper.
This one caught my eye, from Tashi Wangchuk, an official with the Ministry
of Agriculture in Bhutan:

> The [Wildlife] Conservation Society (WCS) and the Nature Conservation
> Division of the Forestry Department in Bhutan signed an MoU in 2004
> for WCS scientists to work in Bhutan. ... One was particularly interested
> in studying the Takin (Budorcas taxicolor), Bhutan's national animal ...
> Little did I know what the reaction of WWF-US would be like. In
> October 2004 I was summoned by Bruce Bunting, a Vice President at
> WWF, on a visit to Bhutan, and shouted and yelled at me for helping
> WCS people. The message was clear, WCS is not to be welcomed to
> Bhutan. Bunting reminded me of our 'professional relationship'. WWF-US
> had given me a scholarship for undergraduate studies in the US to study
> conservation biology in 1990. I was rudely reminded about where my

loyalties should lie. Bunting of course seemed to have forgotten about the bond that I signed with my government on receiving the scholarship. I would pay for the scholarship by working for the Bhutan government on my return. The conversation ended with an implicit threat from Bunting. I was just a puny third world biologist and should not interfere with the agendas of mighty conservation organizations. ...[64]

Denial

In 2009 Friends of the Earth International (FoEI), arguably the world's largest grassroots environmental network that operates with an egalitarian ethic deeply rooted in facilitating the power of local civil society, withdrew their membership of IUCN. FoEI's letter of notification to the Director General of IUCN states the reason for the withdrawal was 'concern about the corporate partnership between Shell and the IUCN' that was silencing IUCN's willingness to critique the negative social and environmental consequences associated with Shell's practices.[65]

> It is of particular concern to FoEI that in our review of IUCN's collective positions regarding Shell's environmental and social performance over the past few years there either is an unnatural silence or no clear articulation from IUCN on many critical aspects of Shell's activities, including: gas flaring, abuse of human rights, environmental degradation, exploitation of tar sands, arctic drilling, and corporate lobbying against European Union climate change policies. ... It is our belief and experience that part-nerships between transnational corporations such as Shell and conservation organizations such as IUCN have a disadvantageous effect on community struggles to protect their environment, health and well-being from corpora-tions. Indeed, these partnerships are used to 'greenwash' harmful corporate activities and distort the reality on the ground.[65]

FoEI's withdrawal followed a failed motion during the IUCN meeting the previous year that sought to direct the IUCN staff to terminate the relationship with Shell. The Nigerian Conservation Foundation and Sierra Club sought to open debate about IUCN relationships with big oil in the Niger Delta and Arctic. Despite securing an overwhelming majority of the vote, the motion 'Termination of the agreement between IUCN and Shell (CGR4.MOT107)' was defeated,[66] because the 'government house' of the membership (IUCN's membership is divided between NGOs and governments) voted against it.

IUCN is not alone in turning a blind eye. In the latest in a long string of damning accusations levelled at WWF, the organisation is being taken to the OECD accused of breaches of OECD Guidelines on the Conduct of Multi-national Enterprises and also the UN Declaration on Human Rights. The complaint alleges that WWF has financed and supported eco-guards that have displaced the Baka tribespeople who have traditionally lived in an area now declared as national park in Cameroon. WWF are accused of forbidding traditional hunting and perpetrating violent abuse, while turning a blind eye to the destruction of Baka land through logging, mining and the trafficking of wildlife. There is concern among tribespeople that their land is being destroyed, even as they are denied access to large parts of it in the name of conservation.[67, 68] Survival International's Director Stephen Corry has said:

> WWF knows that the men its supporters fund for conservation work repeatedly abuse, and even torture, the Baka, whose land has been stolen for conservation zones. It hasn't stopped them, and it treats criticism as something to be countered with yet more public relations.[68]

Tokenism

CIVICUS (The World Alliance for Citizen Participation) reports that in many countries relations between the state and civil society are getting worse. This is certainly borne out in the experiences that José and I share. Where minority world NGOs have no relationships with majority world governments they often hire, mostly on a short-term basis, local activists to represent their interests either in-country for a specific outcome or at international meetings.[11] If these NGOs do fund locals it is mostly to deliver materials and props to government delegations. The local activist plays little or no part in developing materials. They are a veneer of involvement and expected to portray belief in the words on the page. More often than not the local activists fade from the scene soon after the meeting is over. During my interview with José he summed it up well: 'When meetings are in Africa they hire African faces, in South America they hire Latin faces, and in Asia we see Asian faces, but these people are never seen again'.[69]

There are significant costs to this strategy. Foremost, the majority world government and minority world NGO partnership lacks a solid base, and is often deeply reliant on the minority world NGO maintaining a funding flow to the relationship and projects they share. It is also debatable whether these NGOs are effecting real policy change. Indeed, in many cases they might even be hampering it. In recent years many majority world governments have become adept at exploiting the relationship with large NGOs and large foundations to increase funding. But, without a genuine local civil society component there was little or no public engagement – the projects and polices risk poor traction to make real and long-term changes. The NGOs are vulnerable to being duped, because they have no civil watchdog or whistleblower potential. In essence, they undermine one of the most powerful aspects of their own sector.

In contrast to the large salaries and incredible scale of funding for many minority world conservation NGOs, stands the daily struggle of civil society around the world. In March 2016 Phan Sopheak, one of a group of activists awarded the UN Equator Prize at the 2015 Paris Climate Summit, was attacked with the intent to murder. She belongs to the Prey Lang Community Network (PLCN), a grassroots group of Kuy ethnic volunteers who work to protect the Prey Lang Forest, which spans five provinces in northern Cambodia. Phan Sopheak was on forest patrol when she was attacked. Members of the PLCN believe that her assailants were trying to cut her throat.[70, 71] These volunteers had confiscated 85 chainsaws and many cubic metres of wood from illegal loggers in Prey Lang in the previous two months. Like José, they strive to protect what is around them. Like José, they are without mainstream funding. Like José, they produce sophisticated and strategic documentation about their work. At most, they will secure the occasional small grant to cover their costs. They have no living wages. There is no sustained support. We owe them more.

I have significant empathy for conservationists who say that community participation in the Congo Basin, the Amazon and Asia is difficult. In some regions, local civil society is nascent and still quite weak. Social mobilisation can be difficult. Conflicts and power asymmetries between local communities further complicate the picture. And, it is true, that funding for community engagement is limited. However, this does not negate the inherent rightness of trying. Nor will funding always be limited; especially if the large minority world NGOs turn to their funders and declare that it is the new priority. Local communities notice where the money is. They are aware of the game, and the current brand of tokenistic, coopted, neoliberal market environmentalism does little to win their trust and commitment. In a report by Aili Pyhälä, Ana Osuna Orozco and Simon Counsell an indigenous person in South Cameroon is quoted as saying:

> 'Dobi-dobi' [WWF] people have more money than anyone here. They work with all the local big people, the évolués, extractive industries, safaris and even with ministers in Yaoundé. And the whites are behind them, even the Prince of England [sic] and the World Bank.[72]

*** *** ***

A sombre cape has been draped over the world. Beneath the wretched shroud the pressure builds.

Suddenly lightning cracks from left to right, illuminating the field.

The gorilla looks impossibly small and vulnerable, against the vast might of this approaching storm.

References

1   Truda Palazzo Jr, J. 1999. Whose Whales? Developing Countries and the Right to Use Whales by Non-lethal Means. *Journal of International Wildlife Law & Policy*. 2, 1: 69–78.

2   Lewan, T. 1996. Conservationist Doing Right by Threatened Whale. *Los Angeles Times*, 30th June 1996.

3   Carroll, E. L., Baker, C. S., Watson, M., Alderman, R., Bannister, J., Gaggiotti, O. E., Gröcke, D. R., Patenaude, N. and Harcourt, R. 2015. Cultural Traditions across a Migratory Network Shape the Genetic Structure of Southern Right Whales around Australia and New Zealand. *Scientific Reports*. 5: 16182.

4   Global Witness. 2015. *How Many More? 2014's Deadly Environment: The Killing and Intimidation of Environmental and Land Activists, with a Spotlight on Honduras.* London: Global Witness.

5   Global Witness. 2014. *Peru's Deadly Environment: The Rise in Killings of Environmental and Land Defenders.* London: Global Witness.

6   Sá Corrêa, M. 2007. Para quê mais um Instituto Chico Mendes? *Revista ECO 21.*

7   Cortez, H. 2009. 'O pessoal desaprendeu a jogar tomate', diz criador da ONG Projeto Baleia Franca, José Truda Palazzo Jr. *EcoDebate*, 10th August 2009.

8   Friends of the Earth International. 2012. Denouncing the Brutal Murder of Two Fishermen from Rio de Janeiro Friends of the Earth. [online material]

9   Centro di Documentazione sui Conflitti Ambientali. 2012. Rio, Brazil: Killing of Human Rights Defenders. [online material]

10 Frayssinet, F. 2012. Brazilian Environmental Activists Killed in Shadow of Rio +20. Inter Press Service News Agency. [online material]

11 Truda Palazzo Jr, J. 2016. Interview.

12 Dryzek, J. S. 1997. *The Politics of Earth: Environmental Discourses.* Oxford: Oxford University Press.

13 Anheier, H. K. 2004. *Civil Society: Measurement, Evaluation, Policy.* London: Earthscan.

14 Martens, K. 2002. Mission Impossible? Defining Nongovernmental Organizations. *Voluntas: International Journal of Voluntary and Nonprofit Organizations.* 13, 3: 271–285.

15 Charnovitz, S. 2006. Accountability of Non-Governmental Organisations in Global Governance. In *NGO Accountability: Politics, Principles and Innovations.* Edited by Jordan, L., and Van Tuijl, P. London, Earthscan.

16 Donini, A. 1995. The Bureaucracy and the Free Spirits: Stagnation and Innovation in the Relationship between the UN and NGOs. *Third World Quarterly.* 16, 3: 421–440.

17 World Commission on Environment and Development. 1987. *Our Common Future: The World Commission on Environment and Development.* London: Oxford University Press.

18 Wapner, P. 1996. *Environmental Activism and World Civic Politics.* New York: State University of New York Press.

19 Karns, M. P. and Mingst, K. A. 2004. *International Organisations: The Politics and Processes of Global Governance.* London: Lynne Rienner Publishers.

20 Hajer, M. A. 2005. *The Politics of Environmental Discourse: Ecological Modernization and the Policy Process.* Oxford: Oxford University Press.

21 MacDonald, K. I. 2010. The Devil is in the (Bio)diversity: Private Sector 'Engagement' and the Restructuring of Biodiversity Conservation. *Antipode.* 42, 3: 513–550.

22 Daly, H. E. and Cobb, J. B. 1994. *For the Common Good: Redirecting the Economy Toward Community, the Environment and a Sustainable Future.* Boston: Beacon Press.

23   Costanza, R. and Daly, H. E. 1992. Natural Capital and Sustainable Development. *Conservation Biology.* 6, 1: 37–46.

24   Costanza, R., d'Arge, R., de Groots, R., et al. 1997. The Value of the World's Ecosystem Services and Natural Capital. *Nature.* 387: 253–260.

25   Kosoy, N. and Corbera, E. 2010. Payments for Ecosystem Services as Commodity Fetishism. *Ecological Economics.* 69, 6: 1228–1236.

26   Arsel, M. and Büscher, B. 2012. Nature^{TM} Inc.: Changes and Continuities in Neoliberal Conservation and Market-based Environmental Policy. *Development and Change.* 43, 1: 53–78.

27   Cannon, J. 2015. The State of the Market for Ecosystem Services. *Mongabay,* 17th December 2015.

28   McAfee, K. and Shapiro, E. N. 2010. Payments for Ecosystem Services in Mexico: Nature, Neoliberalism, Social Movements, and the State. *Annals of the Association of American Geographers.* 100, 3: 579–599.

29   Maconachie, R. and Hilson, G. 2013. Editorial Introduction: The Extractive Industries, Community Development and Livelihood Change in Developing Countries. *Community Development Journal.* 48, 3: 347–359.

30   Gillespie, A. 1997. *International Environmental Law, Policy and Ethics.* Oxford: Oxford University Press.

31   Gillespie, A. 1997. *The Illusion of Progress: Unsustainable Development in International Law and Policy.* London: Earthscan.

32   Wapner, P. 2003. World Summit on Sustainable Development: Toward a Post-Jo'burg Environmentalism. *Global Environmental Politics.* 3, 1: 1–10.

33   Holmes, G. 2012. Biodiversity for Billionaires: Capitalism, Conservation and the Role of Philanthropy in Saving/Selling Nature. *Development and Change.* 43, 1: 185–203.

34   Sachs, J. D. 2015. *The Age of Sustainable Development.* New York: Columbia University Press.

35   Firmin, A., Tiwana, M., Evanics, R., Hobhouse, E., MacGarry, M. and Sayed, Z. 2015. *State of Civil Society Report: 2015.* New York: CIVICUS: World Alliance for Citizen Participation.

36   Bosworth, D. 2011. The Cultural Contradictions of Philanthrocapitalism. *Society.* 48, 5: 382–388.

37   Aschoff, N. 2015. *The New Prophets of Capital.* London: Verso Books.

38   McGoey, L. 2012. Philanthrocapitalism and Its Critics. *Poetics.* 40, 2: 185–199.

39   Edwards, M. 2008. *Just Another Emperor: The Myths and Realities of Philanthrocapitalism.* London: Demos.

40   Dauvergne, P. and Lister, J. 2013. *Eco-business: A Big-brand Takeover of Sustainability.* Cambridge: MIT Press.

41   Holmes, G. 2015. Philanthrocapitalism, Biodiversity Conservation and Development. In *New Philanthropy and Social Justice: Debating the Conceptual and Policy Discourse.* Edited by Morvaridi, B. Bristol: Polity Press: 81–100.

42   Pearce, F. 2016. *Securing Land Rights and Safeguarding the Earth.* Oxford: Oxfam, International Land Coalition, Rights and Resources Initiative.

43   Ceddia, M. G., Gunter, U. and Corriveau-Bourque, A. 2015. Land Tenure and Agricultural Expansion in Latin America: The Role of Indigenous Peoples' and Local Communities' Forest Rights. *Global Environmental Change.* 35: 316–322.

44   Phelps, J., Webb, E. L. and Agrawal, A. 2010. Does REDD+ Threaten to Recentralize Forest Governance? *Science.* 328: 310–313.

45 Twongyirwe, R., Sheil, D., Sandbrook, C. G. and Sandbrook, L. C. 2015. REDD at the Crossroads? The Opportunities and Challenges of REDD for Conservation and Human Welfare in South West Uganda. *International Journal of Environment and Sustainable Development.* 14, 3: 273–298.

46 Lunstrum, E. 2015. Green Grabs, Land Grabs and the Spatiality of Displacement: Eviction from Mozambique's Limpopo National Park. *Area:* n/a-n/a.

47 Godden, L. and Tehan, M. 2016. REDD+: Climate Justice and Indigenous and Local Community Rights in an Era of Climate Disruption. *Journal of Energy & Natural Resources Law.* 34, 1: 95–108.

48 MacDonald, C. 2008. *Green, Inc: An Environmental Insider Reveals How a Good Cause Has Gone Bad.* Washington, DC: Rowman & Littlefield.

49 Klein, N. 2014. *This Changes Everything: Capitalism vs. the Climate.* New York: Simon and Schuster.

50 Dreiling, M. and Wolf, B. 2001. Environmental Movement Organizations and Political Strategy Tactical Conflicts over NAFTA. *Organization & Environment.* 14, 1: 34–54.

51 Martens, J. and Seitz, K. 2015. *Philanthropic Power and Development: Who Shapes the Agenda?* Bonn: Global Policy Forum.

52 Jarvis, M. and Goldberg, J. M. 2008. Business and Philanthropy: The Blurring of Boundaries. In *Business & Development Discussion Papers.* Washington: World Bank Institute.

53 Aschoff, N. 2015. Exposing the False Prophets of Social Transformation. openDemocracy.

54 Fitzpatrick, C. and Engels, D. 2016. Leaving No One Behind: A Neglected Tropical Disease Indicator and Tracers for the Sustainable Development Goals. *International Health.* 8, suppl 1: i15–i18.

55 Waage, J., Yap, C., Bell, S., et al. 2015. Governing the UN Sustainable Development Goals: Interactions, Infrastructures, and Institutions. *The Lancet Global Health.* 3, 5: e251-e52.

56 El-Zein, A., DeJong, J., Fargues, P., Salti, N., Hanieh, A. and Lackner, H. 2016. Who's Been Left Behind? Why Sustainable Development Goals Fail the Arab World. *The Lancet.*

57 Szabo, S., Renaud, F., Hossain, S., Sebesvári, Z., Matthews, Z., Foufoula-Georgiou, E. and Nicholls, R. J. 2015. New Opportunities for Tropical Delta Regions Offered by the Proposed Sustainable Development Goals. *Environment: Science and Policy for Sustainable Development.* 57, 4: 16–23.

58 Uitto, J. I. and Shaw, R. 2015. *Sustainable Development and Disaster Risk Reduction.* New York: Springer.

59 Wood, S. L. R. and DeClerck, F. 2015. Ecosystems and Human Well-being in the Sustainable Development Goals. *Frontiers in Ecology and the Environment.* 13, 3: 123–123.

60 Fukuda-Parr, S. 2016. From the Millennium Development Goals to the Sustainable Development Goals: Shifts in Purpose, Concept, and Politics of Global Goal Setting for Development. *Gender & Development.* 24, 1: 43–52.

61 Edwards, M. 2009. Why 'Philanthrocapitalism' Is Not the Answer: Private Initiatives and International Development. In *Doing Good or Doing Better: Development Policies in a Globalizing World.* Edited by Kremer, M., van Lieshout, P. and Went, R. Amsterdam: Amsterdam University Press: 237–254.

62 Stevens, C., Winterbottom, R., Reytar, K. and Springer, J. 2014. *Securing Rights, Combating Climate Change: How Strengthening Community Forest Rights Mitigates Climate Change.* Washington: World Resource Institute.

63 Chapin, M. 2004. A Challenge to Conservationists. *World Watch Magazine* November/December: 17–31.

64 World Watch Institute. 2004. Readers' Responses to "A Challenge to Conservationists". [online material]

65 Friends of the Earth International. 2009. IUCN Withdrawal. [online material]

66 World Conservation Congress. 2008. *Proceedings of the Members' Assembly.* Barcelona, International Union for Conservation of Nature and Natural Resources.

67 Vidal, J. 2016. WWF Accused of Facilitating Human Rights Abuses of Tribal People in Cameroon. *The Guardian Online.*

68 Survival International. 2016. Survival International Accuses WWF of Involvement in Violence and Abuse. [online material]

69 Truda Palazzo Jr, J. 2015. Interview.

70 Global Witness. 2016. Machete Attack on Award-winning Cambodian Activist Part of Global Trend of Violence against Forest Defenders. [online material]

71 Prey Lang Community Network. 2016. Statement from the PLCN about the Attempted Murdered on a PLCN Activist Phan Sopheak. [online material]

72 Pyhälä, A., Osuna Orozco, A. and Counsell, S. 2016. Protected Areas in the Congo Basin: Failing Both People and Biodiversity? In *Under the Canopy Series.* London: Rainforest Foundation UK.

4 Thunder rumbles

Night heron – Maximin Djondo

The phone rings. Drawn bleary-eyed from the depths of pre-dawn sleep, Maximin Djondo turns to his clock. It is 5am.

'Mr Bird,' a stranger's voice echoes down the line. 'We hear gunshots. I think they are killing the birds.'

Minutes later, another unknown caller from a second village confirms the report.

To this day he doesn't know how they got his number, but there is pride as he recounts the calls. This is grassroots conservation in action. For decades water-birds on the lake had been hunted. Some hunting was traditional, but more problematic was wealthy sport-hunters with European guides. All that has changed.

A year or two passes, and dawn breaks across Nokoué Lake, southern Benin – this place that Maximin is so committed to.

I imagine that a hoarse call – quawk, quawk, quawk – vibrates across the wetland from black-crowned night herons returning from their nocturnal forage. Pale bellies flash in the morning light, as they settle on mangrove branches. Some of the males sport their breeding plumage – slim, long showy white feathers extend from their heads, their legs and feet in transition from muted yellow to red.

Nearby a manatee and her small dark calf muddle along the lake bed. Her flat paddle-tail gently fans the water – so gentle that the muds and water part without noticing her. Small eyes in a broad, tranquil head blink a welcome to the morning light. Her feeding done, it is time to find a place to rest – shallow water with mangroves as cover is what she now seeks.

Maximin is the Director for Benin Environment and Education Society (BEES), an impressive local NGO which represents so much of what is possible for the future. He is dedicated to facilitating wildlife research and conservation activities in his region, and has spearheaded the development of sustainable income generating opportunities for communities in north and south Benin.

His enlightened perspective has grown from an early programme he worked on for the conservation of the Lama Forest and the red-bellied guenon, a critically endangered monkey found only in Benin. For a time the species was considered extinct, wiped out in a race for its fur. This black-faced little monkey has the misfortune to have an attractive mousey-brown coat with a ruff of white around its throat and a deep red belly. Now rediscovered, these enigmatic little fruit eaters are still very rare and by no means secure. Their habitat is heavily degraded and remaining patches are threatened by timber extraction and conversion to agricultural land. And, these little monkeys are still hunted for bushmeat.

A little over a decade ago, a team of scientists and Benin based conservationists conceived of a programme to create new local business for the local community in return for forest protection. In 2008, BEES created an ecotourism centre in Lama. Maximin and his team now work with the communities who neighbour the forest in an ongoing process where individuals become aware of their environment and acquire the knowledge, skills and experience to enable them to collectively solve the environment problems they face. Residents are organised into a Participatory Forest Management Committee, that oversees their local governance and makes money from offering visitors a tourism service. In return, they care for the forest. Housewives, farmers, artisans and youngsters all participate. This is an excellent example of forest co-management – a partnership between government and a local community, with an NGO as the communicator between. Slowly, but surely, the little guenon's calls are being heard again.

As I set up the computer to call Maximin, the morning over Nokoué has advanced. The lyrical dance of a red-headed malimbe song might be twirling across the water from the forest edge. Perhaps a sitatunga lifts herself up onto a floating island of vegetation. Her shaggy coat, rusty-brown, streams water, like oil off glass. In the morning light, the pale stripes of this wetland-dwelling antelope shine, for just a moment. She has swum through water hyacinth and tall reeds to the safety of this spot. At times she will have submerged herself while predators pass, hooves splayed against the lake bed leaving only her nose above water. She is safe here in Nokoué. Today, no snares have been set.

This is a unique and beautiful region on the margins of survival. Lake Nokoué, 20 km wide and 11 km long, is formed by the deltas of the So and Ouémé rivers in southern Benin. A rich, alluvial region it is the most productive in West Africa. Wetland forests, marshes and flood plains rise and recede with the ebb and flow of seasonal water. Originally farmers, the villagers on and around Nokoué now live from fishing, fish-farming and tourism. To the south sits the city of Cotonou, the economic centre of Benin; to the east, the county's capital, Porto Novo. These waters are relied upon by tens of thousands of fisherpeople.

While comprehensive scientific surveys of the region are still to be completed, so far 168 species of bird and 78 species of fish have been recognised in Nokoué, along with sitatunga, pythons, manatee and tortoises. Close to 100,000 hectares of Lake Nokoué were declared a Ramsar Wetland of International Importance in 2000,[1] yet Benin struggles to overcome some serious problems for the wetland. Mangrove destruction, overfishing, hunting, poaching and pollution are at the heart of their worries; and now, the country must also contend with the impact of rising sea levels.[2, 3] Out of desperation, in 2012 the World Wetland Network (WWN) gave the Ramsar wetland in Benin a grey globe award, calling for an action plan to safeguard the site with the cooperation of local communities.[4] The Wetland Globes were developed by the WWN to encourage best practice in wetland management. They are non-financial awards, nominated and decided by civil society, given to the wetland itself. Wetlands in good condition receive blue globes and wetlands under threat grey.

I was looking forward to my call with Maximin. It had taken us a few weeks to coordinate it. He has been running community workshops and my husband Geoff and I have been immersed in writing. And, while the world forges ahead with almost unfathomable connectivity, the internet in Benin is still unreliable. So, I am thrilled when the connection goes through and his deep, eloquent, francophone accent meets my ear.

I knew of his international wetland work through the grey globe nomination and WWN, but was about to come to understand how community learning, honed with his work with the red-bellied monkeys, was at the core of the programme he was pushing forward for Nokoué.

Dusk is falling in Australia as I settle into my chair to listen the warmth and care of his story about communities, connection and a spirit of cooperation all focused on the wildlife local to these people – elephants, lions, cheetah and buffalo in the north and kingfishers, herons, manatee and sitatunga in the south. Maximin is an adept at applying high-speed hyper-connected global thinking with human scale, person to person, action.

The wetland is suffering, but Maximin's solution is to empower and educate, rather than preach and regulate.

Benin is a country struggling to move forward – the country has few internationally marketable resources, so economic advance is slow. I presumed Maximin would have had to bow to the weight of international funder priorities and I almost dreaded asking who was pulling the strings. So many ecosystem ventures around the world have been set up by minority world NGOs, but, as I was to hear, not so for Nokoué.

Maximin is unique in using phrases like ethics and attitudes when he talks about his work. The programme remains community driven, community managed and the profits raised go directly back into community building projects. As it should be. With this empowerment, the door has opened for Maximin and his team to speak with the community about the other threats than need to be addressed – riparian clearance for agricultural land, heavy pollution loads and traditional fishing growing beyond a scale that the ecosystem can manage. He was pleased to be able to tell me that when people understood most of them changed of their own free will.

The programme is multi-dimensional and mirrors life more realistically. It is balanced to withstand the shocks of international economic ebbs and flows.

He works with women's associations to build sustainable business to catch and process fish. He works with local groups to find sustainable firewood supplies and build stoves that are efficient, but scaled to their needs. Women are being facilitated to weave products out of water hyacinth that is overgrowing the wetland because of high nitrogen levels. BEES provides no-interest loans to help people shift their activities to practices that damage less and benefit the community more.

Maximin's team have been able to educate people about the ecological costs of hunting manatee and sitatunga for bushmeat. Takes of these animals are steadily dropping, not because of laws but because people come to understand.

A modest tourism operation is based in the small lake island Dékanmé with a population of 4,241 people (834 households) and stretches to the famous floating township of Ganvié, with a population of 9,961 as well as Avagbodji and Aguégués with a combined population of 65,000. Dékanmé villagers are trained as skilled bird-guides and in the management of the accommodation and catering infrastructure the community has developed – so the connection to the people and this wetland remains tangible and true.

There are no expat faces calling the shots.

And all of this because of the wildlife around them. This blows apart an often spoken minority NGO myth that local people don't care about the species they live with and that only 'development' or 'protected area' conservation works.

As he speaks, my mind turns over the memory of when we first met a few years earlier when Maximin told me of the struggle he experienced as a national NGO. Working through government can be a barrier to effective activities and involvement. Yet, he is wise enough to know that he needs to bring his Government with BEES in order to be effective in Lama Forest and Lake Nokoué. Part of his success, I think to myself, comes from his tenacity to reach out for the funding and support when and where he needs it. Despite the internet technology challenges Benin faces, Maximin is extremely well connected, and he places BEES at centre of where international decisions are happening. He embodies the role that I believe minority NGOs should facilitate. BEES is so consistently in the room at Climate Change meetings, Ramsar meetings, CBD meetings, African Eurasian Water Bird Agreement meetings and at International Union for the Conservation of Nature (IUCN) Congress that it gives him credibility when it comes to negotiating with his Government counterparts. It is his credibility that opens doors and it is his compassion for the community that makes his brand of conservation work so well.

We talk some more about his other programme of work to build community support against elephant poaching in Benin's north. Like most of my friends, Maximin knows I will never pass up an opportunity to hear about elephants. Pachyderms are my passion. I am surprised to learn that rather than the Government posting border patrols and banning access to parks, civil society has negotiated a cooperative relationship between the community, the elephants and the forest. There is no forced displacement that we hear about elsewhere.

Cultural activities and gathering medicinal plants is a protected right, and like in the south, the villagers are having sustainable business supported and built on a foundation of community ecological knowledge and commitment. When their fledgling ecotourism venture took a hit during the Ebola crisis and poachers tried to move into the region from elsewhere, the local community resisted the poachers. The conservation ethic had already taken root.

With sotto voice Maximin tells me how success comes down to investing in face to face time with people. Respectful communication is valued. Maximin is far too modest to notice his wisdom. He chuckles as he tells me the 'Mr Bird' story and we share light moments of conservation humour. But, in my mind, I am building a strong picture of the power of community.

*** *** ***

Maximin's journey is not as common as we might hope. The minority world NGOs he works closely with, including notably Wetland International and Birdlife International, have a long and distinguished history of commitment to local civil society and empowering local solutions. Too often this is not the situation. In too many cases governments and minority world NGOs fail to recognise and respect the important work carried out by activists and civil society networks working on land and environmental issues, in trying to find a balance between economic development and respect of the environment.[5]

Illuminating the path through the storm

My soul-searching about gorillas in the Virunga raised questions about market mechanisms and the minority world sprinkling money around for small communities to be grateful for.

The more I look, the deeper I delve, the less I believe that the market is the answer. The future of gorillas in the Virunga is currently reliant on two market-based mechanisms – ecotourism and ecosystem services. I have no way to judge the Lama Forest and Lake Nokoué ecotourism model. I have not experienced it firsthand. But, with reluctance I have to say that my experience in Rwanda had a feel of imperialism about it, with the perceived largess of wealthy tourists and the NGOs generating the tourism cast as the heroes. As I described in chapter 3 the neoliberal brand of ecosystem service values nature according to a monetary measurement tuned for the global market. It is not clear if the Virunga has enough to offer that model. And, there are additional questions that must be asked. What happens if a species is too elusive or maybe not interesting for international tourists? What happens if a region is unsuitable for moving people in and out on a mass scale? What happens if a community wants to be left alone? What happens if the global economy takes a nose-dive or the price of travel climbs? What happens if a donor decides to change their focus and move money elsewhere? In my experience, dramatic shifts in funding happen more often than not. Programmes that have been established for a decade are suddenly closed, staff retrenched or moved to other regions and the expectations for conservation management are handed to the community without support. The most recent case that I am aware of is Wakatobi National Park in Indonesia.[6] Market mechanisms are not a solution for all communities and all wildlife, everywhere, and they lead us down a path to a fiercer, more brutal storm. There is another path, one less travelled but perhaps more just. It is a rooted cosmopolitan path made of a myriad of locally conceived and locally owned decisions. It is a path of community empowerment.

In an interview with Sarah Crowe, Danny Sriskandarajah, CEO of CIVICUS, highlights that a transformation, beyond the market, is already taking place for another sector faced with the same dilemma – Development NGOs:

> [W]e are seeing a transformation in who is going to lead social change over the next few decades … the state will retreat, business will have to fundamentally transform how it does business, [and] community and civil society will play a much bigger role in shaping societies around them.[7]

Development NGOs are already shifting their focus, recognising that their relevance will decline if they don't.[8] Conservation NGOs need to think about their relevance as well.

Between 2006 and 2013 Douglas Sheil, Manuel Boissière and Guillaume Beaudoin went, with open eyes and open minds, to learn how the Ijabait hereditary guardians control access to resource-rich lakes and tributaries along the Tariku River, in the Mamberamo-Foja region (Mamberamo Regency) of Papua (Indonesian New Guinea).[9] They found, as others have, that communities in a remote region monitor the environment around them, not because scientists have told them they should, but because it is already an integral part of their lives, livelihoods and cultures. These communities may not have the latest scientific assessments at their fingertips, but they often have generations of invaluable traditional knowledge. And, although local people are often at a disadvantage against powerful external forces, this is not always the case. There is growing recognition that communities oversee, manage and protect natural resources in many ways. It is as if the minority world NGO and scientific community is so focused on its own tools – protected areas, REDD+ and PES – that they can't see what already exists and the great potential inherent in local communities around the world.[9, 10]

> Whether autonomous monitoring is widespread and effective, or rare and ineffective, we need to recognize not only when local people are willing to champion environmental causes, but also when they are already doing so. The potential tragedy of the unseen sentinels is that so much may be lost simply because we failed to open our eyes to look.[9]

Although it has put me at odds with NGO colleagues over the years, I believe that ultimately progress in conservation effectiveness needs to be defined also in terms of equity and the cooperative engagement of local custodians rather than percentage of territories set aside as protected areas or new major new international tourism ventures.

Maximin Djondo and development NGOs are way ahead of minority world conservation NGOs in terms of moving with the times and being responsive to the changes and challenges in the world. I am sure the development sector is fraught with just as many complexities and difficulties as conservation is, and I do not wish to downplay or appear dismissive of any of their struggles. But, I do think the conservation sector can learn from their initiatives, so that we can apply them to our own, often complex problems.

In the first chapter I declared myself as an actor within this subject as well as an observer looking in. I have, until now, maintained a level of observer separation, but from here forward I speak as an actor within the conservation sector, while acknowledging that I am also seeking to learn and change. This involved position allows me to explain some insider perspectives that are not captured well in academic literature.

While conservation is absolutely part of the human rights and development agenda, we have become a separated sector.

This is partially because our focus has a broader sweep. We feel a responsibility to wildlife and nature, as well as people, and we strive to protect whole ecosystems as well as their component parts. As a result, ours has become a science driven agenda that often sees 'the human' as one step removed. I value each and every one of the scientists and conservationists slogging through rainforests, scaling rock faces, scanning endless arctic horizons, or floating in boats waiting to catch that rare glimpse of the species they are seeking to understand. But, we have a challenge to mesh the scope of that science to tangible actions local people can understand – to the human scale. This is a difficult task because decades of international governance have established the ground rules for our engagements – we are required to furnish scientific evidence for every conservation action we promote.

We are also a separated sector because we are being pushed down the neoliberal path – ecosystem services, multi-stakeholder initiatives, sustainable development, protected areas and eco-guards. Governments and funders require our sector to frame activities in support of 'alternative livelihoods' thereby preferencing directions that change community lives, often moving them away, rather than empowering people to stay as a voice for their whole community – human and non-human.

It is really not a surprise that our solutions focus on the species and their needs, after all this is our expertise and our goal is to give a species or an ecosystem much needed respite from the pressure of human activities. Over time, the separation from our sister sectors – human rights and development – has become entrenched, even thought the world is already full of people – people that also need to be respected.

We have become accustomed to the separation. We forget, too often, that the landscape of the minority world was once very different. Our cities and industries have already clear felled whole forests, many species in Europe, North America and Australia are already extinct, many ecosystems are already gone. As I explored in chapter 3, when we look with hopes and prayers at the remnants of wild places and wild things left in the majority world, and we rush to protect what is left, we often cast the people who have lived in these places as the problem to be overcome, forgetting they have lived there without harm for millennia.

The global environmental governance space is now one where governments reject any hint of moral arguments because they are not scientific and any calls for ecological justice are judiciously removed because they are not a conservation matter. Neoliberal market environmentalism language is pervasive. It has been written into the canon by decades of well-funded attention from a handful of minority world NGOs. At the same time, many other minority world NGOs have become used to the narrative, found their own ways to work with it and now rarely question whether it is the right path. In my experience, this pattern manifests across almost all of the discussions and decisions adopted during multilateral environment agreement (MEA) meetings.

Aili Pyhälä and her colleagues have bravely challenged the huge investments sunk into protected areas and eco-guards that have displaced local communities as successful measures:

> Organisations involved in [conservation] work often pose the counterfactual argument that the situation would be much worse had these investments not been in place. This may be true, but it does not substantiate the effectiveness of the present approach, and can be countered with another hypothetical: what would have happened if local communities had obtained ownership and control of these areas?[11]

The physical presence of communities, who depend on healthy ecosystems for their lives and livelihoods, can make them effective stewards. This ethic is about more than hiring local people as park rangers or ecotour guides or systematically enabling them to monitor and blow the whistle on illegal hunting. Truly acknowledging their connection to the place and the animals, recognising that these forests, grassy plains, arctic tundra or wetlands are their home can enhance compliance and cooperation. Driving traditional communities away creates large vacuums where commercial operators find it easy to move in.[11]

This is not just about poachers coming into forests. It means requiring an acceptance of industrialised impact as well. For instance, overfishing in the world's oceans is at the centre of a crisis of sustainability. Nowhere is that crisis more visible than in western Africa. Using 30 years of data from Ghana to link mammal declines to the bushmeat trade, in 2004 Justin Brashares and his colleagues made the firm connection that years of poor fish supply coincided with increased hunting in nature reserves and sharp declines in biomass of 41 wildlife species. Local market data provided evidence of a direct link between fish supply and subsequent bushmeat demand in villages.[12] Industrial fishing vessels from Europe, China and Japan already out-perform local artisanal fishers by at least 20:1. Current rates of fisheries extraction are driving several species towards extinction while jeopardising the livelihoods of artisanal fishing communities across a broad group of countries, including Senegal, Ghana, Sierra Leone, Liberia and Mauritania. Illegal, unreported and unregulated fishing is at the heart of this specific problem.[13]

After a sustained campaign from development NGOs, in 2013 the Twenty-first Session of the United Nations Human Rights Council (UNHRC) reached agreement on the Busan Partnership for Effective Development Cooperation. This agreement established that civil society organisations play a vital role in enabling people to claim their rights, in promoting rights-based approaches, in shaping development policies and partnerships, and in overseeing their implementation.[5, 14]

Each year CIVICUS publishes the *State of Civil Society Report*, offering a comprehensive picture of civil society and the conditions it works in around the world. The 2015 report responds to the Busan Partnership and serves up lots of important information for us to ponder. The call is on NGOs to wean themselves off grant/contract funding, to explore new ways of raising resources, and to design activities that do not need financial support. The really salient message was that civil society is under-represented and marginalised in the web of global governance institutions, which are far more welcoming of large, transnational corporations, but in ways that are not transparent.

The conservation sector has an opportunity to shape the future, but this will mean embracing the fact that the global environmental governance order can only become functional if it is reformed systematically, in ways that reach out to and include a wide range of civil society.

UN governance report agenda

Over a decade ago, the Panel of Eminent Persons on United Nations – Civil Society Relations advocated that:

> constructively engaging with civil society is a necessity for the United Nations, not an option. This engagement is essential to enable the Organization to better identify global priorities and to mobilize all resources to deal with the task at hand. We also see this opening up of the United Nations to a plurality of constituencies and actors not as a threat to Governments, but as a powerful way to reinvigorate the intergovernmental process itself.[15]

The report, *We the Peoples: Civil Society, the United Nations and Global Governance*, otherwise known as the Cardaso Report in honour of the Chairman, had many far-reaching ambitions, but was conflicted and impractical, and still tied itself, modestly in some respects, to neoliberal ideology.[16] It was a brave attempt, but not brave enough.

In 2015, the Report of the Commission on Global Security, Justice and Governance was launched at the Peace Palace in The Hague. It built on the foundation of the Cardaso Report. The report, *Confronting the Crisis of Global Governance*, co-chaired by Madeleine Albright and Ibrahim Gambari, stated: 'The recommendations of the Commission are intended, in this seventieth anniversary year of the United Nations, to encourage a broad-based global policy dialogue and an institutional reform agenda aimed at 2020.'[17] Potential partners from around the world – in governments, civil society organisations, the private sector, media and international organisations – are invited to help build and sustain a coalition for progressive global change, in pursuit of a vision of justice and security for all.

Confronting the Crisis differs dramatically from the Cardaso Report in that it links state fragility and violent conflict, climate and people, and the hyper-connected global economy as focus areas that must be addressed in concert, arguing that 'the intersection of justice and security – or just security – is critical to understanding and tackling today's global governance threats and challenges'. It suggests reform of existing global governance institutions and new forms of collaboration for better governance.[17] It represents the best direction presented to date but is still ideologically torn between neoliberalism and cosmopolitanism. The challenge for the conservation sector is to decide how we will engage with this opportunity.

Understanding the report is an important first step. Specifically, the report reinforces the need to operationalise the Responsibility to Protect (R2P) by strengthening UN agencies, embedding UN mission monitors in all forces participating in R2P implementation and establishing firm goals about preventing, reacting to and rebuilding after mass atrocities. In this suite of recommendations the Commission is placing the United Nations at the centre of governance, while still affirming the role of the state.

It addresses climate and people, recognising that new players are now involved in including the role of corporate initiatives for mitigation and civil society for transparency. Again the role of multilateralism is reinforced, with the United Nations in a central role.

Governing the hyper-connected economy looks at both the risk of financial shocks and also 'illicit financial flows', including trade misinvoicing and aggressive tax minimisation. It is refreshing to see illegal resource extraction also highlighted:

> In fragile and conflict-affected environments, in particular, governments, individuals, multinational firms, and terrorist and criminal organizations compete for finite resources in ways that can prolong armed strife or provoke a relapse into violence. Globally, the activities of large, multi-national carbon-fuel and mineral extraction corporations can have severe environmental consequences, including an acceleration of climate change's harmful effects. Although a potentially large source of public revenue for financing national and global public goods, natural resources can, when

poorly managed, contribute to global insecurity and injustice through negative political, economic, social, and environmental dynamics.[17]

The report outlines steps to address these concern areas, again strengthening UN agencies and establishing new layers of corporate transparency.

It is in the area of governance reform that the report is bravest. It begins by proposing to revitalise the UN General Assembly for the twenty-first century. This includes streamlining the agenda into thematic debates, to focus discussions, input and transparency; creating a Shadow Council of the General Assembly for Security Overnight and establishing a UN Parliamentary Network under UN Charter Article 22 to expand participation in the work of the United Nations, feeding into the UN General Assembly's debates, and complementing the longer-term efforts of civil society organisations to develop a transnational democratic culture.

There are other important and worthy elements to the reform agenda including expanding UN Security Council membership and building greater capacity into the G20 as an accountable coordination body to oversee global economic stability. But for the purpose of this book, it is the refreshing focus on civil society that draws my attention. A proposed UN Parliamentary Network would bring together parliamentarians elected from their national legislatures, to discuss and advise on issues in UN governance that concern citizens worldwide. It would be similar in initial composition to the Parliamentary Network on the World Bank and International Monetary Fund and the Parliamentary Conference on the World Trade Organization, but would have a formal relationship with the United Nations and be focused on the world body's efforts to promote global security and justice, seeking to establish:

> the enhanced participation of nonstate, regional, and local governmental actors in UN and other global institutional matters – beyond their general consultative role – as a critical component for the effective delivery of global public goods. Both policymakers and scholars should look critically at ways to include them in advising policy and decision-making processes, in recognition of their emerging role, in many ways, as a kind of third United Nations.[17]

However, this is also some cause for alarm. Buried deep into the end of the report is a proposal to develop 'new social compacts' to support 'multi-stakeholder solutions to critical governance problems'. This is tempered by the next proposal to establish a UN Global Partnership through meetings of an apex body, the UN Global Partnership Steering Committee, which could take place at least three times per year between the UN Secretary-General, the World Bank President, the head of a new civil society-led Committee on Civil Society–UN Relations, and the vice chair of the UN Global Compact Board of Directors. An annual meeting of the UN Global Partnership, timed to coincide with the opening of the UN General Assembly in September, as well as an interactive and multilingual web portal, would aim to further the engagement of civil society organisations and business groups in the UN agenda, including by giving voice to often under-represented or neglected international policy issues.[17]

As I said, the recommendations are somewhat torn between neoliberalism and cosmopolitanism, but it is a path to work with. The concluding section of the report sets out a strategy for achieving the proposed reform agenda. Key among these is a proposal to convene a World Conference on Global Institutions in 2020. This is the same year the new Paris Agreement will take effect and a mere three years before the first round of Paris Agreement reports.

With *Confronting the Crisis of Global Governance* we have been given an invitation to dream – a gift of shelter from the approaching storm. We can't stop the storm, but we can secure ourselves to survive it and still have what we cherish most on the other side. The task before us is to embrace this gift.

We have much to think about and much to do.

Stepping onto the path through the storm

The first task is to assert the role of civil society. Naghmeh Nasiritousi, Mattias Hjerpe and Karin Bäckstrand surveyed governments participating over a span of four climate change conferences, from 2011 through to 2014. About 40 per cent of the government respondents thought that non-state actors should be included in international policymaking because they represent important stakeholders that are affected by the decisions (they called this a neo-corporatist rationale). Another 40 per cent thought involvement should be to provide information and expertise (neofunctionalist). About 16 per cent believed in a democratic pluralist rationale for non-state actor involvement. What I found particularly interesting was that only 4 per cent thought it was not important to include non-state actors at all.[18] Naghmeh, Mattias and Karin also asked non-state actors for their views, and it is not surprising that more than half of the respondents (who include a combination of corporate actors and NGOs) ascribed to a neocorporatist rationale. Asian and African government respondents attributed more weight to a democratic pluralist rationale than European and North American government respondents.

The stronger support for the neocorporatist rationale may have implications for which types of non-state actors become most actively engaged in international policymaking. The reason it is favoured could either signify a general trend of changing governmental preferences or it could reflect developments that are particular to global environmental governance, where years of gridlocked negotiations have not measured up to the perceived needs.[18]

Naghmeh, Mattias and Karin found similar results in other intergovernmental processes,[18] and my own research supports this trend.[19–21] While on the surface this is a good direction of an evolving political role for stakeholders in representing interests that have a stake in the decisions, there is an important implication that also needs to be considered. Well-funded and well-connected interests will find it relatively easy to make their way into the process and eventually to have a seat at the table. But, the process doesn't distinguish. If widespread support for the neocorporatist rationale means that non-state actors are viewed as political actors in their own right, the evolving practice of non-state actors' participation may favour those organisations that are particularly strong in representing interests and contributing to output.[18] Neoliberal market environmentalism will easily dominate this space. Other non-state actors without such strong representation may well be left in the cold.

Naghmeh, Mattias and Karin's research specifically focused on neocorporatism, neofunctionalism and democratic pluralism, which is a slightly different split to my own research, nonetheless offers important insight. Fuyuki Kurasawa has demonstrated that cosmopolitanism does not need to choose sides between the existing political culture (neocorporatism, neofunctionalism) of international institutions and pluralism, especially when it stems from below.[22] Rooted cosmopolitanism invites a broader, messier, more inclusive community to the table – a community with views that may not be embedded in economic gain and a way for us to develop an understanding of what a participatory governance model might look like.[16, 23] Keeping this front of mind, while considering the current limitations of wildlife governance, is important.

Under pressure of globalisation, there are both theoretical and practical reasons to shift away from a paradigm of global governance in which nation states are the dominant – if not the sole – coordinating power. Civil society should not be seen as a substitute for national governments, because there is much that requires the legality of the current systems to remain in place. Nonetheless, social citizenship both within and beyond the borders of national territories should be recognised.[24]

There is already strong international impetus to move towards more collaborative involvement in environmental governance. Both United Nations Economic and Social Council (ECOSOC) and the newly formed United Nations Environment Assembly (UNEA) grant an additional layer of access and participation to NGOs that have been formally accredited. The first United Nations Conference on Environment and Development (the Earth Summit) in 1992 formalised nine sectors of society (officially called 'Major Groups') as the main channels through which broad participation would be facilitated in UN activities related to sustainable development. The Major Groups are:

- Women
- Children and Youth
- Indigenous Peoples
- Nongovernmental Organisations
- Local Authorities
- Workers and Trade Unions
- Business and Industry

- Scientific and Technological Community
- Farmers

Most accredited NGOs operate through the Major Groups process, although some also seek representation in their own right. Access privileges for accredited NGOs include limited participation in the agenda-setting process and in policy-making and decision-making process. Designated seats are reserved for Major Groups and stakeholders in all public meetings of the Assembly and its subsidiary organs. Accredited stakeholders have access to all public documents, but experience has demonstrated that many documents are withheld from public view by placing them under the restricted agenda items including financial arrangements, so transparency is never quite as comprehensive as the policies make it appear. Both the United Nations Environment Programme (UNEP) and the ECOSOC NGOs branch accept comprehensive written input ahead of meetings and circulate this faithfully to government delegations. Stakeholders have speaking rights, but no voting rights.[25]

This has been an excellent start and on the surface appears to provide civil society access, but in my experience governments still sit around the table as Westphalian sovereign actors protecting their individual economic interest. Even environment delegations adhere, often rigidly, to briefs developed months in advance of the meeting – briefs that have passed review by their economic and foreign affairs ministries and been developed with the aggressive input of economic partners. Very little that is said, by NGOS or other governments, sways positions during meetings. Consequently the gains we celebrate as progress are very often painfully, shamefully small.

The most recent area where Major Group participation is being facilitated is the High Level Political Forum on Sustainable Development (HLPF) – the main UN platform dealing with sustainable development, formally established in July 2013. It meets every year under the auspices of ECOSOC, and every four years under the auspices of the United Nations General Assembly. The coordination of input to intergovernmental processes on sustainable development has been led by the United Nations Department of Economic and Social Affairs (UNDESA)/Division for Sustainable Development (DSD). Major Groups and other stakeholders have been granted significant participatory opportunities in the HLPF through the UN General Assembly Resolution: 'Format and organizational aspects of the high-level political forum on sustainable development'.[26] The Resolution states that, while retaining the intergovernmental character of the HLPF, Major Groups representatives and other relevant stakeholders are allowed to:

- attend all official meetings of the forum
- have access to all official information and documents
- intervene in official meetings
- submit documents and present written and oral contributions
- make recommendations

- organise side events and round tables, in cooperation with Member States and the Secretariat.[26]

UNDESA has been remarkably flexible in the interpretation of the Resolution and the flow of information between Major Groups and the HLPF has been admirable. Major Groups have participated in many meetings with forum delegations and the Chair of the process has remained committed and open to civil society participation.

Although these commitments are positive engagement steps taken by ECOSOC and UNEA/UNEP, and the admirable extension from the HLPF, NGOs are still placed in the outer circle. Their engagement is articulated in principle, but the depth of engagement falls considerably short of the engagement rights of governments. NGOs may be able to influence governance, but they are not genuinely part of the governance process.

The current limitation of global governance for wildlife

Underneath the UNEA, ECOSOC and the HLPF, a staggering number of inter-governmental organisations (IGOs) and MEAs also exist in the global environmental governance space. They have gradually been formed over the past 40 years as governments and NGOs have grappled with large-scale problems that do not restrict themselves to borders and cannot be solved by states alone. This is the world I have worked in for the last 27 years, and I know very well how the ripple of decisions impacts, or not, the laws and priorities at a national level. I also know very well that global governance is a space rife with non-decision-making. This space is notoriously disconnected from the results of decisions and most MEAs engage very poorly with civil society.

For wildlife concerns, the key MEAs are: the Convention on Biological Diversity (CBD), the Convention on International Trade in Endangered Species of Wild Fauna and Flora (CITES), the Convention on the Conservation of Migratory Species of Wild Animals (CMS) and Ramsar. There is another rich layer of dozens of regional agreements beneath many of these as well as important stand-alone instruments that sit to the side. These include 26 CMS species agreements, 17 separate regional fisheries management organisations, Arctic and Antarctic instruments, regional seas instruments, the International Whaling Commission, and of course the climate change negotiations.

Almost all MEAs and instruments express a commitment to work with civil society. Very few actually, tangibly, do.

The science agenda

Each of these MEAs is reliant on the information being deliberated in what could be described as a global biodiversity science network. These include the IPCC, the Intergovernmental Science-Policy Platform on Biodiversity and

Ecosystem Services (IPBES), the IUCN Species Survival Commission (IUCN SSC) and CBD's Subsidiary Body on Scientific, Technical and Technological Advice (SBSTTA). These science bodies provide important advice to influence the policy deliberations of MEAs and governments, and facilitate a suite of tools to help streamline future conservation.

The IPCC is the leading international body for the assessment of climate change. It reviews and assesses the most recent scientific, technical and socio-economic information produced worldwide relevant to the understanding of climate change. Thousands of scientists from all over the world contribute to the work of the IPCC.

IPBES is the intergovernmental body that assesses the state of global bio-diversity and strengthens the science–policy interface for biodiversity and ecosystem services for the conservation and sustainable use of biodiversity, long-term human well-being and sustainable development.

In chapter 3 I referred to IUCN as a quasi-NGO and I retain that definition, because although IUCN has government membership, it also has non-governmental membership, and the decisions it takes are not binding on governments. There are significant sensitivities about this in IUCN circles, but regardless of how it is defined, it is a vitally important body that sits somewhere in between governments and civil society.

IUCN SSC is a science-based network of more than 10,000 volunteer experts from almost every country of the world. The work is divided over 140 species specialist groups, disciplinary groups and task forces. The SSC's major role is to provide information to IUCN on biodiversity con-servation, the inherent value of species, their role in ecosystem health and functioning, the provision of ecosystem services, and their support to human livelihoods. This information is fed into The IUCN Red List of Threatened Species.

SBSTTA is a multidisciplinary body that provides assessments of the status of biological diversity, assessments of the types of measures taken to conserve biodiversity and responses to questions raised by the CBD Conference of the Parties. Thousands of scientists from all over the world contribute to the work of SBSTTA.

There is a connection between the MEAs and each of these major science platforms, but almost no formal, tangible links to local conservation efforts. If links exist it is through the ad hoc participation of scientists that are them-selves committed to local conservation. However, each provides a wealth of detailed and important scientific information that should form a core part of environmental governance deliberations and also community conservation efforts.

Convention on Biological Diversity

In the 1980s there was international recognition that the Earth's biological resources were vital to humanity and that species extinction caused by human activities was happening at an alarming rate. In the late 1980s, the UN convened a number of ad hoc working groups to explore developing a new convention. The Convention on Biological Diversity (CBD) was opened for signature in 1992 at the United Nations Conference on Environment and Development and by June 1993 it had received 168 signatures. The Convention entered into force in December 1993.[27] CBD was important for its time, representing a dramatic step forward in the conservation of biological diversity, the sustainable use of its components, and the fair and equitable sharing of benefits arising from the use of genetic resources. It remains deeply important today, although the complexities of what it now considers have made for a weighty and often impenetrable system.

As the most persuasive international forum relating to wildlife and wild places, it is no surprise that many NGOs attend the full cycle of meetings, but involvement is always as observers and one step removed. Many of the minority world's NGOs attend in their own right; other groups, such as the CBD Alliance that counts 400 members from around the world, attend together. The CBD Alliance brings together civil society organisations to enable better internal communication, and to coordinate work with Parties and CBD bodies. The parallel International Indigenous Forum on Biodiversity (IIFB) brings together indigenous peoples and local communities in the CBD process, and a close relationship exists between the two organisations.[28] But, they represent precious few voices in a sea of dialogue, so their impact is not as great as it deserves to be.

Like most UN Conventions, CBD goes to great pains to make it clear that states are the decision-making authority and that NGOs, or indeed civil society, are invited into the room to listen.[29] Contributions are welcome, when they conform to the agreed direction. I checked again, this week, and the page has been populated with information. So this comment is no longer true.

Convention on International Trade in Endangered Species

Discussions on the need for Convention on International Trade in Endangered Species of Wild Fauna and Flora (CITES) began in the 1960s. International wildlife trade is estimated to be worth billions of dollars and to include hundreds of millions of plant and animal specimens. Because the trade in wild animals and plants crosses borders between countries, the effort to regulate it requires international cooperation. CITES was drafted as a result of a resolution adopted in 1963 at a meeting of members of IUCN. The Convention was opened for signature in 1973 and entered into force in 1975.

CITES works by controlling international trade in specimens of selected species. All import, export, re-export and introduction from the sea of species covered by the Convention have to be authorised through a licensing system. Each Party to the Convention must designate one or more management authority in charge of administering that licensing system and one or more scientific authority to advise them on the effects of trade on the status of the species.

The species covered by CITES are listed in three appendices, according to the degree of protection they need. CITES Appendix I includes species threatened with extinction, and trade of these species is permitted only in exceptional circumstances. CITES Appendix II includes species not necessarily threatened with extinction but that may become so unless trade is closely controlled. Appendix III contains species that are protected in at least one country, and that country has asked other CITES Parties for assistance in controlling the trade. In the case of Appendix I and II species that are taken from the wild at sea and then landed in a specific port, are 'introduced from the sea'. A certificate must be issued by the management authority of the state into which the species is being brought.

There is strength in the rigour required to allow a permit to trade to be issued. This is reinforced by the requirement for the scientific authority of each Party to monitor exports of specimens of Appendix II species and, whenever necessary, to advise the management authority of measures to be taken to limit such exports to maintain the species – throughout their range – to ensure that trade will not be detrimental to the survival of that species. The guidelines for the so-called 'non-detriment findings' have evolved over many years.[30]

Not surprising, this very technical and legalistic agenda requires a high level of understanding for participation. As with CBD, many minority world NGOs participate and an alliance of NGOs does exist – the Species Survival Network – but membership of this network is limited to those who have the capacity for self participation.

Like CBD, CITES itself make no particular effort to involve civil society more broadly.

Convention on Wetlands of International Importance

The Convention on Wetlands of International Importance (Ramsar) is the oldest and the most softly spoken of the modern global intergovernmental environmental agreements. The treaty was negotiated through the 1960s by countries and nongovernmental organisations concerned about the increasing loss and degradation of wetland habitat for migratory waterbirds. Ramsar was adopted in the Iranian city of Ramsar in 1971 and came into force in 1975. The governance culture of this convention is quite different and there is a significant effort to progress conservation actions, rather than push paper around.

Since 1999, the Ramsar has recognised a small group of NGOs as International Organisation Partners (IOPs), conferring an additional participation status to the groups: Birdlife International, Wetlands International, IUCN, the World Wildlife Fund (WWF), the International Water Management Institute, and the Wildfowl and Wetlands Trust.[31, 32]

An important element of the IOP relationship is agreement that both the Secretariat and the IOPs have a responsibility to maintain the relationship and the implicit expectation that progress will be reported upon. This is evidenced in the Memorandum of Cooperation between the Ramsar Secretariat and the IOPs in 2011 and the reports to the Ramsar Standing Committee in 2006 and 2011.[33–35] IOPs play an active role, able to contribute directly to discussions and meetings. They also work together to produce statements from the IOPs as a group and are members of the Scientific and Technical Review Panel (STRP).

In practice the IOPs often act as facilitators between governments, donors, foundations and other bodies and they can, upon request from the Ramsar Secretariat, intervene on its behalf at specific meetings where/when the Ramsar Secretariat can't be directly represented. Importantly, the IOPs provide advice and recommendations on Ramsar processes such as the Montreux Record – wetlands where an adverse change in ecological character has occurred.[36, 37]

Ramsar's recognition and involvement of the IOPs is progressive and very important, although it is key to recognise that IOP status is restricted to large international NGOs.

Convention on the Conservation of Migratory Species of Wild Animals

As a further response to drastic biodiversity declines and a recognition that cooperation was needed between states for the conservation of species that cross national boundaries, the government of Germany enlisted the legal experts of the IUCN's Environmental Law Centre in the 1970s to produce the text which formed the basis of negotiation for the Convention on the Conservation of Migratory Species of Wild Animals (CMS). The Convention was adopted in Bonn in 1979 and came into force in 1983. Migratory species threatened with extinction are listed on Appendix I of the Convention. Migratory species that need or would significantly benefit from international cooperation are listed in Appendix II and the Convention encourages the Range States to conclude global or regional agreements for their conservation. In this respect, CMS acts as a framework convention to develope conservation models that are tailored to the conservation needs of a particular species or group of species across their migratory range.[38]

CMS's relationship with NGOs has been similar to Ramsar in that it pursues partnerships with NGOs and assures them of access to key meetings including the Standing Committee and the Scientific Council,[39] but it is on par with CITES and CBD in others areas. Governments still maintain a firm posture of control and many NGOs have found the partnership status meaningless in practice.[40] However, there are signs that CMS may be prepared to transform.

Can CMS be the first to evolve?

In 2013 CIVICUS conducted a multi-dimensional survey of civil society engagement with ten IGO processes: the Food and Agricultural Organization of the United Nations (FAO), Office of the High Commissioner for Human Rights International Labour Organisation, United Nations AIDS Programme, United Nations Development Programme, United Nations High Commissioner for Refugees, United Nations Women, The World Bank Group, the World Food Programme of the United Nations and the World Trade Organisation (WTO). The resulting CIVICUS message to IGOs and governments is that there is a need to move away from the state-centric model of international governance towards a citizen-oriented model. Their recommendations mirror my own research findings for Ramsar and CMS.[19, 21] New approaches to representation and involvement should be explored. IGOs should consider their ability to respond to and achieve progress on issues identified by people rather than just governments, and to especially make their decision-making processes more open and democratic. Efforts should be made to give civil society delegations a legitimate seat at the table. Civil society involvement should be inclusive of broader worldviews, and not limited to organisations that bring financial resources to the process. New media, including mobile, social media and video streaming, should also be used to encourage participation and the exercise of social accountability. In order to strengthen civil society participation, greater outreach should be offered and dedicated spaces for civil society participation established, with civil society helping to define and govern these, with funding earmarked to enable broad civil society participation. Most importantly, efforts should be made from the local to the global level to ensure that the practical realisation of civil society rights is enshrined in various international treaties and agreements.[19–21, 41]

Such steps require reciprocation. NGOs and civil society organisations should make influencing of global governance institutions a programmatic priority. This will require considerable levels of information sharing and peer learning. The larger, better resourced NGOs with an established presence in key IGOs should take the initiative to democratise the space they hold and involve a wider range of civil society groups in engaging international govern-ance institutions, including by sharing their organisational accreditation and financial resources.[19–21, 41]

CMS and Ramsar provide a conservation policy framework for nearly 600 migratory species, 29 regional species agreements and over 2,000 wetlands of international importance. CMS has 124 contracting Parties with additional governments participating in the 26 regional species agreements that have been concluded under the CMS umbrella. Ramsar has 169 contracting Parties. Both conventions benefit from strong majority representation and commitment.

Over the past three decades, a wide group of NGOs have demonstrated a considerable commitment to all four of the MEAs. For the most part, CBD and CITES keep their NGOs at arms length. Ramsar and CMS have both sought a slightly closer relationship. While CBD and CITES continue to enjoy considerable loyalty and profile generated by NGOs, it is Ramsar and CMS that have grown accustomed to informally using the services of some NGOs for certain activities. For a time this was acceptable, but recently NGOs have come to feel that their commitment has not been matched, in their view, by an institutional commitment within Ramsar or the CMS Family (the parent convention and the 26 species agreements) to implement progress.[20]

To discuss this emerging view I organised a 'Civil Society Dialogue' in the margins of the Tenth Meeting of the Conference of the Parties to CMS (CMS CoP10) in 2012. It was apparent to those participating in the dialogue that NGO commitments to the CMS Family were not well understood by CMS Parties and that NGOs could be more effective contributors if facilitated in doing so.[20] A subsequent review process, in 2013, comprehensively engaged with around 100 wildlife NGOs from around the globe. The review sought to better define the existing relationship between NGOs and CMS in its present form in order to contribute to enhancing that relationship into the future. The NGOs involved came from minority and majority world perspectives. They included organisations who worked closely with the CMS Family right through to critics challenging CMS and its effectiveness.[20]

I conducted a similar survey through the World Wetland Network and the broader wetland conservation community in 2014. The 190 wetland NGOs and civil society organisations involved also came from minority and majority world perspectives.[21]

These two processes were important measures, and both provided similar results. In summary, NGOs from around the world understand that involvement has a cycle: that they must commit to, and participate before and during Ramsar and CMS processes to raise the profile of species issues, such as threats, species conservation status, linkages to other MEAs and the impacts of other decisions. They respect that they must influence these discussions and accords. They know that they may be needed for on-ground implementation support and many of them prepare for this by developing close working relationships with governments as well as seeking funding to facilitate work before, during and after meetings. NGOs judge the value of Ramsar and the CMS Family on implementation of the commitments made by governments, not the number of meetings that have been held or plans that have been developed.[19, 21, 40]

Both reviews found that there is significant scope for NGOs to provide specific types of implementation activity, especially where priority taxonomic or geographical gaps are identified or capacity building is needed in developing regions. NGOs would welcome a more structured and systematic long-term approach to joint planning (and evaluation) so that they could better contribute to Ramsar and CMS implementation.

This is a significant offer from civil society, especially when the practicalities of state capacity are acknowledged. During CMS CoP11, more than half of the assessed 59 Party reports identified a need for financial support to address their commitment to CMS; 27 identified a need for capacity building/knowledge exchange, 23 for technical or material support, 18 for scientific support and 11 for regional or international cooperation.[42]

NGOs have voiced and demonstrated a willingness to step into this capacity breach, offering an opportunity to increase the human resource and financial effort in support of CMS and Ramsar. But, it is clear that progressing greater collaboration in Ramsar and the CMS Family requires a new dynamic to be created where NGOs contribute more systematically, consistently and transparently to the work of these two MEAs. Their work must influence directions. Their views must be legitimately heard. Both reviews emphasised that NGO contributions need to be codified and accepted as a contribution against an agreed plan so that governments recognise the value and build this work more fully into the progression of the Ramsar and CMS agendas. NGOs should be able, for example, to formally represent their own work and have that work accepted and acknowledged as a contribution.[21, 40]

It is clear that progressing NGOs and governments working together requires active dialogue, mutual transparency and accountability, trust building and the development of a shared understanding.[43–46] The tacit agreement underlying any increase in NGO commitment will be that conservation progress must be made – that once policies are established, implementation will follow.[20]

Facing the storm

In the past four chapters I have highlighted the neoliberal path global governance is currently on and who is involved. Some of my reflections have been bruising, but hopefully not fatally so. In the coming chapters I describe how we can embrace a rooted cosmopolitan ethic and prepare for the coming storm of change. If the conservation movement is brave enough to recast the way it works, we can serve the rise of local civil society. We can connect with local communities and provide them with the information they need to understand the wildlife around them; to make their own decisions about how they want to respond to their changing environment; and to buffer them from the external forces pressuring them. We can devolve our grip on how conservation should be done and respond to their wisdom about how to protect wildlife and wild places – how to protect their homes. We can facilitate these voices into international environmental governance and we can demand a seat for these communities at the governance table. We have a lot to offer. Minority world conservation NGOs are skilled and experienced; we have access to science; we understand the cut and thrust of international process.

Like political journalists who have a press gallery 'beat' in Washington, Brussels or London, NGOs who work on MEA issues are similarly tuned. We have a depth of understanding that allows them to intuit what is happening and what words mean. We know 'who is who' and why discussions are moving in particular directions. Many of us have had this focus for longer than the many government officials they observe. Like political journalists, we have expert, detailed, valuable knowledge and they project as authoritative. Like political journalists, our staying power fills their brains with context which informs all kinds of judgments. In the past, this built audience trust.[20] But, NGOs are now faced with a more active and informed civil society community. To continue in the role NGOs need to be worthy of trust and we need to listen to voices and perspectives other than our own.

If we turn ourselves into messengers for communities who are free from corporate pressure and gripping poverty we become stronger than before.

The existential impact of climate change will soon overtake the capacity of the current international system – a system that is already failing to deliver. We need nimble feet and committed capacity if we are to save even a fraction of what we now stand to lose. It is time to face the storm.

*** *** ***

Above our imagined heads the flat base swells into an ominous shaft. The gorilla and I are witness to the inside of a dark churning thunderhead.

A chasm of power. Thunder rumbles.

She stands and turns in frightened, helpless circles, seeking to hide from the might above.

This is bigger than her. It is bigger than me.

Thick, slow drops of rain begin to fall.

I know the storm is just beginning. The world on the other side will not be the same.

Vicious wind whips against my skin. My eyes well with tears.

What have we done?

References

[1] Convention on Wetlands of International Importance. 2007. The Annotated Ramsar List of Wetlands of International Importance: Benin. Gland: Convention on Wetlands of International Importance.

[2] Dossou, K. and Gléhouenou-Dossou, B. 2012. The Vulnerability to Climate Change of Cotonou (Benin): The Rise in Sea Level. In *Adapting Cities to Climate Change: Understanding and Addressing the Development Challenges*. Edited by Bicknell, J., Dodman, D. and Satterthwaite, D. London: EarthScan: 111–127.

[3] Benin Environment and Education Society. 2016. Comprendre le capital naturel. [online material]

[4] World Wetland Network. 2012. Awards 2012. [online material]

[5] Hodenfield, T. and Pegus, C. M. 2013. *Global Trends on Civil Society Restrictions – Mounting Restrictions on Civil Society: The Gap between Rhetoric and Reality.* New York: CIVICUS: World Alliance for Citizen Participation.

[6] Kaye, M. 2015. After the NGOs: Can Wakatobi National Park Survive on its Own? *Mongabay*, 18 November 2015.

[7] Crowe, S. 2016. Interview with Dr Danny Sriskandarajah. UNICEF Innocenti.

[8] Doane, D. 2016. The Future of Aid: Will international NGOs Survive? *The Guardian Online.*

9   Sheil, D., Boissière, M. and Beaudoin, G. 2015. Unseen Sentinels: Local Monitoring and Control in Conservation's Blind Spots. *Ecology and Society.* 20, 2.

10 Orozco-Quintero, A., Burlando, C. and Robinson, L. W. 2015. Just Conservation?: Justice, Conservation and the Protected Areas Establishment Frenzy. *IC Magazine.* [online material]

11 Pyhälä, A., Osuna Orozco, A. and Counsell, S. 2016. Protected Areas in the Congo Basin: Failing Both People and Biodiversity? In *Under the Canopy Series.* London: Rainforest Foundation UK.

12 Brashares, J. S., Arcese, P., Sam, M. K., Coppolillo, P. B., Sinclair, A. R. E. and Balmford, A. 2004. Bushmeat Hunting, Wildlife Declines, and Fish Supply in West Africa. *Science.* 306, 5699: 1180–1183.

13 Daniels, A., Gutiérrez, M., Fanjul, G., Guereña, A., Matheson, I. and Watkins, K. 2016. *Western Africa's Missing Fish: The Impacts of Illegal, Unreported and Unregulated Fishing and Under-reporting Catches by Foreign Fleets.* London: Overseas Development Institute.

14 United Nations Human Rights Council. 2011. Busan: The Fourth High-Level Forum on Aid Effectiveness.

15 United Nations General Assembly. 2005. *We, the Peoples. Civil Society, the United Nations and Global Governance.* Panel of Eminent Persons on United Nations-Civil Society Relations.

16 Willetts, P. 2006. The Cardoso Report on the UN and Civil Society: Functionalism, Global Corporatism, or Global Democracy? *Global Governance.* 12, 3: 305–324.

17 Commission on Global Security, Justice &Governance. 2015. *Confronting the Crisis of Global Governance.* New York: Commission on Global Security, Justice & Governance.

18 Nasiritousi, N., Hjerpe, M. and Bäckstrand, K. 2015. Normative Arguments for Non-state Actor Participation in International Policymaking Processes: Functionalism, Neocorporatism or Democratic Pluralism? *European Journal of International Relations*, 1–24.

19 Prideaux, M. 2015. Wildlife NGOs: From Adversaries to Collaborators. *Global Policy.* 6, 4: 379–388.

20 Prideaux, M. 2014. A Natural Affiliation: Developing the Role of NGOs in the Convention on Migratory Species Family. UNEP/CMS/COP11/Inf.15, Wild Migration.

21 Prideaux, M., Rostron, C. and Duff, L. 2015. *Ramsar and Wetland NGOs: A Report of the World Wetland Network for Ramsar CoP12.* London: World Wetland Network.

22 Kurasawa, F. 2004. A Cosmopolitanism from Below: Alternative Globalization and the Creation of a Solidarity without Bounds. *European Journal of Sociology Archives Européennes de Sociologie.* 45, 02: 233–255.

23 Ling, L. H. M. 2013. *The Dao of World Politics: Towards a Post-Westphalian, Worldist International Relations.* Abingdon: Routledge.

24 Wagner, A. 2004. Redefining Citizenship for the 21st Century: From the National Welfare State to the UN Global Compact. *International Journal of Social Welfare.* 13, 4: 278–286.

25 United Nations Economic and Social Council NGOs Branch. 2011. *Working with ECOSOC – an NGOs Guide to Consultative Status.* New York: United Nations.

26 United Nations General Assembly. 2013. Format and Organizational Aspects of the High-level Political Forum on Sustainable Development. In *A/RES/67/290*. New York: United Nations.

27 Secretariat to the Convention on Biological Diversity. 2016. History of the Convention. [online material]

28 Secretariat to the CBD Alliance. 2016. Our Relation to the CBD. [online material]

29 Secretariat to the Convention on Biological Diversity. 2016. Getting Involved: Information Resources. [online material]

30 Convention on International Trade in Endangered Species of Wild Fauna and Flora. 1973. Washington, United Nations Treaty Series.

31 Convention on Wetlands of International Importance. 2011. Memorandum of Cooperation with The Ramsar Convention's International Organisation Partners (IOPs) Gland: Secretariat of the Convention on Wetlands.

32 Convention on Wetlands of International Importance. 2015. *Conference Report*. Uruguay, 12th Meeting of the Conference of the Parties to the Convention on Wetlands.

33 Convention on Wetlands of International Importance. 2011. *Doc SC42–13: Collaborative review with the International Organization Partners of the Convention's relationships with the IOPs*. Gland, 42nd Meeting of the Standing Committee of the Parties to the Convention on Wetlands of International Importance.

34 Convention on Wetlands of International Importance. 2006. *Doc SC34–33: Meeting of International Organization Partners (IOPs) and the Ramsar Secretariat*, 28 February 2006. Gland, 34th Meeting of the Standing Committee of the Parties to the Convention on Wetlands.

35 Convention on Wetlands of International Importance. 2011. Memorandum of Cooperation with The Ramsar Convention's International Organisation Partners (IOPs) Gland: Ramsar Secretariat.

36 Convention on Wetlands of International Importance. 2010. Ramsar's International Organization Partners (IOPs) – How the IOPs Support the Convention at Global, Regional and National Level: The Case of WWF. Gland, 15th Meeting of the Scientific and Technical Review Panel of the Ramsar Convention.

37 Scientific and Technical Review Panel of the Ramsar Convention. 2015. STRP Members. Ramsar. [online material]

38 Secretariat to the Convention on Migratory Species. 2016. About: Introduction. [online material]

39 Secretariat to the Convention on Migratory Species. 2016. About: Partnerships. [online material]

40 Convention on Migratory Species of Wild Animals. 2014. Inf 15: A Natural Affiliation. Bonn: Secretariat to the Convention on Migratory Species of Wild Animals.

41 Firmin, A., Pegus, C. M. and Tiwana, M. 2014. *State of Civil Society Report: 2014*. New York: CIVICUS: World Alliance for Citizen Participation.

42 Convention on Migratory Species of Wild Animals. 2014. Inf.42: Analysis of National Reports to CMS 2014. Quito, 11th Conference of the Parties to the Convention on Migratory Species of Wild Animals.

43 Benner, T., Reinicke, W. H. and Witte, J. M. 2004. Multisectoral Networks in Global Governance: Towards a Pluralistic System of Accountability. *Government and Opposition*. 39, 2: 191–210.

44 Scholte, J. A. 2004. Civil Society and Democratically Accountable Global Governance. *Government and Opposition*. 39, 2: 211–233.

45 Betsill, M. M. 2008. Reflections on the Analytical Framework and NGO Diplomacy. In *NGO Diplomacy: The Influence of Nongovernmental Organisations in International Environmental Negotiations*. Edited by Betsill, M. M. and Corell, E. Cambridge: MIT Press: 177–206.

46 Bernauer, T. and Betzold, C. 2012. Civil Society in Global Environmental Governance. *The Journal of Environment & Development*. 21, 1: 62–66.

5   Rain pours

Orangutan – Linda Irwin-Oak

In 2012 an infant orangutan was confiscated from a villager in Southwest Aceh, Sumatra. The villager intended to sell him as a pet. He was two when he was found, malnourished, and very thin. His prospects for survival were poor. He was transferred to a quarantine and care centre where he began his recovery and growth.

A year later Linda Irwin-Oak was online campaigning against palm oil. She stumbled on the organisation rehabilitating this little orphan. Linda is a passionate, deeply intelligent and tenacious thirty-something wildlife activist. She comes from an impressive family background of conservation and, pleased to have a way to directly help the orangutan and the local community, she signed up to sponsor him. For her, this signalled the beginning of a three-year connection with this little ape and his journey back to the wild.

I mostly look with disdain on wildlife adoption programmes. I have first-hand experience running them and while I know nongovernmental organisations' (NGOs') intentions are usually good, over time these programmes slip into marketing exercises more so than conservation services. Tough messages are toned down, bad news is disguised. Frequently, there is no actual relationship between the organisation and the animal. If you 'adopt' a wild tiger, or panda, or yes even a dolphin, chances are that animal is part of an existing wild population. The organisation is legitimately campaigning to conserve species habitat, but it is not directly intervening in an individual animal's life. I do not seek to discredit the intended conservation work in any way. I am sure it is noble and valuable; I just wish NGOs would call it conservation. To label this form of fundraising an 'adoption' is disingenuous.

The exception to my disdain are wildlife rehabilitation and re-release programmes – with some strong caveats. When they are done well, with the interest of the animal paramount, they work. These infant orphans – most often apes or elephants – know every bottle they receive is coming from hands of handlers. The process is intensive, one-on-one care for a number of years as the animal grows, learns the skills needed for survival and is eventually facilitated to take back a wild and free life. I applaud these programmes when they work with, employ and listen to the local community. Sadly, too often, this last step is not taken. Even minority world wildlife rescue NGOs, who arguably have the most natural opportunity to work closely with the local community, fall into the destructive trap of believing their worldview is better, treating the local community as an impediment to overcome.

Sadly, there are few wildlife issues more tangled and complicated than orangutan conservation. You would think it would be simple, but the toxic mix of REDD+ and the money it can unlock for conservation release areas, political corruption and minority world NGO blindness to the needs and rights of local communities, mean that the gentle 'person of the forest', is caught in a boiling cauldron of conflict. Orangutan rainforest habitats in Sumatra and Borneo are disappearing at an alarming rate, mostly to clear the land for pulp paper and palm oil plantations. Sumatran orangutans may be extinct in the next few decades, and Bornean orangutans soon after that. The IUCN Red List has declared the Sumatran species critically endangered and the Borneo species endangered.[1, 2] It is very difficult for people from outside the region to know how best to help.

A key decision point for Linda was the knowledge that most of the staff in the centre she supported were from the local villages. The local community also financially benefited from growing and selling the fruits and vegetables for the centre animals. Her assessment was that the programme was built on an equitable foundation. This is actually not a simple thing for an NGO to achieve and should be supported when they do. Linda had specifically made sure that the programme she supported worked with the local community, not against it.

Rescued orangutans in rehabilitation programmes are often very young and require intensive care in specialised sites where veterinary attention and over-sight is viable. When they are old enough and healthy enough to enter the release programme they are moved to the release sites, where their journey back to the wild can be supervised and gradual. Having community support for the programme is vital to long-term success.

When I met with Linda in a small town in rural Australia, near where we both live, the 2015 fires in Indonesia were raging out of control, and danger-ously close to the rescue centre. She told me about her motivation – the little orphan orangutan that was proving himself to be a survivor.

He had regained weight, had been integrated and was socialising with the other orphans. In his second year at the centre he started using leaves as a nest – a vital skill that all orangutans need to have when living in the forest. He was learning cooperative skills, working with another orangutan to open coconuts, and had started to share his nest at night with other infants. By the end of his second year in the centre and in his fourth year of life, he began to naturally wean himself off the milk offered every day. The next year he was introduced to older orangutans and learned the complex social skills of a bigger group. He bonded with an older female orangutan who taught him wilder behaviours and in time he became less interested in interactions with the keepers.

I could see this little orphan was tugging at Linda's heart – he was her motivation. The animal she had adopted would soon be going into the release programme – a process that takes months, and even take years before they are ready. But to survive, they needed habitat. His future home was on fire. And this is where Linda's adoption programme missed a step. They kept the news flowing about the orphans but were shy about communicating the threat of the fires. The shame of it is that their adopters are a tribe of people like Linda, willing and able to join an online activism campaign if asked.

Even without the programme communicating much, Linda's phone was swamped with pictures of rescuers going into the fire zone and hauling animals to safety. She was doing her own research. Spreading her own message. She felt the threat to the one small orphan and was doing what she could from a distance. It was heartbreaking. I felt it as keenly as she did.

I had come to meet with Linda to get some first-hand insight into the growth in online activism. The prism of the Indonesian fires was a poignant example to use. We are from two different activist generations, yet share passion about community and protecting wildlife. There is a familiar language between us – a vocabulary common to activists – but how we work and how we think is miles and miles apart. The difference is harmonious and respected by both generations, but it was a difference I wanted to explore.

Activists can sustain the energy for their work through a bond with the activist community they join. Raging against injustice is strong glue. But, I have often found that activists who work at the heart-felt end of the spectrum – be that poverty, indigenous rights, child slavery or indeed wildlife campaigns – have a lonelier, more difficult road to walk. Despite this she keeps a lightness of spirit that is, without doubt, part of her success. It is a shame her online community don't get to meet her in person. Her eyes literally sparkle with happiness. I admire her immensely.

She has a massive network of online connections and if you didn't know better, looking at her online activity you could easily mistake it for random information sharing. None of the rules I had been taught while working for large NGOs seemed to apply. Years of lecturing from professional commu-nications teams had taught me to 'keep it light, keep it simple', and 'don't post too often'. This was the model being used by her adoption programme. Yet, Linda seemed to be doing the opposite.

Her primary platforms are Facebook and Instagram, so she wasn't a direct part of the #MelawanAsap movement (which predominantly happened on Twitter), but was very much involved with the effort to expose the corruption of the palm oil industry. The love and connection for the wildlife in the fires remained a touchstone through the months I watched her work online, but she very effectively repackaged it, powerfully and quickly, into a palm oil campaign. Her messages were targeted, frank and punchy.

All of this effort was unpaid. Linda had no desire to work for an NGO and had never done so. She enjoyed her autonomy and nimbleness. She respected the work of NGOs and was very happy to work with them, but regarded their constraints and self-focus as an impediment. Her preference was for 'free-style campaigning'. She also wanted to be able to access information as close to the source as possible. It wasn't until I started gathering information from Indonesian campaigners that I realised how strategic and valuable this was, especially at a time when shallow 'clicktivism' generated by the bigger NGOs is being criticised as ineffective.

Linda also had a strong and very solid code how she works. She checked her facts diligently. She documented online activity carefully, so that if pages are taken down she still had records. She screened who she lets into her network and has a rigid policy about who remains in her inner group. Her office was her smartphone. She had honed her system so that individuals in her network receive specific pieces of information directly, capitalising on the fact that social activism information flows so swiftly that any repeats inherent in her system are simply absorbed. It is impressive. Really impressive. Imagine how powerful 100 or 1,000 Lindas could be.

As we sat together she showed me her arsenal specific to her current focus. There were apps for scanning barcodes to determine whether products contained palm oil and lists of palm oil free products. She was gathering the scant English language news and redistributing it as fast as she could. There were a few local groups she had identified as solid targets for donor funds if people wanted to give. She showed me how to put individual messages on people's timelines. She explained what information had to be a graphic and why. Her message was 'share with care – make sure it is real'. It was amazing to see the cornucopia of brands and information all collected together into a remarkably coherent campaign – a whole campaign in a phone. 'One little thing can set off a chain reaction,' she said. 'It's no good just telling someone that they should change. You have to show them what they can do.' Showing meant empowering other people to spread the message too. She felt no sense of ownership of it, and cared little about whose brand had profile. If the message was being spread, and multiplying as it went, that was a good day.

In my mind I was struck by how many campaigns being run by hundreds and hundreds of organisations in Europe and North America were telling not empowering. Sure, NGOs are good at getting messages out, but most often the 'action' is a plea for a donation so that the NGO can do something itself. Sometimes it's a plea to write to a politician. NGOs just can't be nimble enough to do what Linda does – provide individuals with actions that are tuned to them – because so often the best action for that individual is under the brand of another NGO. I couldn't help but chuckle at how the big NGOs would be dismayed with this free-style campaigning. They had absolutely no way to penetrate and dominate it.

When I asked how many people she felt she reached and where they were her reply was about layers. She hadn't met many of her core network in person, and had no idea where they even lived in the world, but they were her tribe. She gave little consideration to national boundaries, economic status, language, gender, colour or religion. What was important was shared values about a subject. When I asked again where they came from, she replied 'the world'! Her reach, when it folded out through additional layers of networks could be to as many as 500,000 people. That is an impressive number. More impressive that it was being fed by a solo activist in a small country town in rural Australia.

A few months after my interview with Linda I had the good fortune to communicate with Armet Memet. It was only then that connection to Linda's decisions about which NGO she supported for orangutan rehabilitation became even more relevant. Armet had worked for a period for an orangutan adoption programme in Borneo. His motivations were a combined love of orangutans, the wider ecosystem and the Dayak communities in the region. Armet's experience was one where a number of international NGOs and research organisations active in the region had put the interests of their programme above the people who had called the Kalimantan home for countless generations. Land was taken from Dayak community control, without their 'free, prior and informed consent' to establish the orangutan rehabilitation centre.[3] I wasn't shocked to hear this, but the confirmation was sad. It is simply not good enough for NGOs to say that the Government had given approval. NGOs should – putting it bluntly – know better than to game the system.

Even after displacing the community, the adoption programme promised the community that their activities would provide an income opportunity, but these gains have not been seen. There was an air of superiority to their relationship with the Dayak that smacked of the bad behaviour I discussed in the previous chapter. As I researched the backstory to Armet's comments I became aware of how many minority world orangutan NGOs were implicated in this behaviour.

The power of online activism cuts both ways. When I reported this to Linda, she responded by immediately notifying her vast network.

*** *** ***

The power of connection

If the corporate elite have motivations that need to be tempered and watched, and governments have no capacity, international NGOs need to find ways to connect with a broader sweep of civil society across the globe. Sticking with brands will limit the potential. But, there is hope.

We are living in an age where new forms of cosmopolitan grassroots revolutions are already being trialled around the world.[4] After decades of frustration with political inaction, communities and activists have taken to electronic communication (social media platforms, blogs, video, citizen journalism sites) to mobilise change.[5] They are using social media as virtual spaces where individuals can learn, evolve and transfer cultural and social capital.[6]

There is an explosion of analysis about the role of social activism, and its success or failure, as a political change agent.[7] The desire for change is not new. Grassroots movements have been alive and well for most of the last century, but their nature has been different. Recent social activism has facilitated mass communication that has been, at times, braver and more international than before. But, it also must be said, as a form of protest online activism is not necessarily pushing the political boundaries very far.[8–11] Indeed, most of the battles that have come to prominence through social activism remain unresolved battle grounds.

Micah White wrote in 2010 that online activism was undermining real-world change. In some respects I agree with his views, but I limit that agreement to online activism in the minority world. Having worked for the conservation movement I am acutely aware that minority world NGO campaigns are increasingly focused on 'easy asks' and 'simple clicks', with the goal of amassing a large volume of signatures and hopefully a member database that can be plumbed for future donations. The soul of the message gets lost in the quest for a high level of online 'exposure'.[12, 13] Many of these campaigns are run by specialised agencies that treat the content in the same way they would when marketing a product. As White says:

> we find ourselves in the bizarre situation where the celebrated international climate change organization TckTckTck with 10+ million members and 350+ partner organizations – including Greenpeace, 350, WWF, OXFAM etc – is covertly run by Havas Worldwide, the world's sixth largest advertising company. Havas' clients include Wal-Mart, Coca-Cola, Pfizer, BP and the rest of the ones who are to blame.[14]

White's concerns are valid when applied to orchestrated campaigns by large minority world NGOs.[4] These campaigns are often about organisational profile and convincing the community to fund the organisation's own professionals to fight the battle. It is a one-way communication, modelled on market capitalism. These campaigns do not represent genuine social movements or the use of the online networks to swiftly communicate messages and disseminate information, across boundaries and across the world.

I concede that social activism has problems inherent in the medium. It does not lend itself to facilitating deliberative discourses on complex, difficult issues. Yet, I want to make the case that judging what is happening based on clicktivism and tangible political change masks important information from view. The diffusion of the internet and social activism in civil society itself is not, and will never be, a black-box process.[15] Face-to-face communication will always be equally, if not more, influential in mobilising people to action. But mobilisation is not the totality of what online activism is. When used to enable people to express shared concern and understanding it can, and does, draw millions of individuals together – to find each other, to collaborate, to learn and be intellectually empowered; and yes, sometimes to organise and act.[9, 13, 16–18]

I am interested to look at the potential of this new frontier of discussions and networking, across borders of many kinds. There are around 280 million people (87 per cent of the population) using the internet in the United States of America, but this pales in comparison to China which has 674 million (49 per cent of the population) and India with 375 million (30 per cent of the population). Perhaps these numbers are not surprising, but the potential for growth in India and China is genuinely staggering.

Brazil has an impressively large number as well with 118 million (58 per cent of the population). Indonesia already has 78 million people using the internet, yet is ranked 110th for human development by the World Bank. Compare this to Germany's 71 million people online and its sixth human development ranking. Indeed, Kenya has more people online at 29 million (63 per cent of the population) than Australia with 21 million (93 per cent of the population).[19]

As connectivity numbers continue to grow in the majority world, and technologies continue to develop to allow larger numbers of people to either receive information or participate in discussions, there is great potential to unite people from different parts of the world, and different cultural and social contexts, under commonly held beliefs, ideals and ideas, transcending the politics of the state.

It is worth picking out a few examples to illustrate that social communication of information, an important element of activism, is flourishing in this new borderless sphere. These examples are deliberately diverse to demonstrate the breadth of expressions and the potential to connect with populations of people not usually drawn into minority world environmental discourse.

Perhaps the most profound recent civil movement – one that will live in the written history of our time – has been the Arab Spring. More accurately it should be called the Arab Revolutions and the Day of Rage. I start with this to illustrate trans-border social activism activity focused on politics. As I write, other movements are erupting and I am sure by the time this book has gone to the publisher there will be more. So, this is a snapshot in time, written from late 2015.

#Jan25 and the Arab Revolutions – an example of mobilisation

#ArabSpring is a phrase that will be synonymous with this time in history. But the issue the hashtag speaks to is not new. It is the western hashtag to describe the revolutionary wave of demonstrations and protests (both non-violent and violent), riots and civil wars in the Arab world that began on 18 December 2010 in Tunisia and proliferated, leading to similar revolts later, in Egypt, Libya, Yemen, Syria, Bahrain and other Arab nations.[20] More accurately, we should call it #Jan25 – the Day of Rage.[21]

The impetus for the protest was born of many problems – dictatorship or absolute monarchy, human rights violation, political corruption, economic decline, unemployment, extreme poverty, and a number of demographic structural factors including a large percentage of educated but dissatisfied youth. Increasing food prices and famine rates associated with climate change were very likely additional stressors that also contributed to unrest.[22] The protests that began in December 2010 united people from across political, economic, class and religious divides in opposition to their autocratic governments.[23]

The Arab online campaigners are the modern incarnation of early twentieth century nationalist networks from this ancient and politically sophisticated region whose broadsheets disseminated strategies for civil disobedience throughout the region in the years after World War I.[24, 25]

Egypt's activists shifted the shared knowledge space into 'the cloud' by witnessing, putting on record and imbuing political meaning to symbolic struggles against social injustice, harassment and censorship as part of a broader movement for political reform.[25–27] Although they shared a common call for personal dignity and responsive government, the revolutions across Tunisia, Egypt and Libya reflected divergent economic grievances and social dynamics. What united them under the label #Jan25 was a shared momentum to build new political institutions. Online communications had little to do with the underlying socio-political and socio-economic factors behind the protest movement, but it helped coordinate the efforts of the different protest groups, under the one banner we now know as the Arab Revolutions.[16]

As Ilhem Allagui and Johanne Kuebler have written:

> If we learned political leadership and coalition building from the Russian Revolution and popular initiative from the French Revolution, the Arab revolutions in Tunisia and Egypt demonstrated the power of networks … people aligned themselves against their enemy, the president, and their attitudes and beliefs changed due to their political engagement. Suddenly, old and young found or discovered themselves to be both patriotic and in revolt. Some did so through the power of the communication technologies they used for informing and freeing themselves; others by responding to the call for taking to the streets. Communication technologies empowered citizens, some of whom used these technologies spontaneously and not strategically.[20]

The protests shared some traditional techniques of civil resistance including strikes, demonstrations, marches, and rallies. They also used social media to organise, communicate, and raise awareness in the face of state repression and internet censorship. Social networking pages that distributed information and content worked codependently with blogs, networking sites, and traditional media institutions. When the Tunisian Government attempted to censor Facebook pages, the hacktivism group Anonymous relayed antigovernment information and provided fax bridges to enable news to spread despite online censorship. When governments blocked and censored opposition websites, internet hosts were moved to other countries.[20] As Manuel Castells puts it – power was shifted from the state to the 'network society'.[28]

The most popular trending hashtags across the Arab region in the first quarter of 2011 were #egypt (with 1.4 million mentions in the tweets generated during this period) #jan25 (with 1.2 million mentions), #libya (with 990,000 mentions), #bahrain (640,000 mentions), and #protest (620,000).[29] In the week before Egypt's Hosni Mubarak resigned (February 2011) related tweets from Egypt – and around the world – ballooned from 2,300 a day to 230,000 a day.[10] The Dubai School of Government reported that in 2011 nearly 9 in 10 Egyptians and Tunisians surveyed said they were using social media to organise protests or spread awareness. In essence, Facebook and Twitter were already enabling a discussion about a historic region-wide uprising.[29] The spike in online revolutionary conversations often preceded major events on the ground.[10] This is an extraordinary level of social organisation beyond state or mainstream media control.

The Internet Society in Tunisia reported that before the revolution there were two million users of Facebook. Three months before Mohamed Bouazizi burned himself in Sidi Bouzid (December 2010) in protest at food prices and political repression, there had been a similar case in Monastir. But no one knew about it because it was not filmed. Yet, because images and video of Bouaziz were put on YouTube and Facebook his action was a powerful, motivating siren. The video alone attracted 152,894 views on YouTube, most within a few days of its upload on 18 December 2010.[25, 30]

Previous protest movements in Tunisia, when social activism penetration was low, had been crushed, but by December 2010, the news of the self-immolation of Mohamed Bouazizi spread easily and freely, triggering mass protests. The Tunisian revolution spilled over into Egypt under the banner of the Jasmine Revolution. There is no question that the social media platforms played a vital role in organising and publicising social protests. Control of conventional media made the role of new media more relevant. During the anti-Mubarak protests, an Egyptian activist put it succinctly in a tweet: 'we use Facebook to schedule the protests, Twitter to coordinate, and YouTube to tell the world'.[25] The movement that spread across Tunisia, Egypt, Libya, Syria, Yemen and Bahrain was fed quality information by traditional media, but gained coordination power through social media.[30]

In 2012, a follow-up report by the Dubai School of Government investigated to what extent individuals felt they agreed with the statement: 'I'm more of a global citizen today' (after interacting with people from around the globe using social media in 2010 and 2011). The positive responses were remarkably high, with many people expressing that social media and, by association, the exposure to a variety of ideas and opinions, led them to become more open and tolerant of broader views.[31]

An important element to draw from this brief summary of these extraordinary events is that #Jan25 – the Day of Rage – was predominantly directed by individual activists, not large well-funded and staffed minority world organisations. I can't quantify my hunch, but I feel certain that a traditional campaign run by a large NGO could not have achieved that level of penetration.

Weibo: an example of discussion

Pollution has become a cornerstone environmental issue in China, and for good reason. China has 16 of the world's 20 most polluted cities. Coal has been the main culprit in annihilating China's air quality. It is the source of as much as 90 per cent of the country's sulphur dioxide emissions and half of its particulate emissions.

Water pollution is also a massive problem. Overuse, contamination and waste in water supplies have produced severe water shortages; approximately two-thirds of China's roughly 660 cities don't have enough water despite the fact that China controls the river water supply of 13 neighbouring countries and has dammed every major river on the Tibetan plateau. Some 300 to 500 million people, mostly in rural areas, lack access to piped water. Almost 90 per cent of underground water in cities and 70 per cent of China's rivers and lakes are now polluted. Combined with negligent semi-industrialised farming practices, the water crisis has turned much of China's arable land into desert, which today claims around one-quarter of China's total land mass.[32]

Despite a rich historical culture of popular protest, social movements, including a sustained environment movement, have been absent from China's contemporary political landscape.[33] Nonetheless, as technology has prospered, internet activism has begun to surface.[34, 35] The messages typically mix text with photography and video, through social activism platforms unique to this region – Weibo and WeChat. Online expressions are often highly emotional, with a subtle undertone about the politics of transparency and accountability, and there is a growing trend for online discussion to begin online and then spill onto the street as protest.

The environmental protests in Xiamen, Dalian, Shanghai and Ningbo in the past five years have all involved intense interactions between online mobilisation and offline protests.[36] Leslie Hook covered an outburst of environmental protest in China in 2013 calling for the halt to the construction of a giant new petrochemical plant. What is interesting about this new wave of protest is the informed nature of the crowd concerned about the release of pollutants. In a region where information has been tightly controlled for decades, government officials have been backfooted by informed questions: Why hadn't the public been consulted before construction began? Why were the local papers not being allowed to write critically about the plant? Why wasn't the public being given a say? These questions have been deeply unsettling for the country's authoritarian officials.

Hook makes the case that this protest and dozens more like it would never have happened if it weren't for China's social-media platforms, the information that is shared and the discussions that build understanding.[37]

Weibo alone has more than 400 million Chinese users.[38] Compare this to Twitter's global 974 million and it is difficult to argue against Weibo's serious social penetration. Chinese activists point to the emergence of social media platforms such as Weibo as a turning point for their causes.[37, 39] Deng Fei, an activist, tells Hook: 'Chinese people were like shattered glass before we had Weibo. There was no way to unite ... [Weibo] has given [activists] more power and more rights, and allows [us] to come together quickly.'[37]

These Chinese-style protests mark a significant social shift. After high-profile protests, the Government's concern over potential public dismay has prompted officials to shelve a series of industrial projects across the country. In 2013, a US$6 billion uranium-processing project in Guangdong province was cancelled the day after a protest against the plan. Later the same year a coal-burning power plant in Shenzhen met a similar end.[37] I was surprised to read that for several years, the only public source of real-time information about Beijing's air quality was a monitoring station on top of the US embassy, which sent readings out every hour on Weibo and Twitter. In 2011, people demanded that Bejing publish hourly pollution data. When the Government complied, it was a landmark victory. People realised the reality of the levels of pollution.[38] Word spread through Weibo and WeChat.

The environmental movement in China is scattered, sporadic, and often located in rural areas and motivated by single incidents rather than more comprehensive agendas that aim at a nation-wide change.[33, 35, 39, 40] It doesn't have obvious leaders and instead operates as a groundswell of people. This is as much because of state regulation as anything else, discouraging the formation of national-level independent NGOs to quell nationwide representation.[41, 42]

Where organised and professional environmental NGOs have formed they have cautiously and carefully reached out to have an increasing involvement in global environmental governance. This movement has successfully built consensus on local and regional environmental issues. With its own form of networks, Chinese environmentalism has achieved a significant impact on both domestic and international public opinion.[40]

Weibo serves this movement as an effective communication platform. Most messages articulate critical opinions, requesting and sharing information, questioning the credibility of sources, and calling for action.[33]

These are early days for a movement that is still not sure if the Government will allow it to survive. Activists can be arrested in China for words alone. But, social activism will continue to grow and will itself adapt to the changing forms of control.[18, 34, 43]

The example of Chinese environmentalism illustrates how social media can support communication flexibility, if tuned to a region.

#MelawanAsap: an example of reproach

My final example loops back to Linda, the orphan orangutan and the role of social activism in Indonesia and Malaysia.

In their corporate quest for more profit and volume, and safe in the knowledge that their illegal activity will be unchecked in lawless regions, pulpwood and palm oil giants have been burning tropical rainforest, opening up massive peat swamps and installing extensive networks of canals across Indonesian and Malaysian rainforests for decades. Their effort is concentrated in Sumatra and Borneo. Peat canals lower the water table and dry out the land. Fires burn in areas where they would never naturally occur, smouldering for weeks in underground peat deposits.

Plantation clearance activities are the largest sources of carbon pollution in the world today. The World Resources Institute estimates that the 2015 Indonesian fires produced more carbon pollution than the emissions from the whole of US economic activity over the same period. By the end of October 2015 emissions had reached 1.62 billion metric tons of CO_2 – bumping Indonesia from the sixth-largest emitter in 2015, up to the fourth largest in just six weeks.

Indonesia already provides 52 per cent of the world's palm oil supply, and with investment support from Malaysia and Singapore the country aims to continue to be the world's largest supplier of the commodity. Almost 11 million hectares of oil palm plantations – owned by Indonesian, Malaysian and Singaporean companies – are exporting 33 million tons of palm oil, reaping revenues of US$18.4 billion in 2014. Indonesia further plans to allocate millions of hectares of land for agricultural development, including 9 million hectares for smallholders that include palm oil. So, just as Singapore and Malaysia share the profits of Indonesia's palm oil, so they share the responsibility for fire and haze.[4] Linda, and many activists like her, argue that manufacturers using palm oil in products must also share responsibility, along with consumers of the many processed foods and household products that use this cheap and poorly regulated oil source.

The big palm oil companies have engaged in marketing spin, suggesting the blame for the fires mostly lies with small farmers and villagers. In truth, a number of actors – large and small – are involved in burning land and forest, including communities whose forest-dependent subsistence livelihoods have been disrupted by plantation development. Because of complex and profoundly unjust land tenure arrangements in Indonesia, they are forced to clear new land just to survive, but theirs is a small contribution. Large corporations levelling blame in their direction is profoundly unjust. It is corporations in close cooperation with the Indonesian, Singaporean and Malaysian Governments that are complicit in complex patronage networks and tiered revenue streams for illegally burning land to clear it for large-scale agriculture.[44, 45] The human cost of this battle is tragic, but there is another innocent caught in cross-fire – the gentle 'person of the forest', Indonesia's orangutan.

Responding to the annual fires in Sumatra and Borneo that had spiralled out of control in late 2015 Indonesian activists from Wahana Lingkungan Hidup Indonesia (WALHI or The Indonesian Forum for Environment) launched a dramatic, locally focused effort to force decision-makers to act.

With reports, from 29 June to 5 October 2015, of more than 300,000 people in six Indonesian provinces seeking medical treatment for respiratory problems and other diseases caused by smoke or haze, civil society took to Twitter and created a storm of their own. It was remarkable to watch the campaign unfold, with most of the international coverage spreading virally through Twitter and indie journalism websites like Mongabay. Mainstream English language media, for the most part, gave the fires only a passing glance.

Indonesian activists trended Twitter coverage a number of times in the 30 days to 27 October with #MelawanAsap (#FightSmoke) and clocked up around 100,400 messages in this short window. For the public protest in the capital of Indonesia's Riau province on 12 October they focused on #RevolusiLangitBiru (#BlueSkyRevolution) spreading another 2,600 messages. The outrage continued and from 19 October onwards through #EvakuasiKami (#EvacuateUs), #HazeYouJokowi and #StopTheFires a further 30,000 messages went out. Most of these messages were in Indonesian, with international English messages picking up the #StopTheFires tag late in the month.[46]

This social activism didn't stop the fire. Indeed, the fires were simply too large to be stopped except by the monsoon rains that fell some months later. But for the first time it shone a sharp spotlight on the Indonesian Government and was a firm expression of public anger.

Yanuar Nugroho has studied the role of online technology and civil society adoption in Indonesia for more than a decade. He has found that online technology has empowered Indonesian activists in organising their movement, widening their perspectives, expanding their network, and, to some extent, increasing their bargaining position when dealing with other actors in Indonesian politics.[47, 48] Despite problems with levels of remote connectivity, Indonesian civil society uses the technology dynamically. Together with his colleague Shita Laksmi, Yanuar Nugroho has identified that the strong sense of community in the Indonesian culture facilitates trends to spread quickly. The relatively low costs of the technology also meant that its penetration to some rural – although not yet all – communities was high. They found that activism in Indonesia is characterised not only by the use of the technology (one-direction) but also by the co-evolution between technology use and the development of activism itself – a two-way relationship where each shapes the other.[15]

Since the close of the Suharto era in Indonesia many groups have emerged, both formal and informal, networking with national and international organisations alike. They have both shaped and been shaped by the social, economic and political development of the country. Internet and social activism effectiveness is determined by other factors than just 'use' and adoption. Yanuar and Shita recall a remark made during a reflective workshop in Jakarta (FC, Jakarta focus group discussion, 21 October 2010):

If you ask us why we use the Internet, the answer is clear: it reaches globally and it is interactive. These two features enable you to get feedback from wide ranging of audience when you communicate an idea. It also functions as communication media, even when we are absent … Because the Internet connects people, if we use it for education, it will become much more effective as it can help share our limited knowledge resources to many more communities and network providers. That way, we collaborate and network with others.[15]

In the aftermath of the fire I received feedback from Dayak activists in Borneo who had been active throughout the #MelawanAsap campaign. Norhadie Karben and the late Itan Kussaritano are from the Dayak Indigenous Peoples of the Kalimantan Forests. Dayak is a European name to encompass the 200 or so riverine and hill-dwelling indigenous groups in the interior of Borneo, each with their own dialect, customs, laws, territory and culture. Not only are these brave and wonderful people, but they are tenacious communicators.

Through a translator, Itan Kussaritano told me that in his experience social activism has become an important means to provide information about campaigns. Often it was the primary source of news, spreading interpretation about print or electronic media.[49] Norhadie Karben added that social media and other online tools help them maintain communication with other networks that support the struggle of his people and in turn help them to influence government policy.[50]

They both consciously use social activism to ensure that their network is empowered with information and important facts, and they find that this information quickly spreads through people's private social relationships. They still face impediments, including the cost of internet access, but they are convinced that social activism is a core empowerment tool.[49, 50] Norhadie organises his Facebook account in a remarkably similar way to Linda. His networks are in layers, based on interests and similarities.

Both Itan and Norhadie strive to build conversations or discussions between people, instead of people just being served information as is the case with traditional media. It was deeply important to them that these conversations involved people from outside their region. They both recognised the power of being part of a bigger movement and consciously positioned their work in that context.[49, 50]

I was struck by Norhadie's final comment:

> Surely we as a society that live to take care of peatlands which have been a store of natural resources for generations of our ancestors, are eager to involve and communicate with people from elsewhere, particularly people in developed countries which use the raw materials, so that natural biodiversity can be kept and preserved.[50]

Their sentiments were echoed strongly by other local Kalimantan activists on the frontline during the #MelawanAsap campaign and all the way to the Paris Summit. Arie Rompas and Aryo Nugroho are also members of the Dayak community and represent WALHI Kalimantan Tengah. WALHI is the organisation at the frontline of many of the legal challenges over illegal burning of peatlands and land grabbing for palm oil. The distinct difference between WALHI and many of the international orangutan NGOs, is that they act for the forest and all who live in it – people and orangutans alike.

Again through a translator, Arie and Aryo both said they saw social activism as a means to encourage people's involvement, rather than telling people what they should think. They felt that the community and the media came to understand, in their own time and their own way. This is a subtle difference, but I think an important one. Sharing information was seen by both as valuable, even if the sharers didn't connect formally to the campaign. Aryo added that when they wanted feedback from the community they specifically used mediated campaigns and their website for this.[51, 52]

Arie told me that he saw a middle-class audience as the core group he needed to connect with – they understood the technology and were active users of social media. This audience wasn't only Indonesian, but he was constrained by language beyond Indonesia's shores. Aryo agreed, adding it was important to build a sense of solidarity with the global activist community, especially as many of the problems WALHI worked on did not stem from Indonesia, but from abroad. They both felt that reaching audiences in Europe was fundamental to their success.[51, 52]

They may not know each other. They may never meet. But Linda Irwin-Oak, and hundreds of activists like her, responded to Arie, Aryo, Itan and Norhadie's calls for support in 2015. Linda loves orangutans with a deep passion, but her activism was about palm oil. She was drawn to the epicentre of a series of legal battles aimed at stopping agribusiness from undermining this critical ape habitat – habitat that her orphan may one day call home.

New opportunities

I have tried to demonstrate that the very essence of the internet and social activism is its ability to network; to reach those who are usually unreachable. Yet, the potential to network individuals or groups will not be harnessed unless the users themselves engage in networking activities. Networking should empower civil society. Participatory action should not be 'manufactured' or 'captured' from above by politicians, minority world NGOs or elites seeking to use it for their own ends. It should decentralise knowledge and enable knowledge sharing.[15] Where participatory action has occurred but turns out to be simply legitimating decisions perceived to have already been made by other powerful actors, the trust deficit is significant.[53] Engaged people benefit from a thickening of alliances and relationships, which in turn can strengthen their participation.[53]

What interests me most about these examples, and numerous others not mentioned, is that people are becoming attuned to thinking about what someone else, somewhere else, is saying. They are connecting with like-minded individuals despite traditional boundaries. They are becoming accustomed to messages outside of the normal channels we use – formal political process and the media. They are operating as rooted cosmopolitans.

Jill Hopke indentified two mutually supportive but separate ways the activists communicated through online technology. Twitter and Facebook serve as real-time curated and episodic news feeds, through hashtag indexing, allowing both core activists and more casual tweeters to engage with the day of action in-the-moment as events took place in widely disparate geographical locations on a transnational scale. The activists communicated and reported in more detail in more durable longer-term, organised structures of closed listserves. She identified that listserves (or websites) helped the movement to persist over time and space by enabling activists to enhance trust in diffused networks. They used the listserves (or websites) to make sense of complex scientific and technical information, as well as to connect with experts.[54]

Social media platforms are themselves grappling with what this all means. During the Arab Revolution, technology firms 'leaned forward' with new tools or applications introduced to serve an eager public (and in doing so, capture market share), such as Google's speak-to-tweet service, an application designed to translate voicemails into tweets that was used by the activists as a means of bypassing Mubarak's Twitter blockade. Several tech firms built dedicated portals to allow in-country users to share content. Others, such as Facebook, responded poorly – working against the campaign by shutting down one of the protest-group pages because they used a pseudonym to avoid government harassment. Supporters eventually persuaded Facebook to reinstate the page, but the incident showed how businesses such as Facebook, YouTube and Twitter may not fully appreciate the way in which their majority world users engage with these tools as public-information infrastructure and not just as 'cool', minority world applications in the service of personal amusement.[27]

Of course, we should remain critical and of implying cyber-utopianism or 'internet centricity' and should also remain alert to how a given technology might negatively affect a network or group. Internet and social activism are not detached from daily lives. Scholars should continue to debate the extent to which social activism facilitates actual action. These discussions are worthy, but are not my core focus. My interest lies in how social media can be used for borderless communication to help civil society better communicate and participate in environmental governance in the future.[15, 47]

Governance is inevitably a long-term process. It requires a commitment to layers of procedure and consultation. The challenge is to evolve long-term institutionalised decision-making processes to be systematically influenced where there is no organisational structure to aggregate people's opinions.[7] There is a need to network participation and widen the involvement, to capture the views of organisations and communities who are ultimately the bene-ficiaries of the governance.[55] The internet does not solve all obstacles to collective action, but it can provide a networked infrastructure and tools for organising, coordinating and campaigning. Indeed, technically skilled, and sometimes resource poor, actors can take advantage of networked collaboration to discover, learn about and challenge policy-making.[56] The internet and social activism has to be appropriated so that it helps create relationships between individuals and the civil society movements in which they participate.[15] These concerned groups should be deliberately – and strategically – facilitated to contribute to cosmopolitan governance.

As we look into the approaching storm, we can garner strength about what is to come with our knowledge that our technological age connects us across the world. We can, if we choose, agree to work together, to share goals and aspirations, and learn from each other's experiences. But, we need the international governance system to evolve to allow for organic and adaptable cultural expressions of conservation and protection. This requires leaders who can facilitate our voices to be heard against the wind and rain as it lashes around us.

*** *** ***

The wind of the imagined storm has become so strong it pushes against my balance.

Hail pounds the ground, flattening the wheat and gouging the soil.

The gorilla stumbles through the pellets of ice to take shelter beneath an old tree. A sentinel of time, it offers her what comfort it can. She crouches, head bowed and eyes tightly closed.

A thick, powerful torrent of rain melts the hail and fills the air.

I struggle through the wall of water to stand beside her. She doesn't move, but I see the rise and fall of her breath.

As I lower myself to sit beside her, our backs both press against the trunk. This tree has watched generations of our kind come and go.

The storm rages around us, as sorrowful as my soul.

References

1 Ancrenaz, M., Marshall, A., Goossens, B., van Schaik, C., Sugardjito, J., Gumal, M. and Wich, S. 2008. Pongo pygmaeus. In *The IUCN Red List of Threatened Species 2008: e.T17975A7640635.* IUCN SSC Primate Specialist Group.
2 Singleton, I., Wich, S. A. and Griffiths, M. 2008. Pongo abelii. In *The IUCN Red List of Threatened Species 2008: e.T39780A10266609.* IUCN SSC Primate Specialist Group.
3 Memet, A. 2016. Personal communication, facilitated by Lee Tan, February 2016.
4 White, M. 2016. *The End of Protest: A New Playbook for Revolution.* Toronto: Alfred A. Knopf.
5 Firmin, A., Tiwana, M., Evanics, R., Hobhouse, E., MacGarry, M. and Sayed, Z. 2015. *State of Civil Society Report: 2015.* New York: CIVICUS: World Alliance for Citizen Participation.
6 McEwan, B. and Sobre-Denton, M. 2011. Virtual Cosmopolitanism: Constructing Third Cultures and Transmitting Social and Cultural Capital through Social Media. *Journal of International and Intercultural Communication.* 4, 4: 252–258.

7   Vissers, S. and Stolle, D. 2013. How Do I Change Politics? Evaluating the Effectiveness of Political Participation Modes. Paper presented at the Annual Meeting of the Canadian Political Science Association.

8   Shirky, C. 2011. The Political Power of Social Media: Technology, the Public Sphere, and Political Change. *Foreign Affairs*, January–February 2011: 28–41.

9   Štětka, V. and Mazák, J. 2014. Whither Slacktivism? Political Engagement and Social Media Use in the 2013 Czech Parliamentary Elections. *Cyberpsychology*. 8, 3.

10 Howard, P. N., Duffy, A., Freelon, A., Hussain, M., Mari, W. and Mazaid, M. 2011. Opening Closed Regimes: What Was the Role of Social Media During the Arab Spring? In *Project on Information Technology and Political Islam Data Memo 2011.1*. Seattle: University of Washington.

11 Miller, V. 2015. Phatic Culture and the Status Quo: Reconsidering the Purpose of Social Media Activism. *Convergence: The International Journal of Research into New Media Technologies*: 1354856515592512.

12 Chaua, L. 2015. Orangutans Need More Than Your Well-meaning Clicktivism. *The Conversation*. [online material]

13 Lim, M. 2013. Many Clicks but Little Sticks: Social Media Activism in Indonesia. *Journal of Contemporary Asia*. 43, 4: 636–657.

14 White, M. 2010. Rejecting Clicktivism. [online material]

15 Nugroho, Y. and Laksmi, S. 2011. *Citizens in @ction: Collaboration, Participatory Democracy and Freedom of Information – Mapping Contemporary Civic Activism and the Use of New Social Media in Indonesia*. Jakarta Selatan: Manchester Institute of Innovation Research/HIVOS Regional Office Southeast Asia.

16 Stepanova, E. 2011. The Role of Information Communication Technologies in the 'Arab Spring'. *Ponars Eurasia*. 15: 1–6.

17 Juris, J. S. 2012. Reflections on #Occupy Everywhere: Social Media, Public Space, and Emerging Logics of Aggregation. *American Ethnologist*. 39, 2: 259–279.

18 Sullivan, J. 2014. China's Weibo: Is Faster Different? *New Media & Society*. 16, 1: 24–37.

19 Internet World Statistics. 2015. Usage and Population Statistics. [online material]

20 Allagui, I. and Kuebler, J. 2011. The Arab Spring & the Role of ICTs: Introduction. *International Journal of Communication*. 5: 8.

21 Alhassen, M. 2012. Please Reconsider the Term "Arab Spring". In *The Blog*.

22 Korotayev, A. and Zinkina, J. V. 2011. Egyptian Revolution: A Demographic Structural Analysis. *Entelequia: revista interdisciplinar* 13: 139–169.

23 Foreign Affairs Committee. 2012. The Arab Spring Uprisings. London: Commons Select Committees: United Kingdom Parliament.

24 Anderson, L. 2011. Demystifying the Arab Spring. *Foreign Affairs*. 90, 3: 2–7.

25 Khondker, H. H. 2011. Role of the New Media in the Arab Spring. *Globalizations*. 8, 5: 675–679.

26 Radsch, C. C. 2013. Digital Dissidence & Political Change: Cyberactivism and Citizen Journalism in Egypt. Doctoral Dissertation, American University, School of International Service.

27 Howard, P. N. and Hussain, M. M. 2011. The Role of Digital Media. *Journal of Democracy*. 22, 3: 35–48.

28 Castells, M. 2007. Communication, Power and Counter-power in the Network Society. *International Journal of Communication*. 1, 1: 29.

29 Mourtada, R. and Salem, F. 2011. Arab Social Media Report (Volume 1, Number 2). Dubai: Dubai School of Government.

30 McGarty, C., Thomas, E. F., Lala, G., Smith, L. G. E. and Bliuc, A. M. 2014. New Technologies, New Identities, and the Growth of Mass Opposition in the Arab Spring. *Political Psychology*. 35, 6: 725–740.

31 Mourtada, R. and Salem, F. 2012. Arab Social Media Report (Volume 2, Number 1). Dubai: Dubai School of Government.

32 Xu, B. 2014. China's Environmental Crisis. Council on Foreign Relations. [online material]

33 Sukosd, M. and Fu, K. 2013. How Chinese Netizens Discuss Environmental Conflicts? Framing and Functions on Sina Weibo. Framing and Functions on Sina Weibo (June 11, 2013).

34 Yang, G. 2014. Internet Activism & the Party-State in China. *Daedalus*. 143, 2: 110–123.

35 Yang, G. and Calhoun, C. 2008. Media, Civil Society, and the Rise of a Green Public Sphere in China. In *China's Embedded Activism: Opportunities and Constraints of a Social Movement*. Abingdon: Routledge.

36 van Rooij, B. 2010. The People vs. Pollution: Understanding Citizen Action against Pollution in China. *Journal of Contemporary China*. 19, 63: 55–77.

37 Hook, L. 2013. China's Environmental Activists. *FT Magazine*, 23rd September 2013.

38 Kay, S., Zhao, B. and Sui, D. 2015. Can Social Media Clear the Air? A Case Study of the Air Pollution Problem in Chinese Cities. *The Professional Geographer*. 67, 3: 351–363.

39 Sima, Y. 2011. Grassroots Environmental Activism and the Internet: Constructing a Green Public Sphere in China. *Asian Studies Review*. 35, 4: 477–497.

40 Xie, L. 2011. China's Environmental Activism in the Age of Globalization. *Asian Politics & Policy*. 3, 2: 207–224.

41 Matsuzawa, S. 2012. Citizen Environmental Activism in China: Legitimacy, Alliances, and Rights-based discourses. *ASIANetwork Exchange: A Journal for Asian Studies in the Liberal Arts*. 19, 2: 81–91.

42 Van Rooij, B., Lora-Wainwright, A., Wu, Y. and Zhang, Y. 2014. Activist Acquiescence: Power, Pollution and Access to Justice in a Chinese Village. UC Irvine School of Law Research Paper 2014–2022.

43 Reese, S. D. 2015. Globalization of Mediated Spaces: The Case of Transnational Environmentalism in China. *International Journal of Communication*. 9: 19.

44 Purnomo, H. 2015. Playing with Fire: The Economics and Network of Fire and Haze. *The Conversation*. [online material]

45 Edwards, S. 2015. Why Indonesia Can't Stamp Out Fires That Have Cast a Haze over South-East Asia. *The Conversation*. [online material]

46 Topsy. 2015. #MelawanAsap/#FightSmoke. Topsy Labs, Inc. [online material]

47 Nugroho, Y. 2012. Localising the Global, Globalising the Local: The Role of the Internet in Shaping Globalisation Discourse in Indonesian NGOs. *Journal of International Development*. 24, 3: 341–368.

48 Nugroho, Y. 2010. NGOs, the Internet and Sustainable Rural Development. *Information, Communication & Society*. 13, 1: 88–120.

49 Kussaritano, I. 2016. Personal communication, facilitated by Lee Tan, January 2016.

50 Karben, N. 2016. Personal communication, facilitated by Lee Tan, January 2016.

51 Rompas, A. 2016. Personal communication, facilitated by Lee Tan, February 2016.

52 Nugroho, A. 2016. Personal communication, facilitated by Lee Tan, February 2016.

53 Gaventa, J. and Barrett, G. 2010. So What Difference Does it Make? Mapping the Outcomes of Citizen Engagement. *IDS Working Papers*. 347: 1–72.

54 Hopke, J. E. 2015. Hashtagging Politics: Transnational Anti-Fracking Movement Twitter Practices. *Social Media + Society*. 1, 2.

55 Theocharis, Y. 2015. The Conceptualization of Digitally Networked Participation. *Social Media + Society*. 1, 2.

56 Breindl, Y. 2013. Assessing Success in Internet Campaigning. *Information, Communication & Society*. 16, 9: 1419–1440.

6   Through the storm

Snow Leopards – Yash Veer Bhatnagar and Kulbhushansingh Suryawanshi

The small Buddhist town of Kibber, in the Spiti Valley of northern India's Trans-Himalaya, offers important insights about a new role for nongovernmental organisations (NGOs) as conduits between government and the community.

Finding effective ways to conserve large carnivores is challenging in almost every region of the world – in the Himalaya large home ranges and the threats the animals themselves pose to livestock makes coexistence with humans difficult. In other parts of the world, programmes designed by minority world NGOs have tended towards a command and control approach – hunting bans, eco-guards and pushing communities off their land. This worldview causes conflict and understandable resistance. In many cases it is ethically bankrupt. In this wild Himalayan region the Nature Conservation Foundation in India, working closely with the international Snow Leopard Trust, has walked a road less travelled. Their path has been informed by their experience with snow leopards and the rugged, noble people who live alongside them. Their example illustrates a way out of the conflict with morality and grace.

In researching the Nature Conservation Foundation's work I discovered that India fosters a rare talent for narrative writing, lost to many other parts of the world. Despite the hot Australian summer outside, as I read about their science and their discoveries I am transported to a Himalayan landscape by two committed conservation scientists: Yash Veer Bhatnagar and Kulbhushansingh Suryawanshi. Before I had even spoken to these gentlemen, I had already come to love snow leopards.

Snow leopards are often called the 'grey ghosts' of the Himalaya. Rarely seen, these elusive animals have an indivisible presence in crevices on rock faces or shadows in the snow. Their white-grey coats, spotted with large black rosettes, blend perfectly with the harsh mountain landscape. Snow leopard researchers are a tenacious bunch, undaunted that the animals they long to see stay resolutely just beyond view. They invest rugged, difficult months beyond comfort and safety for tiny glimpses of these big cats. The animals seem to hover moments ahead, leaving behind mere traces of their meal – some scattered bone and the hide of an ibex, argali or bharal. Time after time, their writing builds excitement at finding pug marks in sand or snow, only to be crashed against the rocks of the writer's soul as the animals remain tangibly beyond sight.

When a snow leopard does come into view, it imprints deeply:

> There was no sign of the leopard. But then it happened. I heard a few rocks tumbling and suddenly, only a few feet in front, a very surprised snow leopard screeched to a halt just in time to avoid bumping into me.
>
> It happened quickly, but my mind slows the scene each time I think of it: startled round eyes, screeching forelegs, tail drawn to a huge arc above its head, the sudden whiff of its approach, and a distinct feline odour.
>
> Before I could collect my senses it turned and dashed across a narrow grassy patch to the edge of a cliff, looked around for a second, and disappeared.
>
> We rushed down but all we saw was a blank cliff. The 'grey ghost' had vanished.[1]

These endangered leopards[2] are an integral part of Central and South Asia. They range from Afghanistan in the east to Kazakhstan, Russia in the north and across to China in the west. Their habitat is fragmented with little connection in between. Human communities across this region have a similar sparse and disconnected pattern.

Yash Veer, Kulbhushansingh and their colleague Charudutt Mishra focus their conservation research in the Spiti, a desert mountain valley located high in the mountains in the north-eastern part of the Indian state of Himachal Pradesh. The name Spiti means 'Middle Land'. Quite literally, this is the land between Tibet and India. The region's Buddhist culture is similar to that found in the nearby Tibet Autonomous Region and the Ladakh region in India. The Kibber village has around 80 homes, made by hand of stone. Life here is modest, harsh but proud.

I called Kulbhushansingh early in my evening. The sun was setting over our farm, yet through the phone the world came alive with the mid-day hustle and sound of southern India outside the Nature Conservation Foundation offices. He was tentative about telling me his story at first, but I learnt that he was a mountaineer and drawn to the wilds of the Himalaya. He was a loner, so community conservation was something he had to learn from Charudutt – an adept in that cultural setting. As the discussion grew, he opened up about how he had developed a strong connection with the people of the Spiti. We discussed his scientific work, and then I asked if he had any snow leopard stories. With an affable, resonant timbre, he told me his tales. I was hooked.

In 2008 he was researching the foraging behaviour of bharal, or Himalayan blue sheep, an important prey species for snow leopards in the region. He was in the Spiti Valley. It was cold and the snow was deep. These are tough conditions to work under, especially when you are investing days and nights trekking, watching and taking meticulous notes about mountain sheep habits.

The invisible leopards were always palpably nearby. He found fresh kills and pug marks, but the snow leopards remained beyond sight. After months of this routine, he was taking a rare day of rest in the village. The sun was out and so he sat outside his hut to relax. He wasn't looking for wildlife so was surprised when a snow leopard and her cub suddenly appeared across a deep gorge, just a few hundred metres from the village.

Exhaustion and pain were banished. He scrambled to a position where he could watch the leopards, but not be seen. He was joined by other research colleagues in the village and some of the local children. The group's excitement was high. Hours went by while they watched this rare and mysterious mother and her cub lying and playing in the sun.

To see two snow leopards together was already extraordinary. Then a third leopard appeared high on the ridge. Kulbhushansingh and the other researchers could feel the electric tension between the animals. The cub hid behind a rock while the two adults studied each other across the distance. Dusk fell and darkness slowly masked the drama, to continue beyond human gaze.

Seeing these animals was a rare moment in a researcher's life, but then Kulbhushansingh's tale of wonder took an unexpected, very human twist. When he stood his feet were dangerously cold, after hours without movement. Frostbite was a real threat. He struggled back down to the village, his mind bouncing between jubilation and concern. Villagers bundled him inside and cut his now frozen boots from his feet, warming his limbs back to safety. While the commotion clattered around him he recounted the day. An old woman sat quietly nearby. Perhaps she was compelled to speak to soothe the mixture of emotions flashing across his face. He expected admonishment for risking himself to see wild animals. Instead, her words touched his heart and in turn, years later, reached out and touched mine. 'In my 80 years of living in this village and walking these hills I have never seen a snow leopard,' she said. 'It is through your work and your pictures that I hope I can.' In that moment Kulbhushansingh recognised the deep desire we all share to see what is wild.

Kulbhushansingh had another tale to tell me. A few years later he received a report of a man who had shot a snow leopard near his home. The community had agreed not to kill snow leopards, so there was implied accusation of wrong-doing in the message. Kulbhushansingh knew there were many layers of motivation in these circumstances. So, he went to see the herder, to collect data and to understand what had happened.

The leopard had found a way into the herder's livestock pen during the night and had killed 20 goats. This was a significant loss for the man, and they both knew it could have become far worse. As Kulbhushansingh was telling me the story, I knew that snow leopards in these circumstances can easily kill an entire herd. Had the man not taken action, the loss could have been absolute.

The herder told Kulbhushansingh he had no choice but his voice was conflicted – deep vulnerability and anger, mixed with regret. This single night would impact on his family's wellbeing for months. But that didn't diminish the man's compassion. The herder understood the leopard needed to eat to survive. Kulbhushansingh had heard this often – a respect for the sameness between man and leopard.

He helped the herder to fix the enclosure to prevent further night attacks. Over the day they became friends and Kulbhushansingh would speak with him often in the years to come. There was a humorous twist to the story. The enclosure had a small window in it and another snow leopard was often seen looking through the window at the goats inside. The man would invite people to come and see 'his snow leopard' through this little window. The predator had become a familiar, a relationship with peaceful equilibrium.

These relationships and insights are only possible with time. It was through Yash Veer that I came to understand the depth of continuous work that had been invested in Kibber since 1995. The Nature Conservation Foundation and Snow Leopard Trust researchers had become part of the village family – with all the various tensions and differences that come with working in groups of people, even those who share a bond. This was a measure of Charudutt's commitment to the snow leopard project. Yash Veer recounted how Charudutt had lived in the village for extended periods, had helped the local school with teaching mathematics, played sports, shared their celebrations and sadness, and become a part of the community. The children Charudutt had taught were now the adults making village decisions. Over time a deep trust, friendship and respect had developed.

This allowed new insights and understanding to be uncovered. Each in their own way, Yash Veer and Kulbhushansingh explained that wildlife conservation must have context for people who are caretakers of this wildlife. This means understanding the layers and permutation of people's perspectives and motivations.

Decades of minority world assumptions have been made about people's relationships with predators. Presumptions are reinforced by simple surveys that seek people's thoughts, without necessarily overlaying other factors. Too often these shallow investigations simply reinforce what the researcher believes, without checking whether that belief is actually true.

The Nature Conservation Foundation had taken a different route and invested the time to really understand the problem. This understanding helped them to work more constructively and collaboratively with the community to build long-term solutions tuned to the community's needs. Kulbhushansingh is now leading work to investigate an even deeper picture. He has discovered that individual attitudes are influenced by different factors at different levels of social organisations. He now knows that gender, education and age, income sources in the family, agricultural production and type of livestock holder are all factors that influence perspectives. With this information, overlaid with numbers of livestock taken, new patterns have started to emerge.

Charudutt, Kulbhushansingh and Yash Veer, and their many colleagues, believe the future of snow leopards is in the hands of the people that share the region – the people who look across the same landscape, share the same seasons and feel the same wind, rain and snow. They strive to empower the community to forge a harmonious relationship with snow leopards (and wolves).[3] They have developed solutions that address their real-world problems. Rather than simply campaigning for a massive park to be declared and re-locating the people out of the region (a frequently used minority NGO solution), they work on better enclosures to protect smaller livestock. They work with the community to change herding practices like moving bigger livestock to areas where they are not as easily preyed upon. They have created an insurance scheme to compensate the community when snow leopards (or wolves) kill livestock. They are backing these plans with sustained research to confirm how many snow leopards and wolf kills there actually are, and what livestock is actually being taken and when. They are also exploring new problems such as why snow leopards take large livestock.

At times the Nature Conservation Foundation has discovered that their science doesn't match community perception. At other times their science has revealed uncomfortable conservation truths, like the discovery that an increase in wild prey has not meant a decrease in livestock kills. Because this is a partnership between the Nature Conservation Foundation and the community all information is shared and discussed. They build solutions together.[4–7] They know they have decades of work ahead of them to solve new conundrums.

The Nature Conservation Foundation village level insurance programme is a particularly novel solution, designed to both offset economic losses from livestock depredation and to reduce the extent of depredation by providing financial rewards for anti-predatory solutions to herding. The insurance programme began with just one village. Three years later, overcoming initial scepticism, the villages of Gete, Tashigang and Kee also joined the programme. The Nature Conservation Foundation has now started a new insurance programme for the larger village of Chichim. More than 100 herding families are participating across the Spiti, and similar programmes have been developed in four villages in the Gya-Miru region of Ladakh as well.[4] Not only is this solution important in recognising that snow leopards cause significant economic hardship for people, but it is an instructive example that doesn't rely on wealthy tourists trekking into the region. The programme creates its own financial support and is beautifully self-contained.

With these solutions and relationships, the attitude of people towards wildlife conservation has also evolved. Most villagers have stopped killing carnivores or driving them away from kills.[4, 5] It is a remarkable story of tenacious decades-long commitment to these villagers and these species. Indeed, in speaking with Yash Veer, I discovered that the Nature Conservation Foundation is coming to understand there may be no exit point for their involvement. The community needs their permanent presence to be a voice for the snow leopards.

So, how does an NGO sustain such a commitment? This has been Yash Veer's focus for a few years now. Early on, they had assumed the insurance scheme would become self-funded, eventually. But, inflation and the reality that the predator–prey relationship was changing in the Spiti, forced the Nature Conservation Foundation to reconsider. They now understand they will be there for many years to come, perhaps even permanently. So, the Foundation has tapped into the creativity the sub-continent possesses in spades, and conceived 'Project Snow Leopard'. The programme has been embraced by the Indian Government as part of the National Indian High Altitude Programme, and with this has come institutional funding and support. It took a lot of work and time but they developed a *Management Plan for the Upper Spiti Landscape including the Kibber Wildlife Sanctuary* based on the philosophy of community landscape conservation.[8]

As Yash Veer described the management plan, I was also hearing an example of the longer-term role of civil society in wildlife conservation.

He might not use this turn of phrase, but Yash Veer was describing their role with the Spiti community as an interpreter or conduit between the community and government. The Nature Conservation Foundation effectively acts as a telescopic connection, that carries the community landscape conservation plan, up through each level of local and regional government, retaining the community's connection throughout and into the national government discussions. It builds participation from the ground up, flowing from village level 'wildlife committees', through 'landscape committees' and finally to national level management. The Foundation has a seat at the table to speak for the snow leopards, alongside community representatives and government officials.

The Project Snow Leopard Management Plan is profoundly different from many others I have read. For a start it is designed and developed by an NGO and the community. It inherently recognises the value and role of traditional, democratic village councils and the presence of traditional land use rights. It establishes a new NGO specifically to carry out day-to-day coordination of the plan. This is groundbreaking in and of itself. The Indian Government is agreeing that civil society should remain in control. The plan cements the role of important existing NGOs, such as the Nature Conservation Foundation, to support, advise and represent the wildlife.

The implications are breathtaking; this is a perfect real-world example of rooted cosmopolitanism. The plan's vision – which has the buy-in of government and communities alike – speaks to community empowerment, connections with wildlife and a desire to become a 'globally outstanding example of endangered species conservation'.[8]

When I started to write this book, I knew the case I wanted to make, but I had no example for demonstrating that it was possible. But in listening to the soft, expressive voice of Yash Veer – a gentleman of the snow leopards – I was being given a tangible, real-world illustration. It was a gift.

While Yash Veer was clearly proud of what they had achieved, I could see the Nature Conservation Foundation had achieved something far bigger. They were laying the foundation stones for civil society to project a genuine, unpasteurised voice of the Kibber Village – the old women who tended to Kulbhushansingh's frostbite, the herder with the 'snow leopard window' – and many other villagers around the world, into the halls of the United Nations in New York.

*** *** ***

I sometimes hear from minority world NGOs, and often from the general public in North America and Europe, that the majority world doesn't care about wildlife – that intervention from the 'enlightened north' is needed 'before everything is gone'. Nothing more completely quashes that claim than the achievement of the Nature Conservation Foundation and the Snow Leopard Trust in the Spiti. I have always believed that people everywhere care about the world around them. What they don't care for is being told by someone, half a world away, what they should do.

After the interview with Yash Veer I read all 299 pages of the Project Snow Leopard Management Plan in detail. It is a significant flagship programme of the Indian Government[8] and, while not unique, it provided a useful illustrative example to chart what might be possible.

It achieves conservation through two elements. The first is the identification of key areas that are of core importance for wildlife. Across the broader landscape they find ways for people and wildlife to co-exist, to reduce people's dependence or use, so these core areas can be left for wildlife. Outside these core areas they find management balance between community use of the landscape's resources and wildlife needs. No-one is being moved; no villages are being relocated. The community is the root of the wildlife management plan from the start.

Project Snow Leopard functions through decentralised decision-making. Four levels are identified. Discussions and decisions begin at the village or village cluster level, through Village Wildlife Conservation Committees. These Village Committees include representatives of the gram sabha (village councils) and Gompa (monasteries) as well as youth, women, local NGOs, the scientists and government officials. The deliberations of the Village Committees are communicated into Landscape-Level Implementation Committees that have oversight for a number of areas. The Village Committees have representatives in the Landscape-Level Committees to ensure that there is consistent communication and equitable agreement. These Landscape-Level Committees communicate their deliberations to the national level through a Project Snow Leopard National Steering Committee.

The Project Snow Leopard National Steering Committee, within the Ministry of Environment and Forests, is ultimately legally responsible for oversight of the plan. The Nature Conservation Foundation has been identified as the 'anchor institution' assisting the Ministry with all technical aspects related to the programme.[8] It is no coincidence that it is also the Nature Conservation Foundation that is on the ground working with the local communities at the village level as well. This is what Yash Veer was referring to when he recognised there was no exit point. They would remain involved as this important conduit, in perpetuity, or would facilitate others into their role.

The Project Snow Leopard Management Plan contains a series of recommendations to address the issues that the scientists have identified as important, including:

- livestock depredation by snow leopards and other species
- retaliatory persecution for loss of stock
- excessive grazing by local livestock and migratory herders
- poaching
- pressure from roads
- immigrant labour
- uncontrolled tourism
- other human disturbances
- climate change.

At the base of the conduit, the plan builds local capacity to carry out areas of management, and involves the local Buddhist religious institutions that already promote protection of all sentient beings.[8] At the far extension of the channel the Government takes responsibility for ensuring that all other government departments complement and support the plan. Research organisations (Nature Conservation Foundation and Wildlife Institute of India) are tasked to monitor snow leopard abundance and distribution, and to bring forward the needed science.[8]

A particularly novel element worth mentioning is the Government recognises this management plan requires resources and funds need to be available to allow work to continue. Rather than centralising financial access, or requiring village communities to fundraise for their effort, the Government has established a not-for-profit body into which they deposit funding for implementation. The five-year budget for the whole plan is a modest US$400,000. This way funds are available as needed and can be distributed with ease and less bureaucracy.[8]

Imagine if this communication of information and empowered management, rooted at the local level, channelled through the various levels of government, was conveyed beyond the state and directly into international conservation discussions – that the views of communities who look upon snow leopard footprints every day were heard.

I investigated to see how well it was reflected in the CMS Central Asian Mammals Initiative. This CMS programme formally involves Afghanistan, Bhutan, China, India, the Islamic Republic of Iran, Kazakhstan, Kyrgyzstan, Mongolia, Nepal, Pakistan, the Russian Federation, Tajikistan, Turkmenistan and Uzbekistan. It has a focus on Bukhara deer, wild camel, wild yak, saiga, argali, Mongolian gazelle, goitered gazelle, kulan, kiang, chiru, Przewalski's horse, Tibetan gazelle, and chinkara as well as snow leopard and cheetah.

I found that CMS defers to the Global Snow Leopard & Ecosystem Protection Programme – a World Bank supported intergovernmental agreement with an ambitious goal to protect 20 healthy populations of snow leopards across the cat's range by 2020.[9] On the surface it all sounds good, but as I read through the report of the first Steering Committee meeting there was absolutely no grassroots information publically represented. Instead, the focus seemed to be on governments seeking funding. I can't be sure what informal discussions transpired. I was not in the room for this meeting or a follow up held in 2016 in Germany. The concept of local empowerment may be alive and well, but in the record of the meeting it wasn't a good sign.

I can only hope that in the years to come the important work of the Spiti Village Wildlife Conservation Committees and the Nature Conservation Foundation, as rooted cosmopolitanism, directly and publically influences decisions.

The Nature Conservation Foundation and Snow Leopard Trust story I provide is one example. There are others equally meriting mention. Some I know like the mangrove rehabilitation work by the Zoological Society of London (ZSL) and the International Union for the Conservation of Nature (IUCN) SSC Mangrove Specialist Group in the Philippines began in 2007, where over 50 per cent of mangroves have been lost. ZSL established a community-based mangrove rehabilitation project, empowering local communities to protect remaining mangrove forests and developing science-based methods for communities to rehabilitate lost forest sites, especially through fishpond reversion, helping to ensure greater food security, improved protection against natural disasters and increased household incomes for local communities.[10]

Another inspiring example is the Wechiau Community Hippo Sanctuary which protects a 40km stretch of the Black Volta River in Ghana's upper west region through a community managed scheme, created by local elders in 1999. Fearing alienation from their land, the community leaders had previously rejected proposals by the Government to establish a government-run hippopotamus reserve in the area. Instead, they worked with the Calgary Zoological Society and EarthWatch to establish a community-managed sanctuary that is zoned to protect the hippopotami and the habitat, while enabling the traditional uses of the forest to be maintained. The community has relocated farms away from the river, allowing for forest regeneration and minimal human-hippo conflict. Fishing is regulated to protect hippopotamus wallowing zones. Livestock encroachment on riparian habitats has been limited thanks to alternative water access via boreholes. A fire belt now surrounds the core zone. This is a rooted cosmopolitan model that has demonstrated strong conservation and community benefits and has created a number of community owner businesses, including a shea nut cooperative.[11, 12]

A great many other organisations are quietly progressing fine community-driven work. Their work should also come forward, and would have far greater traction, visibility and influence if it were to become part of internationally tuned cosmopolitan approach.

Conservation goals should be set by governments, but the conservation form should be born out of the community – their home, their solution, their management. In the case of the snow leopards in the Indian Himalaya, the goal was to 'safeguard and conserve India's unique natural heritage of high altitude wildlife populations and their habitats by promoting conservation through participatory policies and actions'. The community and the Nature Conservation Foundation designed a comprehensive management plan with Village Wildlife Conservation Committees at its core.[8] In the case of the Volta River in Ghana's upper west region the motivation was to retain autonomy in their management of local natural resources, and to sustain their environment.

Imagine if the Spiti Villages were actively connected to other similar communities elsewhere in the world. Or, if the community of the Black Volta River in Ghana was able to support a community in Latin America to mirror their model. Information flows when people who share a focus or an understanding feed their views and information through an extendable channel that connects local to global discourse. Voices collected in this way can be powerful. They help build identity and understanding. They help us to move beyond the boundaries constructed by money and power, and create communities of connected political life.[13]

Facilitating these voices to be present at the decision-making table is where MEAs can show leadership and perhaps pressure the World Bank as well. But MEAs won't pay attention until civil society raises a collective voice. International NGOs need to become rooted cosmopolitan pathfinders and advocates as well.

In 2014, the Government of Ghana and I presented the findings of the review of more than 100 NGOs from across the world that had wildlife as their focus the Tenth Meeting of the Conference of the Parties to CMS (CMS CoP10). These NGOs were big and small, from the minority and majority world, and had a broader spectrum of views from animal welfare through to sustainable hunting. In summary, the review findings were that:

- civil society – both NGOs and local civil society groups – are the implementers and sometimes even the coordinators of work under the convention and its agreements.
- most CMS agreements are poorly linked to other MEAs (the Convention of Biological Diversity – CBD, the Convention on International Trade in Endangered Species of Wild Flora and Fauna – CITES, the Convention on Wetlands of International Importance – Ramsar and the United Nations Environment Assembly – UNEA) and consequently NGOs often find their agreement-focused work is not reflected in the policy developments of other fora – either by CMS or governments.
- civil society programmes are necessarily localised – this is the scale where conservation takes place. Without the means to draw these efforts together, acknowledgement about them quickly becomes scattered. Governments frequently overlook them.
- there is significant scope for civil society to provide additional specific types of implementation activity (such as scientific, technical, practical, local, popular, capacity-related) especially where priority taxonomic or

geographical gaps are identified or capacity building is needed in developing regions.

- civil society wants a formal mechanism to inform/report on their activities so that efforts made by civil society are seen as relevant and respected. It is important that civil society contributions are codified and accepted as a contribution against an agreed plan, so that Parties or Signatories recognise the value, and build this work more fully into the progression of the CMS agenda. At present, only a fraction of NGO/civil society CMS-related activities are reported into CMS processes.
- CMS needs a monitoring and evaluation process that defines and tracks the main benchmarks for the convention's work – a legally enforceable peer review mechanism (compliance regime) – that civil society should have access to.
- the CMS Family offers unique attributes by providing for high-level policy discussions (through the CMS CoP) as well as detailed and region-specific species actions plans and activities coordinated through agreements. If facilitated properly, CMS could usefully draw local activities into the CMS Family to build a better picture of what is being done and where the gaps are.

The review was, in effect, a first tentative step taken by these wildlife NGOs towards a closer working relationship with the CMS Family. We recommended that CMS convene a regular NGO forum to discuss priority areas and invite or solicit NGO formal contributions. We suggested that this would help to build continuity between CMS and other MEAs where NGOs were much more active than the CMS Secretariat. We urged the Secretariat to foster strong and lasting relationships between governments and NGOs. We suggested that CMS develop a mechanism to enable NGO-facilitated work to be formally and consistently reported, to provide a more accurate picture of CMS progress. We asked that CMS explore formalised models for NGO involvement like Ramsar's International Organisation Partners (IOPs). We requested the creation of a formalised focal point for NGOs to assist them to understand and contribute to the CMS CoP process. Along with a number of other technical issues, we specifically asked that CMS review the NGO Partnership agreements to ensure there is a reciprocal benefit established. Many of the CMS Partner NGOs reported the Partnerships amounted to little more than paper.[14]

In 2015, I also worked with the World Wetland Network – a global network of over 2,000 small to medium NGOs and civil society organisations focused on wetlands – to explore how their relationship could also grow with the Ramsar convention. We received more than 190 responses from all over the world.[15] The main findings of this second process mirrored those from the CMS review very closely, with these additions from Ramsar civil society:

- Ramsar's Communication, Education, Participation and Awareness programme activities require greater advocacy and technical/financial support. Many NGOs have skills that could be more actively used in this process.

- some governments appear to discourage efforts for Ramsar site designations. Important wetlands are eligible for Ramsar listing but nominations are stalled by bureaucracies or government policy. A means for civil society to highlight potential nominations is required.[15]

We recommended governments should recognise that NGOs often create a longer-term and more continuous link for Ramsar than government representatives. There was a strong need to develop more structured guidance for Ramsar Parties, and National Focal Points, on how to engage civil society. We suggested that Ramsar should explore options to expand on the IOP status to include more NGOs and civil society organisations. We recommended that Ramsar invite NGO and civil society input into reporting on the state of wetlands, as well the wetland nomination process and inclusions in the Montreux Record. We made the case that governments should acknowledge that a great proportion of the Ramsar work was being done by civil society, often with no funding or support. We urged Ramsar to prioritise funding and support for NGOs and civil society organisations that are working on Ramsar-listed wetlands.[15]

Ramsar did not progress anything during the meeting directly after we released the review, but this could easily be because the NGO community didn't aggressively seek it. The World Wetland Network (WWN) NGOs decided to tread softly during the meeting, to avoid government concern about an IOP application that was being considered at the time. Perhaps at the next Ramsar CoP the agenda can be more forcefully put.

A cosmopolitan form of wildlife governance

Andrew Strauss and Richard Falk have long championed a Global Peoples Assembly – a global parliamentary body established independently of the United Nations.[16] Dieter Heinrich proposed a World Parliamentary Assembly within the UN structure.[17] For me, these ideas are the ultimate manifestation of this connected political life. Indeed, many scholars have hoped that a worldwide, popularly elected, legislative assembly would be established at some point in the future.[18–20] Until recently, such a prospect reeked of utopianism. Yet, a question always sat in the back of our minds: if democracy is so appropriate in the state setting, why isn't democracy just as important in the global setting?[16] In 2012 Joseph Schwartzberg published a persuasive roadmap for how a World Parliamentary Assembly might form[19] and the release in 2015 of the *Report of the Commission of Global Security, Justice and Governance* offers a tangible hope that the dream might still come true.

In today's world, states retain their authority by delegation from their citizens. If people choose to circumvent the state and create an elected authority themselves – a Global Peoples Assembly – and then delegate powers to this new assembly, there is little states can do. If it happens, they will no longer be able to claim that they are the sole authority.[20] As Andrew Strauss has carefully described, this assembly doesn't automatically change the system or solve the inherent problems we currently face, but over time its influence would grow. The more details the assembly addresses, the more relevance it will hold.[20] The centre of political gravity will eventually shift towards it. Its role in law making will be mainstreamed.

While I am philosophically on board with the Global Peoples Assembly project, I am also someone who has spent a long time in the storm shelter and I have two fundamental reservations about its viability at this point in history.

Setting aside the major shift required by the entrenched national elites, I believe we don't have time to wait for the project to unfold. Purely from a wildlife and environment perspective we are on the brink of irreversible collapse, right now. The storm is upon us and we have to take definitive steps towards a new form of global environmental governance in this decade.

My second reservation relates to the level of detail and deliberation that needs to be facilitated to genuinely overcome the world's current list of global problems – climate change, nuclear weapon possession along with other weapons of mass destruction, pandemics or world trade gone wrong to name just a few. The world is far too complex to have all governance matters deliberated by one body of people, no matter how large.[21]

We are already in a post-Westphalian world, even if many international relations scholars are reluctant to acknowledge it. There is an alarming resurgence of popular nationalism, but the neoliberal agenda is still transferring power incrementally to the corporate elite (chapter 2), away from multilateralism and towards multi-stakeholderism. International NGOs are complicit in the shift (chapter 3) without recognising the implications of the model they are promoting. The *Report of the Commission of Global Security, Justice and Governance* comprehends the storm that is coming and attempts a reset for 'just peace', proposing to revitalise the UN General Assembly and developing a transnational democratic culture that brings non-state actors into governance discourse. The MEA structures we already have – CBD, CITES, Ramsar and CMS – can respond to this agenda if they choose to (chapter 4).

The notion of developing a transnational democratic culture might have been difficult to conceive 20 years ago. Governance by the people requires different political communities for different issues to be formed. Today, civil society discourse develops organically, connecting people with shared views and concerns across the world (chapter 5). Our local understanding is changing, even now. Angel Parham and Danielle Allen call this our 'sociospatial imagination'. They have investigated how we imagine the globally distributed localities to which we have connections, and the social relations that are overlaid on those geographical conceptions in our current digitally connected age.[22] People around the world now routinely encounter the stories and appeals of 'distant others' with a frequency and intensity unknown in the pre-internet era. This exposure is already shaping how we think of ourselves in relation to these others who are socially, culturally, and geographically far removed from us.

Digital connectivity supports the development of our sociospatial imagination in three directions. First, we can see ourselves as mutually dependent on faraway others. Second, we have opportunities to share knowledge and experience with these faraway others. This raises our appreciation in a third direction of the kinds of cultural, political, and environmental goods that can be realized only by working collectively at the global level. These three orientations prepare our sociospatial imaginations to change our experience and dependence on proximity so that we can appreciate and understanding narratives from all corners of the globe.[22]

In the right hands and with the right intent, digital connectivity can provide rich, multilayered portraits on complex issues, cultivating conscious, globally oriented equitable interest that remains rooted in local experience. It can expand the boundaries of the self while also equipping rooted cosmopolitans with tools and resources that help them to enter the worlds of others to more fully experience and more effectively interpret unfamiliar narratives. It provides an opportunity for communities to participate in framing directions and decisions.[22–24]

Harnessing and directing this potential is important. David Held suggests that states should assume the role of facilitator and enabler, rather than that of a top-down agency, while 'energiz[ing] a diversity of groups to reach solutions to collective action problems.'[25] For wildlife and environment issues, at least, I believe this enabling governance should continue to be facilitated through CBD, CITES, Ramsar and CMS and that these MEAs should be evolved into inclusive and broadly representative global decision-making channels.

NGOs are now recognised and consistent observer participants in these MEAs.[26–30] The significant step forward from this current arrangement would be for a representative delegation to be formally at the table, as a conduit to convey local voices on matters that directly affect them. This would require an alliance of local civil society (community landscape conservation bodies) that share a perspective on an issue. This is unashamedly a rooted cosmopolitan proposal – a radical localisation of power and authority. Forming such alliances overcomes the democratic accountability and legitimacy concerns about NGO participation, in that representation is on behalf of a clearly defined group and doesn't extend to speak for all civil society, everywhere.[29, 31] I advocate that individual community programmes should combine across regions to form a series of cosmopolitan delegations. These delegations should have input in the international law-making process, with formal standing and a vote. My proposal does not impinge on any state sensibilities about interference in national law-making. States would retain the same rights and responsibilities they currently hold when they engage in any international process. They can commit, withdraw or lodge a reservation.

Establishing these new delegations in CBD, CITES, Ramsar and CMS would be the smoothest process for NGOs to create. These MEAs retain the best of what we already have – the structures and the iterative progress of conservation decisions. The caveat is that NGOs would need to play a brave and central role as conduits and advocates, representing local community voices. I don't advocate for international NGOs to gain more individual power or a seat for self-representation.

Anthony Burke, Stefanie Fishel and their colleagues have proposed an Earth System Council, with representation of Earth system scientists, major ecosystems (the Amazon basin, the Arctic and Antarctic, etc), species groups, and states as a new level of governance with similar standing to the UN Security Council. Their proposal acknowledges that the Earth is shared by human communities and a huge collective of non-humans who also have a right to existence. We are entangled. No being is truly autonomous or separate and we ignore the destruction of and our severance from the non-human world at our peril. They argue, and I agree, that trusting states to 'discharge their responsibilities' according to the 'old bargaining rituals of diplomacy' will fail.[32]

Their proposal has strong merit and deserves to be explored fully. I don't believe it is the full solution. I still maintain that the complexities of what must be discussed, decided and managed requires a detailed tier of intervention, even if it becomes a first step towards the grander visions of a Global Peoples Assembly or an Earth System Council.

In the next chapter I will describe more about how this might work, but first it is important to establish the core principles that would need to be applied. Combining the example of Project Snow Leopard, the discussions of the previous chapters, useful recommendations developed by the Rainforest Foundation[33] and IUCN's Environmental and Social Management Framework[34] with the philosophy of rooted cosmopolitanism, I propose three initial principles of future cosmopolitan wildlife governance:

- building connectivity up from community landscapes, to ecoregions and to biomes
- establishing monitoring and transparency from the start
- committing to perpetual capacity.

Community landscapes, to ecoregions, to biomes

The foundation principle I propose is to tune wildlife conservation to community landscape conservation that respects cultural identity and expression and the connectedness of human and non-human members of the community, and to channel this to international discussions.

Building on the excellent leadership demonstrated by the Nature Conservation Foundation, the Snow Leopard Trust and the people of the Spiti in the Himalaya, I suggest similar tiers of management conduits, beginning at the village level and iteratively forming collective agreement at the landscape level. Once this is reached the views and preferences of the landscape level information are fed to ecoregional discussions, before being captured by biome level cosmopolitan delegations.

David Olson and his colleagues have defined 14 terrestrial biomes, with 867 terrestrial ecoregions,[35] reflecting extensive collaboration with over 1,000 biogeographers, taxonomists, conservation biologists, and ecologists from around the world. There is corresponding analysis for the marine environment as well. The terrestrial biomes are:

- tropical and subtropical moist broadleaf forests
- tropical and subtropical dry broadleaf forests
- tropical and subtropical coniferous forests
- temperate broadleaf and mixed forests
- boreal forest/taiga
- tropical and subtropical grasslands, savannas and shrublands
- temperate grasslands, savannas and shrublands
- flooded grasslands and savannas
- montane grasslands and shrublands
- tundra
- mediterranean forests, woodland and scrublands
- deserts and xeric shrublands
- mangroves.[35]

As there are no fully marine dwelling human communities (that I am aware of), I would suggest that the marine biomes are appended to their terrestrial counterparts. For the past 15 years this work has been the foundation for scientists and a number of groups to prioritise hotspot regions, and protected area designations.[36, 37]

I propose the terrestrial biomes have a different, more rooted cosmopolitan value. They can be the foundations grouping for the cosmopolitan

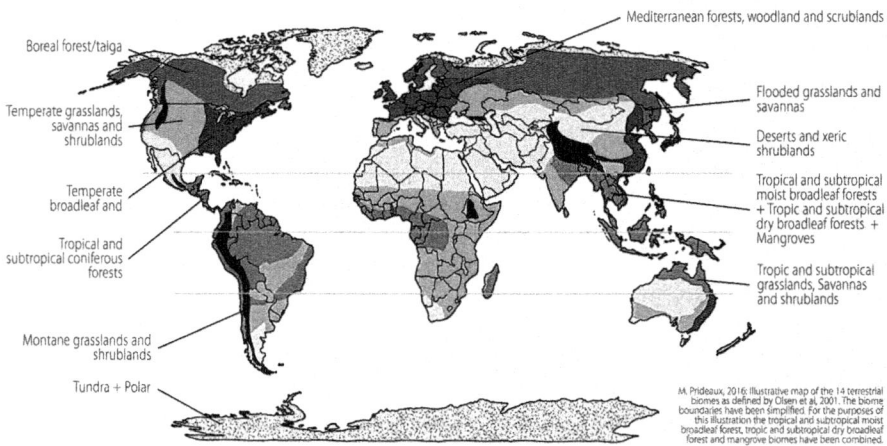

Figure 6.1 14 Terrestrial Biomes

delegations. Ecoregions and biomes are well defined for the terrestrial and management environment, and are able to capture the view and information of people's connections to their landscape and wildlife community, unimpeded by state boundaries or politics. Ecoregions reflect the distribution of species and communities. Communities living in similar biomes across the world can share information and learnings, based on their similar ecological experiences.

Facilitating so many localised discussions will require considerable commitment from international NGOs. They will need to redirect their current focus, time and resources to assume the role of ecoregion and biome advocates, a role often referred to as 'bridging organisations' in governance literature.[38] Communities will need skilled and committed facilitation and support. This is a role that NGOs, with their pre-existing expertise, experience and resources, can embrace. To build enough trust to advocate for a community necessitates commitment and considerable participatory work before a community will genuinely give 'free, prior and informed consent' to wildlife conservation actions on their lands and waters. The presumption should be that the community remains, and they develop proposals for how their activities can adapt, modify or evolve. They should have the option for voluntary area closures, or of considering if new activities should start.

Garnering this level of commitment takes time and trust. But, the community gains empowerment to manage the place where they live. They can stand as the recognised guardians of the wildlife who share the same space, through access to processes they previously couldn't influence. What everyone else gains is certainty of permanent and unconditional conservation.

This principle requires a new leap of faith and commitment from minority world NGOs and government actors, to devolve decision-making to the community level and to adapt the MEA system to embrace a multitude of expressions – a tapestry of conservation diversity.

Monitoring and transparency

The second principle is to establish monitoring and transparency. This is how certainty and commitment is maintained. Monitoring of scientific indicators and conservation progress is absolutely necessary to communicate into the process. Monitoring community compliance is equally important. This information must be regularly presented to the community landscape conservation management bodies and government agencies, and should be the foundation of discussions about ongoing progress and necessary adaption.

Equally, this information should be channelled to the other important intergovernmental processes that are deliberating science – IPCC, IPBES, IUCN SSC and SBSTTA.

People are complicated, and the dynamics of groups inevitably mean that disagreement and tension occurs. Recognising this, government agencies should provide independent and transparent grievance mechanisms with which to handle conflict. Equally, governments should provide detailed information on how funding is being used, and by whom, to ensure financial accountability and maintain confidence.

Communicating outwards is another important element of monitoring and transparency. Community landscape conservation management committees and their NGO conduits and advocates need to be able to communicate broadly with surrounding communities, communities elsewhere, individuals and civil society organisations around the world who want to support their conservation management. The networks must grow organically and include everyone who wants to be involved.

Perpetual capacity

The third principle is that cosmopolitan wildlife governance needs to be adaptive and perpetual. This requires continual capacity in community landscape conservation management committees and conservation science programmes.

Funding should be directed to civil society and local communities to strengthen their capacity and ownership of conservation activities. Active conservation science designed to deliver systematic, transparent, independent monitoring and evaluation of conservation projects is also vital.

The final element of this principle is that partnerships between NGOs and local communities need to be invested in. Trust needs to be built so that NGOs can serve as conduits and advocates for the community.

Advocacy

The fourth element is not a principle, but instead is a precondition in two parts.

The governance I propose is a complex and diffuse logistical programme that requires skill and resources to reach out to communities across the world to help them frame the future. Minority world NGOs must step forward to be the pathfinders and community advocates to ensure that community landscape conservation is communicated effectively through the tiers of ecoregions and biomes into international processes. Maintaining such connectivity takes commitment. This is a long-term role. Without NGOs it simply won't happen. Indeed, without NGOs it simply can't happen because the other options further subjugate communities to politics or the market. There is a humility involved in what I propose as well, because it is a programme of service to wildlife and communities – to the entangled reality that Anthony Burke, Stefanie Fishel and their colleagues have called us to acknowledge[32] – to cosmopolitan wildlife governance.

MEAs must also adapt to welcome NGO/civil society delegations at the table of global environmental governance to provide input into the law-making process with formal standing and a vote, and as much right to direct the administrative support for the MEAs as any government has.

This two-part precondition is as important as the three core principles.

Imagine another future

Traditional governance approaches are proving incapable of addressing the changes we face.[32, 39] They have led us down a path where those that govern are increasingly self-interested, and those that are governed are pushed outside of any legitimate collaboration. Even in the face of popular nationalism, the Westphalian system is crumbling, by design and by force. Social policy literature for other sectors already foresees a future where governments and their agencies play an essential leadership and strategic function role, while relying on civil society as the 'delegated implementers'.

To be successful, governance that collaborates in this way must construct an institutional framework that facilitates a complex mix of policy, discourse, negotiation and arbitration. History of conflict or cooperation, power and resource imbalances, leadership, institutional design and incentives for participation are all factors that must be consciously known.[39–43] It sounds complicated, but the evidence shows that collaborative governance arrangements already extend government resources, developing new solutions, and enabling decisions that go beyond mere compliance.[44–46]

The principles for cosmopolitan wildlife governance that I propose are not such a leap beyond what already exists.[45, 47] What is novel is connecting local issues directly to international governance, where the profound decisions about our future are already being made and triage decisions will be discussed in the near future.

If we don't connect local wisdom to these discussions, those in charge will make arbitrary decisions without the full knowledge of what is possible – about what we value and want to save for the other side of the storm now upon us.

*** *** ***

My imaginary journey with the gorilla in the storm continues.

The tempest rages. We are exhausted, soaked and bruised.

Her coat hangs wet and water streams off her body. She shakes with fear and holds herself tight. Powerless, all she can do is wait for the nightmare to pass.

This storm is not of her making and the shelter she deserves is stripped away. The rain is like bullets, scarcely broken by the bare branches above us.

The only sound is the scream of the wind.

With deep sadness, I can do nothing but ride through hell with her. I silently pledge to do better on the other side.

References

[1] Bhatnagar, Y. V. 2012. From Ricefields to Snowfields. In *Snow Leopard: Stories from the Roof of the World*. Edited by Hunter, D. Boulder: O'Reilly Media: 49–53.

2 Jackson, R. M., Mallon, D., McCarthy, T., Chundawat, R. A. and Habib, B. 2008. Panthera uncia. *The IUCN Red List of Threatened Species.*

3 Jackson, R. M. 2015. Successes and Shortcomings of Approaches to Global Snow Leopard Conservation. *Human Dimensions of Wildlife: An International Journal.* 20, 4: 310–316.

4 National Conservation Foundation. 2015. People, Livestock and Snow Leopards. [online material]

5 Suryawanshi, K., Bhatia, S., Bhatnagar, Y. V., Redpath, S. and Mishra, C. 2014. Multi-scale Factors Influencing Human Attitudes towards Snow Leopards and Wolves. *Conservation Biology.* 28, 6: 1657–1666.

6 Suryawanshi, K., Bhatnagar, Y. V., Redpath, S. and Mishra, C. 2013. People, Predators and Perceptions: Patterns of Livestock Depredation by Snow Leopards and Wolves. *Journal of Applied Ecology.* 50, 3: 550–560.

7 Bagchi, S. and Mishra, C. 2006. Living with Large Carnivores: Predation on Livestock by the Snow Leopard (Uncia uncia). *Journal of Zoology (London).* 268: 217–224.

8 Himachal Pradesh Forest Department. 2011. Management Plan for the Upper Spiti Landscape including the Kibber Wildlife Sanctuary. Edited by Ministry of Environment and Forests. New Delhi: Government of India.

9 Global Snow Leopard & Ecosystem Protection Programme. 2016. The First Step: 20 by 2020. [online material]

10 Zoological Society of London. 2016. Rehabilitating Mangroves in the Philippines. [online material]

11 Sheppard, D. J., Moehrenschlager, A., Mcpherson, J. M. and Mason, J. J. 2010. Ten Years of Adaptive Community-governed Conservation: Evaluating Biodiversity Protection and Poverty Alleviation in a West African Hippopotamus Reserve. *Environmental Conservation.* 37, 03: 270–282.

12 Asase, A., Oteng-Yeboah, A. A. and Mason, J. 2006. Engaging People in the Wechiau Community Hippopotamus Sanctuary in Ghana. Paper presented at the Nature of Success: Success for Nature, Oxford.

13 Walker, R. B. J. 2002. After the Future: Enclosures, Connections, Politics. In *Reframing the International: Law, Culture, Politics.* Edited by Falk, R., Ruiz, L. E. J. and Walker, R. B. J. London: Routledge: 3–25.

14 Convention on Migratory Species of Wild Animals. 2014. *Inf 15: A Natural Affiliation.* Bonn: Secretariat to the Convention on Migratory Species of Wild Animals.

15 Prideaux, M., Rostron, C. and Duff, L. 2015. *Ramsar and Wetland NGOs: A Report of the World Wetland Network for Ramsar CoP12.* London: World Wetland Network.

16 Falk, R. and Strauss, A. 2000. On the Creation of a Global People's Assembly: Legitimacy and the Power of Popular Sovereignty. *Stan. J. Int'l L.* 36: 191.

17 Heinrich, D. 2010. *The Case for a United Nations Parliamentary Assembly.* Berlin: Committee for a Democratic UN.

18 Falk, R. and Strauss, A. 2001. Toward Global Parliament. *Foreign Affairs.* 80, 1: 212–220.

19 Schwartzberg, J. E. 2012. *Creating a World Parliamentary Assembly: An Evolutionary Journey.* Committee for a Democratic UN.

20 Strauss, A. J. 2002. Overcoming the Dysfunction of the Bifurcated Global System: The Promise of a People's Assembly. In *Reframing the International: Law, Culture,*

Politics. Edited by Falk, R., Ruiz, L. E. J. and Walker, R. B. J. London: Routledge: 83–106.

21 Falk, R. 2011. The Promise and Perils of Global Democracy. In *Global Democracy: Normative and Empirical Perspectives.* Edited by Archibugi, D., Koenig-Archibugi, M. and Marchetti, R. Cambridge: Cambridge University Press.

22 Parham, A. and Allen, D. 2015. Achieving Rooted Cosmopolitanism in a Digital Age. In *From Voice to Influence: Understanding Citizenship in a Digital Age.* Edited by Allen, D. and Light, J. S. Chicago: University of Chicago Press.

23 McAfee, N. 2015. Acting Politically in a Digital Age. In *From Voice to Influence: Understanding Citizenship in a Digital Age.* Edited by Allen, D. and Light, J. S. Chicago: University of Chicago Press.

24 Kahne, J., Middaugh, E. and Allen, D. 2015. Youth, New Media, and the Rise of Participatory Politics. In *From Voice to Influence: Understanding Citizenship in a Digital Age.* Edited by Allen, D. and Light, J. S. Chicago: University of Chicago Press.

25 Held, D. 2010. *Cosmopolitanism: Ideals and Realities.* Cambridge: Polity Press.

26 Corell, E. and Betsill, M. M. 2001. A Comparative Look at NGO Influence in International Environmental Negotiations: Desertification and Climate Change. *Global Environmental Politics.* 1, 4: 86–107.

27 Betsill, M. M. and Corell, E. 2001. NGO Influence in International Environmental Negotiations: A Framework for Analysis. *Global Environmental Politics.* 1, 4: 65–85.

28 Raustiala, K. 1997. States, NGOs, and International Environmental Institutions. *International Studies Quarterly.* 41, 4: 719–740.

29 Tallberg, J. and Uhlin, A. 2011. Civil Society and Global Democracy: An Assessment. In *Global Democracy: Normative and Empirical Perspectives.* Edited by Archibugi, D., Koenig-Archibugi, M. and Marchetti, R. Cambridge: Cambridge University Press.

30 Prideaux, M. 2015. Wildlife NGOs: From Adversaries to Collaborators. *Global Policy.* 6, 4: 379–388.

31 Beauzamy, B. 2010. Transnational Social Movements and Democratic Legitimacy. In *Legitimacy Beyond the State?* Edited by Erman, E. and Uhlin, A. London: Springer: 110–129.

32 Burke, A., Fishel, S., Mitchell, A., Dalby, S. and Levine, D. J. 2016. Planet Politics: A Manifesto from the End of IR. *Millennium – Journal of International Studies.* 44, 3: 499–523.

33 Pyhälä, A., Osuna Orozco, A. and Counsell, S. 2016. Protected Areas in the Congo Basin: Failing Both People and Biodiversity? In *Under the Canopy Series.* London: Rainforest Foundation UK.

34 International Union for the Conservation of Nature. 2015. The Environmental & Social Management System: An Intrinsic Part of IUCN's Project Cycle. [online material]

35 Olson, D. M., Dinerstein, E., Wikramanayake, E. D. and Burgess, N. D. 2001. Terrestrial Ecoregions of the World: A New Map of Life on Earth. *BioScience.* 51, 11: 933.

36 Hoekstra, J. M., Boucher, T. M., Ricketts, T. H. and Roberts, C. 2005. Confronting a Biome Crisis: Global Disparities of Habitat Loss and Protection. *Ecology Letters.* 8, 1: 23–29.

37 García, L. M. C., Arreola-Lizarraga, J. A., Mendoza-Salgado, R. A., Galina-Tessaro, P., Beltrán-Morales, L. F. and Ortega-Rubio, A. 2015. Applying Ecological Diversity

Indices with Ecosystem Approach at Ecoregional Level and Prioritizing the Decree of New Protected Natural Areas. *Interciencia*. 40, 3: 179.

[38] Berkes, F. 2009. Evolution of Co-management: Role of Knowledge Generation, Bridging Organizations and Social Learning. *Journal of Environmental Management*. 90, 5: 1692–1702.

[39] Reddel, T. 2004. Third Way Social Governance: Where is the State? *Australian Journal of Social Issues*. 39, 2: 129–142.

[40] Emerson, K., Nabatchi, T. and Balogh, S. 2012. An Integrative Framework for Collaborative Governance. *Journal of Public Administration Research and Theory*. 22, 1: 1–29.

[41] Ansell, C. and Gash, A. 2008. Collaborative Governance in Theory and Practice. *Journal of Public Administration Research and Theory*. 18, 4: 543–571.

[42] Fung, A. and Wright, E. O. 2001. Deepening Democracy: Innovations in Empowered Participatory Governance. *Politics and Society*. 29, 1: 5–41.

[43] Deacon, B., Ollila, E., Koivusalo, M. and Stubbs, P. 2003. *Global Social Governance: Themes and Prospects*. Helsinki: Ministry for Foreign Affairs of Finland, Department for International Development Cooperation.

[44] Rogers, E. and Weber, E. P. 2010. Thinking Harder About Outcomes for Collaborative Governance Arrangements. *The American Review of Public Administration*. 40, 5: 546–567.

[45] Kettl, D. F. 2002. Conclusion: The Next Generation. In *Environmental Governance: A Report on The Next Generation of Environmental Policy*. Edited by Kettl, D. F. Washington DC: Brookings Institution Press: 177–190.

[46] Karkkainen, B. C. 2004. Post-Sovereign Environmental Governance. *Global Environmental Politics*. 4, 1: 72–96.

[47] Wilson, G. K. 2002. Regulatory Reform on the World Stage. In *Environmental Governance: A Report on The Next Generation of Environmental Policy*. Edited by Kettl, D. F. Washington DC: Brookings Institution Press: 118–145.

7 Birdsong after the storm

'We the peoples'

The UN Charter begins 'We the peoples',[1] evoking a democratic ideal of popular, genuinely representative governance implying a role for everyone, not just an elite few. There is a legion of fans for this phrase. Academics have written significant and important books about it. Careers have been forged around it, including mine. But the phrase means little unless it is interpreted well.

A few brave and influential souls have kept the dream alive. In 1996, the late Secretary-General Boutros Boutros-Ghali stated:

> Our global society must invent rules which take into account not only the wishes of political actors, namely States, but also the behaviour of economic agents and the aspirations of social and cultural actors. These new actors in international life are the guarantors of an open, living democracy ... I have said repeatedly that I would like to see non-State institutions and non-governmental organizations accorded an increasing role within the United Nations itself.[2]

In 2000 Kofi Annan captured the hearts and minds of my sector when he said:

> I see a United Nations keenly aware that if the global agenda is to be properly addressed, a partnership with civil society is not an option; it is a necessity. I see a United Nations which recognizes that the NGO revolution – the new global people-power – is the best thing that has happened to our Organization in a long time ... Civil society organizations have already given new life and new meaning to the idea of an international community. The desire to participate in the management of a changing world, and the need to engage in areas where governments are unable or unwilling to act, have driven you to action.[3]

The grip of government control has curtailed the progress, but not the dream. They have focused on the other part of the preambular language that 'representative governments' hold the power and will always hold the power. Theirs is an agenda of intention. When nongovernmental organisations (NGOs) have been discussed it has often been from a perspective of NGO accountability and representativeness, casting civil society as a dangerous alliance. These accusations have been eloquently answered, in full, by Helmut Anheier[4–6] and Jan Aart Scholte,[7] Margaret E. Keck and Kathryn Sikkink,[8, 9] as well as Margaret P. Karns and Karen A Mingst.[10] I feel no need to rehearse them again.

To be fair, civil society does present governments with a messy policy landscape that governments are often ill-equipped to navigate.[11, 12] NGOs do have the capacity to marshal pressure on negotiations and so it is not surprising that many government bureaucrats perceive NGOs as operating on contested ground.[13, 14] It would be spurious to suggest that all elements of civil society are entirely benign. There is good and bad in all sectors of human society. I am confident that the UN Secretary-Generals Boutros Boutros-Ghali, Kofi Annan and Ban Ki Moon[3] would all agree that tarnishing every aspect of this sphere with distrust negates an important opportunity.

At a time of funding pressure and agendas growing ever larger, it is an opportunity to consider carefully.[15, 16] In 2011, many of the specialised agencies including United Nations Educational, Scientific and Cultural Organization (UNESCO), FAO and the World Health Organization had annual budgets ranging from US$300 million to over US$2 billion. This is nowhere near the budgets these agencies require to continue their important work. Even so, they dwarf the 2014 budget for the Convention on Biological Diversity (CBD) set at US$28 million.[17] The Convention on Wetlands of International Importance (Ramsar), the Convention on International Trade in Endangered Species of Wild Flora and Fauna (CITES) and the Convention on Conservation of Migratory Species of Wild Animals (CMS) are an even lower-order political priority, with their budgets each hovering around the US$5 million mark.[18–20]

In sharp contrast to their meagre budget allocations, CBD, CITES, Ramsar and CMS each address specific details that cannot be overlooked. Their agendas have grown long and complex for a reason – the world is a complicated place and working out solutions requires specialised, careful and detailed deliberations. Yet, the Secretariats of each of the four MEAs have such low capacity that very often it is skilled NGO diplomats that are the repositories of institutional memory, who are able to connect and complement issues and deliberations.[15, 21] Without civil society being involved, the system already risks losing track of the subtleties.[22]

Ensuring that this specialised information can be communicated through an already complex system is a challenge. It will not be met with superficial answers. Motherhood statements cannot capture the detail of forest and savannahs, of tundra and wetlands and the millions upon millions of interwoven human and non-human relationships. As the impact of climate change creeps around the world, shifting seasons and rainfall, creating storms and fire, melting ice and flooding deltas, we need to be able to address the collision and change at the level of the impact – where people and wildlife live. Simply allowing minority world NGOs to be in the room is not enough. Relying on two global Sustainable Development Goals (SDGs) – Goal 14: Conserve and sustainably use the oceans, seas and marine resources for sustainable development; and Goal 15: Protect, restore and promote sustainable use of terrestrial ecosystems, sustainably manage forests, combat desertification, and halt and reverse land degradation and halt biodiversity loss[23] – is just not detailed enough.

This book has sought to make the case that intergovernmentalism should be retained and evolved to include local civil society at the global environmental governance table. Those who live in proximity to the wildlife issues being discussed should be involved. It is their human and non-human community that is being discussed. It is their ecological region of the world that is affected. They share the wind and the rain, the dawn and the dusk, the ebb and flow of the seasons of their region with their wildlife community kin. They share the pain when their home is destroyed. People around the world reflect wildlife in their myths, symbols and rituals. Many call it a kinship with all life. Thomas Berry beautifully calls it a communion of subjects.[24] Their information and community perspective should inform discourse. This is what 'we the peoples' should come to mean.

This doesn't suggest that other voices are not important and needed. International NGOs, a whole range of scientific, economic and policy experts and yes, corporations, all need to input as well, but civil society is the missing link.

There are many ways this might be possible. Multi-stakeholder governance is the most popular solution being proposed at present, but I believe cosmopolitanism and the cosmopolitan delegations to be a more appropriate path.

Resisting the world becoming a commodity

There is an agenda afoot for the legal recognition that NGOs and transnational corporations have both developed a de facto status in global decision-making; that global institutions should adapt to incorporate an appropriate political balance between these sectors, as a replacement for the existing UN system.[25, 26]

There are some elements of this that I agree with, in that pluralism as a philosophy recognises and affirms diversity within a political body. It permits the peaceful coexistence of different interests, convictions and lifestyles. For pluralism to function and to be successful in defining 'common good', all groups have to agree to a minimal consensus that shared values are at least worth pursuing. Pluralist governance (in whichever form) acknowledges that there are overlapping and non-exclusive communities in the international space. The overlaps cross the traditional boundaries of states.[27] In practice this will mean more multi-stakeholder initiatives.

As I discussed in chapter 2, the neoliberal proposal is to bring 'stakeholders' together on specific subjects, because of their interests and their capacity, and for these stakeholders to agree on sets of rules and objectives, unshackled by democratic oversight. The aim is to have market solutions that are lean and regulated by market choice. For example, in the climate change policy round, we see emerging climate partnerships, which live in the nexus between climate diplomacy and the global carbon market.[12, 28] Another is the stakeholder community with a strong interest in palm oil industry regulation involving actors from across the world including the palm oil production companies, manufacturing consumers of palm oil, communities in proximity to plantations, individuals and organisations interested in the wildlife in proximity to the plantations, and governments who must make regulatory decisions about the industry. In this instance, they have developed the Roundtable on Sustainable Palm Oil. They have established themselves as a not-for-profit association that proposes 'to transform markets to make sustainable palm oil the norm'. They seek to 'unite stakeholders from the palm oil industry to develop and implement global standards for sustainable palm oil'. Their '2000 members globally ... represent 40 per cent of the palm oil industry, covering all sectors of the global commodity supply chain'.[29] As a market mechanisms I am confident that they have impact, and are playing an important role in the moulding of industry behaviour, even if the regulation is not as pervasive as some wish.[30, 31] But, their process has already subjugated communities, including their non-human members, who have lived for thousands of years where palm oil plantations wish to clear the landscape, reducing their claim to one stakeholder among many, and with very little power.

Shifting the decision-making into a pluralist space, where all the stakeholders – about palm oil or climate change – are at the table sounds great. It sounds like governance by 'We the peoples'. But, depending on which way you tilt your head, it also sounds like Davos Multi-stakeholder Governance discussed in chapter 2, especially if it is a private system with no governance checks and balances. The evidence tells us that multi-stakeholder initiatives usually involve a limited group, with limited views.[27] Sandra Moog, André Spicer and Steffen Böhm have found that multi-stakeholder initiatives often become platforms for commercial strategy, dominated by commercial concerns. Relying on stakeholder self-selection for engagement depends on their capacity and material circumstances. Without some oversight it is easy to imagine that, over time, stakeholders that are not able to self-fund their involvement eventually drop away.

In the case of the Roundtable on Sustainable Palm Oil, the missing connection is palm oil discussions on all the other governance issues that relate to it – especially those that have little or no market relevance, such as indigenous land rights and critical habitat for wildlife.[30–33] At the moment, the focus is very much on the regulation and growth of the palm oil industry.

I respect the work of practitioners advocating the multi-stakeholder initiative road. But, there are risks inherent in such a system. I have reservations about applying these amorphous arrangements to an area with no direct link to the market. I am sure there are successful multi-stakeholder initiatives. I am just not sure they should become the default solution. I have little confidence that they can be equitably applied to situations where there is little or no relevant economic benefit, and therefore the market isn't a force to bring into play.[34]

Cosmopolitanism

Throughout this book I have sought to make the case that Westphalia – a system of sovereign states co-governing the world – is already falling apart and being replaces by a neoliberal agenda. It is being destroyed by self-interest and corruption, and it is failing to address the existential, global issues of our time.

Decades of negotiation have been invested and yet climate change remains tokenistically addressed. Nuclear weapon possession is still a problem, even today. World trade is cementing huge global inequities. The powerful continue to lord it over the powerless. Communities are disenfranchised from decisions. This book has sought to trigger us all to ask questions about the neoliberal worldview that is creeping in to dominate every aspect our lives.

I don't suggest that we need to turn the clock back, to go without electricity, telecommunications, medical advances and wear 'hair shirts' (a common accusation thrown at people who speak from a green conscience). I value and respect the great innovations of our time and I genuinely hope human ingenuity and innovation will continue. I don't, however, believe that the world should be governed by 'boardrooms and business plans'. Too much that we value falls outside of that system of thinking. Too much of what is important to our being – the sublime and powerful connections we have to the non-human world around us – will be lost.

I have suggested that we face a storm of our own making and that the choices we make in the coming decades will shape the future in profound ways. We will lose much, but we also have an opportunity for transformative gain.

We already have an international body founded on the principle of human dignity – the United Nations. While we have yet to dent poverty, we have growing levels of global education and health. We have greater connection to each other than at any time in history, through worldwide telecommunications. In chapter 5 I have tried to demonstrate how this connectivity offers the opportunity to collaborate, to understand and form agreement. Such opportunity was not possible even two decades ago. Our home – Earth – is a complex place. She deserves more from us, as do all who live and breathe on her surface, in her air and in her waters. We need to harness the opportunity ahead of us and channel it effectively, for the sake of the 'communion of subjects'.

To embed cosmopolitan principles to the real world of politics requires consciously building full participation into what David Held calls 'democratic public law'.[35] At the moment, the world order is pulling in the opposite direction. The opposing force is apparent in the behaviour of governments, transnational corporations and even some minority world NGOs as I detailed in chapters 2, 3 and 4.

I salute the Commission on Global Security, Justice & Governance for forging a path for us all to confront the crisis of global governance, as was discussed in chapter 4. The Commission has called for 'just security', acknowledging that this means more than simply an absence of war. It means forging mutually supportive systems of accountable, fair and effective global governance.[36] It is not a report of pleasant platitudes and gentle implications. There is a sharp tone of warning peppered throughout the text. The final paragraph leaves no room for doubt about their message:

> We, the members of the Commission on Global Security, Justice & Governance, call upon all peoples and nations to rise to this challenge. Our structures of global governance are merely a reflection of how we choose to govern ourselves across borders and entire regions. Powerful states and other increasingly influential global actors have a special responsibility to work toward a shared analysis of global problems and to seize opportunities to remedy them. Further still, we must all refuse to accept mediocre solutions that rely on institutions and mindsets from another era. Only when men and women from diverse places and backgrounds rally around a shared, inherent need for security and justice – always felt locally but created at many levels – can these powerful actors be nudged toward what is needed, as well as what is right.[36]

My contribution to both the Commission on Global Security, Justice & Governance invitation and the Global Peoples Assembly project is to propose achievable reforms to a focused area of global environmental governance. These changes could have significant impact on justice and sustainability, by creating a space for cosmopolitan voices to be included in deliberation and democratic decision-making in the global domain. Perhaps, with time, they could become examples to follow elsewhere.

In the previous chapter I proposed initial principles of a rooted cosmopolitan form of wildlife governance and suggested that cosmopolitan delegations from each of the world's biomes would be the smoothest process for civil society to create. This proposal serves the cosmopolitan ideal by decentralising information, empowering localised decision-making, while also creating higher-level cosmopolitan political power. It creates a conduit connecting the local to the global.

The principles I have suggested are to:

- tune wildlife conservation to landscape level community driven management, in perpetuity;
- support active and adaptive, permanent community management;
- invest in scientific, programmatic and financial monitoring and reporting, and to transparently communicate this to civil society around the world.

These principles are not new, and echo documents from the United Nations, the International Union for the Conservation of Nature (IUCN) and international development NGOs. Indeed a great many of the smaller and medium conservation NGOs already ascribe to them in some form.

Principles are nothing without a framework to facilitate them. Facilitating the conduit from the local to the global ensures that the landscape level community wildlife management is communicated effectively in international processes where they can have influence and power. The first essential part of the framework requires international minority world NGOs to step forward and assume the role of conduits. Maintaining such connectivity takes skill and resources. This is an important and challenging role to embrace in partnership with the community management bodies. The second essential part of the framework is that MEAs must adapt to welcome NGO/civil society cosmopolitan delegations into the law-making process with formal standing and a vote. They should have as much right to direct the administrative support for the MEAs as any government has.

My proposal does not impinge on any state sensibilities about interference in national law-making. As I stated earlier, states retain the same rights and responsibilities as they currently hold when they engage in any international process. They can commit, they can withdraw or they can lodge a 'formal reservation'. What I propose is to develop political institutions at the global level that responds to rooted cosmopolitan direction and serves as a constructive supplement to the laws of the state.

Rooted cosmopolitan governance in CBD, CITES, Ramsar and CMS

Establishing cosmopolitan delegations

At first glance it might seem that the cosmopolitan delegations should be modelled on the principles behind the Major Group process in UNEA and ECOSOC. The nine Major Groups are the sectors: Women; Children and Youth; Indigenous Peoples; Non-Governmental Organizations; Local Authorities; Workers and Trade Unions; Business and Industry; Scientific and Technological Community; and Farmers.[37] I have proposed (in chapter 6) that instead of separate groups according to sectors for engagement with the MEAs, it would make more sense to assemble according to biomes especially for CBD, Ramsar, CMS and CITES.

It would be necessary for governments to first agree on what constitutes a legitimate cosmopolitan delegation and the diplomatic standards that must be met. This book has attempted to make the case that the constituency should be sufficiently broad to encompass a fair and reasonable representation of civil society interests from across a region, or if appropriate, across the globe. Once agreed, cosmopolitan biome delegations could be invited to self organise according to these standards.

Governments normally legally sign an MEA, as a written commitment to abide by the principles of the MEA and the goals and principles it establishes; they are then obliged to reflect this intent in domestic laws. This sounds like a high bar, but in practice it is a fairly loose arrangement that the states themselves often disregard. The cosmopolitan biome delegations could also be required to sign the MEAs and their governing documents to also reflect their intent, with the understanding that their commitment takes a different form, but is nonetheless a significant commitment.

Once the cosmopolitan biome delegations have signed the MEA, and are given approval by the MEA administrative processes, their engagement would be facilitated in the same way that any government currently engages. This is where the proposal for the cosmopolitan biome delegations differs dramatically from the UNEA and ECOSOC Major Groups format. The objective is for these delegations to have a formal seat at the table as equals – not as observers at the back of the room, who must defer to everyone else.

These cosmopolitan biome delegations would contribute in the spirit of the evolving commitments reflected through the evolution of Resolutions and work programmes, in exactly the same way that governments do. They would contribute equitably to the financial base that supports the agreement (according to the established UN contribution system) and be eligible to receive financial support for attendance if their financial resources were below a set limit – exactly the same way that governments do.

Cosmopolitan biome delegations would meet collectively with their representative bases, in exactly the same way that regional blocs of governments currently engage (teleconference between meetings) and as delegations in face-to-face negotiation sessions in the margins of meetings.

In essence, each cosmopolitan biome delegations would become a full Party to the MEA. But, they would bring a significant cultural difference to the table. Their direction would emerge from the local level and their perspective would be 'ecological place', not 'political space'.

Civil society in CBD, CITES, Ramsar and CMS

The suggestion that cosmopolitan biome delegations become Parties to each of the MEAs is not quite as far-fetched as it might first appear.

It is already a well-established practice for NGOs seeking involvement in international policy to participate in intergovernmental processes. Many NGOs already consciously nest themselves within the processes in which they are working. Over time effective wildlife diplomacy has become more coordinated, consistent, and influential. As a consequence, many NGO diplomats have a longer history of direct experience with key environment conventions and more technical knowledge about the issues being discussed than some of their government counterparts.[16] I have been in dozens of meetings where, if the badges were removed, it would be difficult to distinguish between government and NGO delegates. NGOs as observers at the Conference of the Parties for CBD, CITES, Ramsar and CMS are an absolute norm now.

In both Ramsar and CMS a close working relationship between NGOs and the Secretariat has formed. NGOs have become trusted and useful allies and partners, as a de facto extension of the Secretariat.

Ramsar has gone one step further and formally recognised a small group of NGOs as International Organisation Partners (IOPs) since 1999. This status has been given to Birdlife International, Wetlands International, IUCN, the World Wildlife Fund (WWF), the International Water Management Institute and, recently, the Wildfowl and Wetlands Trust.[38, 39] CMS has similarly recognised the value of the NGO community in resolutions since 1994[27] and also progresses Partnership, albeit less formally, with NGOs. In 2002, during CMS CoP7, the Secretariat was urged to progress '... *partnerships with interested organizations specialized in the conservation and management of migratory species for the provision of secretariat services for selected [agreements]*'[40] and it has done so both for agreement support and to increase capacity on a range of issues over the past 14 years.[22]

An important element of the Ramsar IOP relationship is that both the Secretariat and the IOPs have a responsibility to maintain the relationship and the implicit expectation of reporting on progress.[38, 41, 42] IOPs play an active role, contributing directly to discussions and meetings; they also work together to produce statements as a group. IOPs are permitted as observers in all activities of the Convention including the CoP, Standing Committee and with formal roles in the STRP.[43] In practice the IOPs often act as facilitators between governments, donors, foundations and other bodies and they can, upon request from the Ramsar Secretariat, intervene on its behalf at specific meetings where/when the Ramsar Secretariat can't be directly represented. Importantly, the IOPs provide advice and recommendations on Ramsar processes such as the Montreux Record,[44] a list of Ramsar wetland sites facing threats. However, no NGOs, including the IOPs, have a formal vote in Ramsar.

CMS's relationship with its NGOs is also strong, and CMS has involved NGOs in various ongoing and *ad hoc* advisory groups. This has been an important avenue for close and effective cooperation between the CMS Family Secretariats and experts within the NGO community. In some instances NGOs provide coordination and technical support of Advisory Groups to various agreements, as well as providing ongoing cooperation between CMS agreement Secretariats and regional experts within the NGO community.[22] CMS Partner NGOs are permitted to attend the Scientific Council and Standing Committee meetings as observers. Like Ramsar, no NGOs, including Partners, have a formal vote.

Ramsar's IOPs and CMS's Partnerships are both progressive and very important, although restricted to large international NGOs at this stage. CBD has also been building this area for a number of years, with CBD CoP12 in 2014 placing an emphasis on 'active participation of stakeholders' in the development of policies and plans.[25, 26]

CITES, for the most part, has been content for its NGOs to remain observers. The CITES mandate linked to trade has effectively kept civil society in the bleachers. Their input is limited to restricted speaking rights in meetings and their contribution is as lobbyists.

A close working relationship with a Secretariat is an important achievement for the conservation sector, but it also carries a functional limit. The Secretariat serves the governments, and therefore so too do the NGO efforts. Shifting to a collaborative governance role is not possible by working through the Secretariats, as it exceeds their mandate. It is time to stand in the full glare of the sun and claim a seat at the table, as a Party. As an equal.

Rooted cosmopolitanism requires a shift to collaboration

Bringing new voices to the table will change the dynamic and challenge the status quo of historical power relationship between governments. It will also shift the focus of which agenda are the priorities to discuss and when. Suddenly the voiceless will be heard. Collaborative governance is already a well-explored path and there is a significant amount already to draw upon.

Chris Ansell and Alison Gash have developed an important model for successful collaborative governance arrangements that provide a useful structure for the MEA evolution I propose. Their model has four broad variables – starting conditions, leadership, institutional design and collaborative process.[45]

Starting conditions set the basic level of trust, conflict and social capital that become resources or liabilities during collaboration. Power/resource imbalances must be addressed, and in this proposal are overcome by minority world NGOs assuming a facilitation role for cosmopolitan biome delegations. The history of involvement between the actors must be transparently known. This develops the incentive to participate.[45] I believe this history is now well understood between the actors in CMS and Ramsar.

Leadership provides essential mediation and facilitation for the collaborative process and is a critical ingredient in bringing parties to the table and for steering them through the rough patches of the collaborative process.[45, 46] In my proposal, that leadership needs to be provided by the MEA Parties – governments – in assessing and permitting the entry of cosmopolitan biome delegations, as well as in overseeing the institutional design and maintaining the collaborative process.

Institutional design provides direction to the institutional body (in this case the MEA Secretariat), establishes basic protocols and ground rules for collaboration, which are critical for the procedural legitimacy of the collaborative process. Access to the collaborative process itself is the most fundamental design issue. Participation should not be simply tolerated. It must be actively sought.[45]

Building on Chris Ansell and Alison Gash's design, a model for the proposed collaborative governance arrangements can be illustrated this way:

The collaborative process itself should be highly iterative and non-linear, and should operate as a cycle. It should be built on a foundation of principled

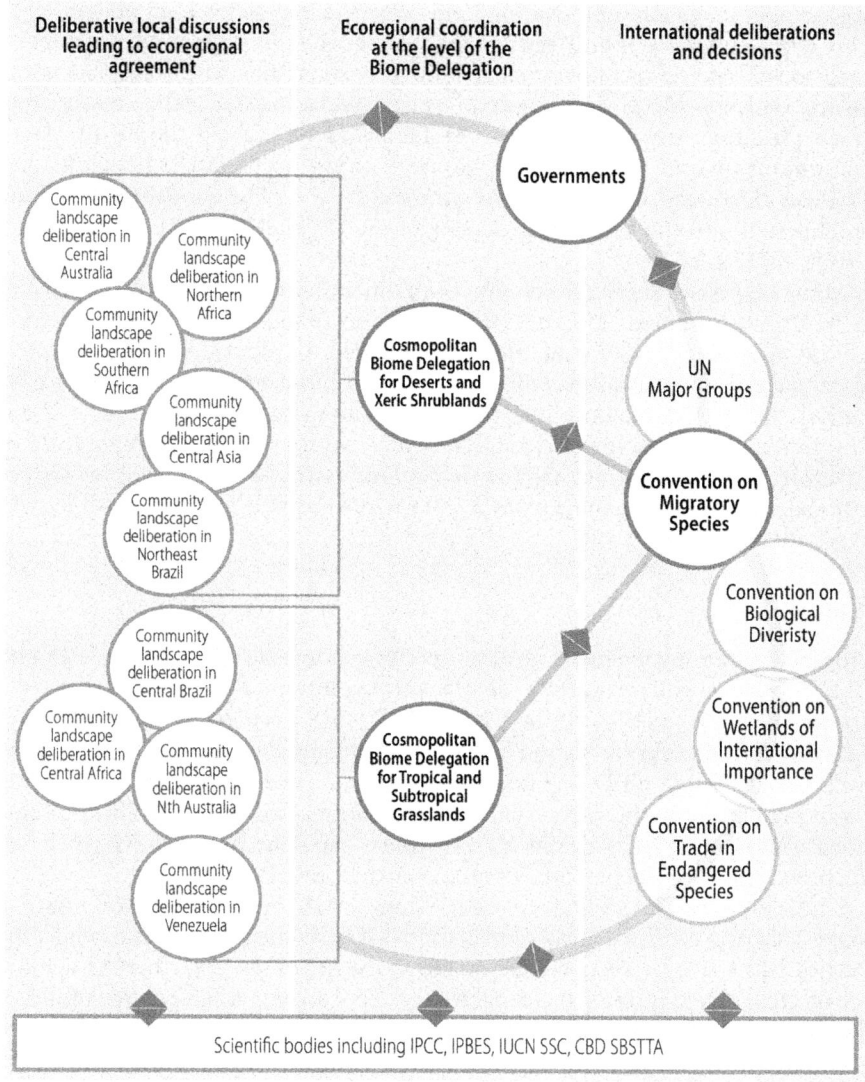

Deliberative local discussions leading to ecoregional agreement

Ecoregional coordination at the level of the Biome Delegation

International deliberations and decisions

Community landscape deliberation in Central Australia

Community landscape deliberation in Northern Africa

Community landscape deliberation in Southern Africa

Community landscape deliberation in Central Asia

Community landscape deliberation in Northeast Brazil

Community landscape deliberation in Central Brazil

Community landscape deliberation in Central Africa

Community landscape deliberation in Nth Australia

Community landscape deliberation in Venezuela

Cosmopolitan Biome Delegation for Deserts and Xeric Shrublands

Cosmopolitan Biome Delegation for Tropical and Subtropical Grasslands

Governments

UN Major Groups

Convention on Migratory Species

Convention on Biological Diveristy

Convention on Wetlands of International Importance

Convention on Trade in Endangered Species

Scientific bodies including IPCC, IPBES, IUCN SSC, CBD SBSTTA

M. Prideaux, 2016: Illustrative diagram of Cosmopolitan Biome Delegations, with a small representative sample of the community landscape contributions. This illustrative example would need to be scaled up to include at least the 14 terrestrial biomes and 867 ecoregions (as defined by Olsen et al, 2001) as well as corresponding marine biomes and ecoregions.

Figure 7.1 Cosmopolitan Wildlife Governance

engagement and shared motivation, and provide capacity for joint action.[45, 47] This will require a cultural shift in the MEAs. The participation parameters need to be tailored to allow greater remote participation and staggered information delivery to enable wider civil society discussion and deliberation,[22] in much the same way as the UNDESA/DSD has progressed the HLPF. Here the minority world NGOs have some work to do, to form the networks and alliances they need with local communities.[46, 48–50] The model should draw on and feed into the scientific processes of the IPCC, IPBES, IUCN SSC and CBD's SBSTTA.

Many others are calling for a new commitment to deep collaboration.[5, 46, 47] Lisen Schultz, Andreas Duit and Carfl Folke reviewed 146 Biosphere Reserves in 55 countries and found that stakeholder participation and adaptive co-management practices were linked to positive management performance.[51] Indeed, 'the term "collaborative governance" promises a sweet reward. It seems to promise that if we govern collaboratively, we may avoid the high costs of adversarial policy-making, expand democratic participation, and even restore rationality to public management'.[45] That reward will only be possible with hard work and agreement.

Radical dreams

Progressing the involvement of cosmopolitan biome delegations in CBD and CITES would still require a significant evolution of the current access arrangements for NGOs. Both CBD and CITES need to initiate discussion between their Parties about the benefits of drawing civil society closer. Of the two, it is likely that CBD will do this first, because the body is already moving down the path of 'indigenous rights' and 'traditional knowledge'. These discussions should be promoted and NGOs should seize the opportunity whenever it arises to ask for deeper consideration of their involvement.

Leadership is more likely to come from CMS or Ramsar. Both have a longer history of direct involvement of NGOs in their work, and while the Parties still strive to keep NGOs in the space of 'observers', there is a more substantive recognition of the capacity that civil society already contributes to the work of each body.

Within the formality of the Eleventh Meeting of the Conference of the Parties to CMS (CMS CoP11) in 2014 Ghana presented the NGO request for this dicussion to begin. The CMS Parties reciprocated with an agreement to formally explore options for furthering the relationship including *inter alia*:

1 mechanisms to enable NGO-facilitated work to be formally and consistently reported across the CMS Family and to be considered by the Parties and CMS Family agreement bodies;
2 models for further NGO involvement in CMS processes; and
3 modalities for further strategic engagement with NGOs to provide implementation and capacity building expertise.[52]

These options are to be developed through the formality of CMS process by the CMS Standing Committee for presentation and discussion during a future CMS CoP.

So, the recommendations to both CMS and Ramsar stand, and I now add another to this list. Ramsar and CMS should both investigate options for facilitating cosmopolitan biome delegations to formally participate as legitimate delegations, with formal seats at the table – to have formal standing and a vote.

Through this book I have sought to make the case that there is a path forward through the storm we have made if we choose to take it – a rooted cosmopolitan path that reflects that we are 'a communion of subjects not a collection of objects'.[24] In fact, considerable groundwork has been laid already, at least in CMS and Ramsar. But, taking the next step down the path I propose requires two things to happen.

The first is that international NGOs need to acknowledge their role in the current system and take active steps to develop respectful relationships with civil society conservation actors and facilitate these genuine, unpasteurised voices into international process. This is possible and viable, and there many NGOs already with these relationships in place. They are already tuned to take on this role, they just need the MEA system to evolve to accommodate them.

The second step is that governments need to loosen their grip on governance and invite new perspectives, and new actors, to legitimately sit at the governance table. They need to make space for cosmopolitan biome delegations to be a voice for local conservation and to respectfully include those voices in their deliberations as equals.

The United National General Assembly can assist this progression, by acknowledging the steps NGOs, Ramsar and CMS have already taken, and voicing support for this work to continue.

I believe we are on the cusp of a transitional moment in human history and I believe we have to be conscious about the decisions we make in the near future. The past decade has witnessed scientific publication after publication being released that calls out with distress and anguish at the rate of species and ecosystem loss. Governments have committed to a series of biodiversity targets for the last two decades, but they are never met and are simply renegotiated forward in the next round. The most recent are the Aichi Targets and the new Sustainable Development Goals (SDGs).

In 2006 Paul Crutsen called our current age the Anthropocene to highlight that human activities are exerting impacts on the environment. On all scales we are outcompeting our home.[53] Alarmingly, Colin Waters and his colleagues have made the case that humans have pushed the Earth into a new epoch.[54] There is no new language available to emphasise the urgency with greater clarity. It has been said, time and time again.

Something must change. The thunderhead fed by climate change and broken politics is forming above us. Very soon the gusts of wind will begin to whip and wail. Some of us, on the very margins of the storm are already feeling the tempest's bite. It will get worse before it gets better. And, it will only get better if we take steps now.

The cosmopolitan wildlife governance I propose is not polished, nor finished. It is the product of one mind and one point of view. It deserves to be robustly debated, pulled apart and built anew – for that is also what cosmopolitanism requires. I hope it will contribute to a path through the storm and that when we emerge we will still hear birdsong.

As I finish this book I have scanned through the latest United Nations General Assembly Resolutions. Buried deep, as document A/RES/70/208, almost obscured between Resolutions on 'financing of the International Criminal Tribunal', 'telecommunications in the context of international security', 'oil slick on Lebanese shores', and 'external debt sustainability and development' sits a Resolution entitled *Harmony with Nature*. It was adopted by the General Assembly in all its wisdom on 11 December 2015. It wasn't the first time this gem had been on the agenda. The principle of harmony with nature has been quietly agreed each year for the past five years, but seeing it again gives me hope. In its briefest summary it says:

> [G]ross domestic product was not designed as an indicator for measuring environmental degradation resulting from human activity and the need to overcome this limitation with regard to sustainable development and the work carried out in this regard ...
>
> [M]any ancient civilizations, indigenous peoples and indigenous cultures have a rich history of understanding the symbiotic connection between human beings and nature that fosters a mutually beneficial relationship.
>
> [The UN General Assembly calls] for holistic and integrated approaches to sustainable development, in its three dimensions, that will guide humanity to live in harmony with nature and lead to efforts to restore the health and integrity of the Earth's ecosystems.
>
> [The UN General Assembly will initiate] a virtual dialogue on Harmony with Nature among, inter alia, experts on Earth jurisprudence worldwide, ... in order to inspire citizens and societies to reconsider how they interact with the natural world in order to implement the Sustainable Development Goals in harmony with nature, ... and requests that the experts submit a summary to the General Assembly at its seventy-first session and that the virtual dialogue be hosted on the website on Harmony with Nature.[55]

The invitation has been given. Radical dreams can foster new belief and ideas about how we should organise our lives and society. Instead of limiting ourselves to the way we have been taught to see the world, we can dare to think beyond capitalism; beyond states as the ultimate power; beyond the notion that in order to to save what we love we have to monetise it.

I invite you to embark on such radical dreaming. Richard Falk has invited normative thinkers to inhabit a 'shadowland' – a conceptual space where we are outraged by contemporary conditions, mindful of past realities and devoted to exploring future possibilities.[56] Slavoj Žižek, a radical philosopher, has dared us to assume that the catastrophic future we dread has already happened and to work backwards to work out what we should have done. Both of these great thinkers have implored us to mobilise ourselves to change that destiny.[57]

In 2014 I stood in the shadowland and imagined my version of a catastrophic future. It was one where the world is monetised and wildness is gone. Tiger's footprints are not seen in snowdrifts or the deep, pungent smell of elephant musth is not carried on the wind. Cranes no longer walk with grace across shallow pools of water. Ancient trees that have borne witness to hundreds of human generations no longer cast their welcome shadow. Soaring albatross are not seen cresting waves hundreds of miles from land. The black nose of polar bear no longer emerges from blizzards of snow. A child does not stand on a river bank and squeal with delight under the spray from a hippopotamus' surfacing nostrils. A gorilla's eye no longer catches our hearts and our souls propelling us to be better than we are right now. The twirling song of the red-headed mallimbe is only a silent echo across the wetland.

In my catastrophic future all of these precious moments, and millions of others as well, are only stories we tell our grandchildren. If our people came from the forest or the mountain or the desert or the sea we tell the stories with added sadness for our place has also been lost to time. Humans may have survived, but the world is brittle and harsh.

That catastrophic future does not need to happen.

Each of us has a short flash of time on Earth, yet we carry a profound responsibility for all who call this place home, now and in the future. I have stood in the shadowland and dreamed a path. I offer it to you.

Spark your own dreaming.

The storm is upon us now.

*** *** ***

My imaginary journey through the storm concludes.

The gorilla and I still sit together under the ancient tree. Our sentinel of comfort is stripped of its leaves, but it still presses against our back with what comfort it can give.

The sky gently opens to illuminate the world, making visible a new, deeper pain – the damage of the storm.

Trees are blown over. Branches torn from trunks are scattered around us. Thrown across the landscape like small twigs.

Those left standing have no leaves.

Water streams across the ground, gathering leaves and debris, scouring it clean.

I look at the gorilla and her deep ache. She is doubly bruised from the assault of the storm and the loss of her world.

Eyes closed, her head is still bowed, her arms still around her body in protective embrace.

Her gift was to become my muse, to propel me to write, with hope that birdsong will be there for generations to come.

In time wind becomes breeze and whispers from a new direction, drawing with it a gentle dryness. The whisper murmurs about what is gone, what is swept away.

Then, in the distance, a small song begins. It twirls and flits, and begins again.

She lifts her eyes to see. The pirouetting song answers the whisper of loss in the breeze.

With heartbreak I watch my gorilla muse for a long, precious moment, then I follow her gaze to the promise of birdsong.

References

[1] United Nations. 1945. Charter of the United Nations. In *1 UNTS XVI*. San Francisco: United Nations.
[2] Boutros-Ghali, B. 1996. Secretary-General Emphasizes That Global Relations Must Be Governed by Democratic Principles. [online material]
[3] Annan, K. A. 2016. Secretary-General, at Arab Regional Conference, Stresses Important Role of Civil Society in Advancing Sustainable Development Agenda. [online material]
[4] Anheier, H. K. 2004. *Civil Society: Measurement, Evaluation, Policy.* London: Earthscan.
[5] Anheier, H. K., ed. 2013. *The Governance Report 2013: Hertie School of Governance.* Oxford: Oxford University Press.
[6] Anheier, H. K. 2009. What Kind of Nonprofit Sector, What Kind of Society? *American Behavioral Scientist.* 52, 7: 1082–1094.
[7] Scholte, J. A. 2004. Civil Society and Democratically Accountable Global Governance. *Government and Opposition.* 39, 2: 211–233.
[8] Keck, M. E. and Sikkink, K. 1999. Transnational Advocacy Networks in International and Regional Politics. *International Social Science Journal.* 51, 159: 89–101.
[9] Keck, M. E. and Sikkink, K. 1998. *Activists Beyond Borders: Advocacy Networks in International Politics.* Cambridge: Cambridge University Press.
[10] Karns, M. P. and Mingst, K. A. 2004. *International Organisations: The Politics and Processes of Global Governance.* London: Lynne Rienner Publishers.

11 Dimitrov, R. S. 2005. Hostage to Norms: States, Institutions and Global Forest Politics. *Global Environmental Politics.* 5, 4: 1–24.

12 Gale, F. 2014. Four Models of Interest Mediation in Global Environmental Governance. *Global Policy.* 5, 1: 10–22.

13 Florini, A. M. 2001. Transnational Civil Society. In *Global Citizen Action.* Edited by Edwards, M. and Gaveenta, J. London: Earthscan Publications Ltd: 29–43.

14 Florini, A. M. 2008. Making Transparency Work. *Global Environmental Politics.* 8, 2: 14–16.

15 Prideaux, M. 2015. Wildlife NGOs: From Adversaries to Collaborators. *Global Policy.* 6, 4: 379–388.

16 Prideaux, M. 2014. Wildlife NGOs and the CMS Family: Untapped Potential for Collaborative Governance. *Journal of International Wildlife Law & Policy.* 17, 4: 254–274.

17 Convention on Biological Diversity. 2014. Document 12.7: Report of the Executive Secretary on the Administration of the Convention and the Budget for the Trust Funds of the Convention. Pyeongchang, 12th Conference of the Parties to the Convention on Biological Diversity.

18 Convention on International Trade in Endangered Species. 2013. Document 8.3: Budgetary Proposals for 2014 to 2016. Bangkok, 16th Conference of the Parties to the Convention on International Trade in Endangered Species of Wild Fauna and Flora.

19 Convention on Wetlands of International Importance. 2012. Resolution XI.2: Financial and Budgetary Matters. Bucharest, 11th Conference of the Parties to the Convention on Wetlands.

20 Convention on Migratory Species of Wild Animals. 2014. Resolution 11.1: Financial and Administrative Matters. Quito, 11th Conference of the Parties to the Convention on Migratory Species of Wild Animals.

21 Prideaux, M., Rostron, C. and Duff, L. 2015. *Ramsar and Wetland NGOs: A Report of the World Wetland Network for Ramsar CoP12.* London: World Wetland Network.

22 Convention on Migratory Species of Wild Animals. 2014. *Inf 15: A Natural Affiliation.* Bonn: Secretariat to the Convention on Migratory Species of Wild Animals.

23 United Nations. 2015. Sustainable Development Goals. Division for Sustainable Development, UN-DESA. [online material]

24 Berry, T. 2006. Prologue: Loneliness and Presence. In *A Communion of Subjects: Animals in Religion, Science, and Ethics.* Edited by Waldau, P. and Patton, K. New York: Columbia University Press: 5–10.

25 Gleckman, H. 2016. Multi-stakeholderism: A Corporate Push for a New Form of Global Governance. In *State of Power 2016.* Amsterdam: Transnational Institute.

26 Gleckman, H. 2014. Multi-stakeholder Governance Seeks to Dislodge Multi-lateralism. In *State of Civil Society Report: 2014.* Edited by Firmin, A., Pegus, C. M. and Tiwana, M. New York, CIVICUS: World Alliance for Citizen Participation: 183–189.

27 Macdonald, T. 2008. *Global Stakeholder Democracy: Power and Representation Beyond Liberal States.* Oxford: Oxford University Press.

28 Bäckstrand, K. 2008. Accountability of Networked Climate Governance: The Rise of Transnational Climate Partnerships. *Global Environmental Politics.* 8, 3: 74–102.

29 Roundtable on Sustainable Palm Oil. 2016. Roundtable on Sustainable Palm Oil. [online material]

30 Marin-Burgos, V., Clancy, J. S. and Lovett, J. C. 2015. Contesting Legitimacy of Voluntary Sustainability Certification Schemes: Valuation Languages and Power Asymmetries in the Roundtable on Sustainable Palm Oil in Colombia. *Ecological Economics.* 117: 303–313.

31 Pesqueira, L. and Glasbergen, P. 2013. Playing the Politics of Scale: Oxfam's Intervention in the Roundtable on Sustainable Palm Oil. *Geoforum.* 45: 296–304.

32 Laurance, W. F., Koh, L. P., Butler, R., Sodhi, N. S., Bradshaw, C. J. A., Neidel, J. D., Consunji, H. and Mateo Vega, J. 2010. Improving the Performance of the Round-table on Sustainable Palm Oil for Nature Conservation. *Conservation Biology.* 24, 2: 377–381.

33 Offermans, A. and Glasbergen, P. 2015. Boundary Work in Sustainability Partner-ships: An Exploration of the Round Table on Sustainable Palm Oil. *Environmental Science & Policy.* 50: 34–45.

34 Moog, S., Spicer, A. and Böhm, S. 2014. The Politics of Multi-Stakeholder Initia-tives: The Crisis of the Forest Stewardship Council. *Journal of Business Ethics.* 128, 3: 469–493.

35 Held, D. 2010. *Cosmopolitanism: Ideals and realities.* Cambridge: Polity Press.

36 Commission on Global Security, Justice & Governance. 2015. *Confronting the Crisis of Global Governance.* New York: Commission on Global Security, Justice & Governance.

37 United Nations. 2016. Major Groups and Other Stakeholders. [online material]

38 Convention on Wetlands of International Importance. 2011. *Memorandum of Cooperation with The Ramsar Convention's International Organisation Partners (IOPs).* Gland: Secretariat of the Convention on Wetlands.

39 Convention on Wetlands of International Importance. 2015. *Conference Report.* Uruguay, 12th Meeting of the Conference of the Parties to the Convention on Wetlands.

40 Convention on Migratory Species of Wild Animals. 2002. *Resolution 7.7: Imple-mentation of Existing Agreements.* Bonn, 7th Conference of the Parties to the Convention on Migratory Species of Wild Animals.

41 Convention on Wetlands of International Importance. 2011. *Doc SC42–13: Colla-borative Review with the International Organization Partners of the Convention's Relationships with the IOPs.* Gland, 42nd Meeting of the Standing Committee of the Parties to the Convention on Wetlands of International Importance.

42 Convention on Wetlands of International Importance. 2006. *Doc SC34–33: Meet-ing of International Organization Partners (IOPs) and the Ramsar Secretariat,* 28 February 2006. Gland, 34th Meeting of the Standing Committee of the Parties to the Convention on Wetlands.

43 Scientific and Technical Review Panel of the Ramsar Convention. 2015. STRP Members. Ramsar. [online material]

44 Convention on Wetlands of International Importance. 2010. *Ramsar's Interna-tional Organization Partners (IOPs) – How the IOPs support the Convention at Global, Regional and National Level: The Case of WWF.* Gland, 15th Meeting of the Scientific and Technical Review Panel of the Ramsar Convention.

45 Ansell, C. and Gash, A. 2008. Collaborative Governance in Theory and Practice. *Journal of Public Administration Research and Theory.* 18, 4: 543–571.

46 Berkes, F. 2009. Evolution of co-management: role of knowledge generation, bridging organizations and social learning. *Journal of Environmental Management.* 90, 5: 1692–1702.

47 Emerson, K., Nabatchi, T. and Balogh, S. 2012. An Integrative Framework for Collaborative Governance. *Journal of Public Administration Research and Theory.* 22, 1: 1–29.

48 Chataway, C. J. 1998. Track II diplomacy: From a track I perspective. *Negotiation Journal.* 14, 3: 269–287.

49 Hahn, T., Olsson, P., Folke, C. and Johansson, K. 2006. Trust-building, knowledge generation and organizational innovations: the role of a bridging organization for adaptive comanagement of a wetland landscape around Kristianstad, Sweden. *Human Ecology.* 34, 4: 573–592.

50 Menkel-Meadow, C. 2007. Getting to Let's Talk: Comments on Collaborative Environmental Dispute Resolution Processes. *Nev. LJ.* 8: 835.

51 Schultz, L. 2009. *Nurturing Resilience in Social-ecological Systems: Lessons Learned from Bridging Organisations.* Stockholm: Stockholm University.

52 Convention on Migratory Species of Wild Animals. 2014. *Resolution 11.11: Enhancing the Relationship Between the CMS Family and Civil Society.* Quito, 11th Conference of the Parties to the Convention on Migratory Species of Wild Animals.

53 Crutzen, P. J. 2006. The 'Anthropocene' In *Earth System Science in the Anthropocene.* Edited by Ehlers, E. and Krafft, T. Heidelberg: Springer: 13–18.

54 Waters, C. N., Zalasiewicz, J., Summerhayes, C., et al. 2016. The Anthropocene Is Functionally and Stratigraphically Distinct from the Holocene. *Science.* 351, 6269.

55 United Nations General Assembly. 2015. Resolution 70/208: Harmony with Nature. In *A/RES/70/208.* New York: United Nations.

56 Falk, R. 1983. *The End of World Order: Essays on Normative International Relations.* London: Holmes & Meier Publishers.

57 Žižek, S. 2009. *First as Tragedy, Then as Farce.* London: Verso.

Index